Volume I

Reminiscences

of

Admiral John Smith Thach
U. S. Navy (Retired)

U. S. Naval Institute
Annapolis, Maryland

November, 1977

PREFACE

Volume I of the Reminiscences of Admiral John Smith (Jimmy) Thach, USN (Retired) contains the manuscript of five taped interviews with the Admiral at his home in Coronado, California in 1970-71. These interviews were conducted by Commander Etta Belle Kitchen, USN (Ret.) for the Oral History program of the U. S. Naval Institute. Admiral Thach has reviewed and corrected the manuscript. It has since been re-typed and indexed.

Admiral Thach is well known as one of the Navy's finest aviators in World War II. He is also master of a lively narrative style that makes his story both readable and entertaining. Thach developed a number of innovative techniques for dealing with the enemy in aerial combat. The 'Thach Weave' is perhaps the best known. He talks about all of them in some detail in this volume - a volume which ends with the final raids against the Japanese mainland in 1945.

John T. Mason, Jr.
Director of Oral History
U. S. Naval Institute

ADMIRAL JOHN S. THACH, U. S. NAVY, RETIRED

John Smith Thach was born in Pine Bluff, Arkansas, on April 19, 1905, son of James H. and Jo Bocage (Smith) Thach. He attended the Fordyce High School before his appointment to the U. S. Naval Academy, Annapolis, Maryland, from his native state in 1923. As a Midshipman he participated in football and wrestling. Graduated and commissioned Ensign on June 2, 1927, he subsequently attained the rank of Rear Admiral, to date from November 1, 1955, was promoted to Vice Admiral, to date from January 6, 1960 and to Admiral, to date from March 25, 1965.

Admiral Thach has flown all types of naval aircraft including heavy multi-engined patrol bombers and high performance jet fighters.

Graduated from the Naval Academy in 1927, he remained there during the summer for the short course in aviation and on July 14, was assigned to the battleship MISSISSIPPI, then operating with Battleship Division FOUR of the Battle Fleet. On June 7, 1928, he was transferred to the USS CALIFORNIA, Flagship of the Battle Fleet, and served on board until detached in March 1929 for flight training at the Naval Air Station, Pensacola, Florida, where he was designated Naval Aviator on January 4, 1930. In March of that year he reported for duty with Fighting Squadron ONE, the famous "High Hat" Squadron. This squadron was well known for demonstrating formation flying skill by taking off in a nine-plane formation with the wing tips of each plane tied by a manila line to the next plane in formation. After performing various maneuvers, this formation was able to land and taxi off the field with all planes still tied together.

Continuing duty involving flying, he soon became recognized as one of the Navy's aerial gunnery experts, repeatedly shooting "E" scores in each type of combat aircraft assigned. In July 1932 he reported for duty in the experimental division of the Naval Air Base, Hampton Roads, Virginia. As a test pilot of new experimental aircraft, he flew rough water tests of seaplanes and carrier arresting gear, tests of landplane types. In June 1934 he was assigned to Patrol Squadron NINE, based on the USS WRIGHT. While in that assignment he was ordered by the Navy Department to a special test project in command of the Navy's large experimental seaplane, the XP2H-1. This four-engined giant, completed in 1932, was at that time the largest airplane ever constructed in the United States. It was the second largest in the world (the German DO-X being slightly heavier). He flew this experimental plane on a non-stop twenty-five hour test flight from Norfolk, Virginia, to the Panama Canal on January 15-16, 1935. For this feat, he received a "Well Done" from the Chief of Naval Operations.

Adm. J. S. Thach, USN, Ret.   Page 2

In June 1936 he joined Scouting Squadron SIX-B, attached to the USS CINCINNATI, and a year later reported for duty with Patrol Squadron FIVE-F, based at the Fleet Air Base, Coco Solo, Canal Zone. In June 1939 he was ordered to Fighting Squadron THREE as Gunnery Officer. "For exceptional skill and technique in aerial gunnery and bombing; efficient and meticulous operation of the squadron gunnery department; marked ability to train other pilots in fighting plane tactics and gunnery..." during the period 1939-1940, he received a Letter of Commendation. He was commanding that squadron when the United States entered World War II in December 1941.

He evolved the theory that a two-plane fighter formation would be superior in combat to the old established three-plane formation and developed special offensive and defensive tactics for them. In the South Pacific, Admiral (then Lieutenant Commander) Thach got a chance to put his new theory into practice. His Fighter Squadron THREE rose from the carrier LEXINGTON to meet twenty Jap planes, and knocked down nineteen. The "Thach-trained" Butch O'Hare in this battle shot down six bombers in six minutes.

The tactics he taught the men of his squadron worked so well he was sent back to Pearl Harbor to teach young Army Air Force, as well as Navy pilots what had become known in the Pacific as the "Thach Weave." From Pearl Harbor he went to the Navy's Operational Training Command to indoctrinate new pilots with his war-proven tactics, and from Jacksonville he was sent to the Fast Carrier Task Force as Air Operations Officer, first under Admiral Mitscher, then under Admiral McCain. He developed the system of blanketing enemy airfields with a continuous patrol of carrier-based fighters that prevented the land-based planes from taking off, and systematically destroyed them on the ground. It was he who planned and directed, under Admiral McCain, the Navy's final offensive blows against the Jap homeland. Under his skillful planning, the planes of Admiral McCain's Task Force THIRTY-EIGHT were destroying hundreds of aircraft a day.

In recognition of Admiral Thach's brilliant work, he was invited by Admiral Halsey to come aboard the USS MISSOURI to witness the Surrender ceremony.

Returning to the United States soon after the Japanese surrender, he served the two succeeding years as Director of Training, on the Staff of the Chief of Naval Air Training, and two years as Special Assistant to the Chief of Naval Air Training. He remained at Pensacola until June 1950, when he assumed command of the USS SICILY.

Ten days later, war broke out in Korea. The SICILY departed within a few days for the Far East and was the first carrier to arrive in Korean waters to augment the VALLEY FORGE, which was the only carrier in the Far East at the outbreak of Korean hostilities. During the fourteen months Admiral Thach had command of the SICILY the aircraft of this ship provided close air support of ground forces during many crucial battles, including the Inchon landing and the fight to the sea at Hungnam from the Chosin Reservoir area.

In August 1951 he reported as Chief of Staff and Aide to Commander Carrier Division SEVENTEEN and in December of that year came to Washington, D. C., to serve as Naval Aide to the Assistant Secretary of the Navy for Air. He commanded the USS FRANKLIN D. ROOSEVELT (CVA-42) from May 1953 to April 1954, after which he was in command of Naval Air Bases in the Sixth Naval District, with headquarters at the Naval Air Station, Jacksonville, Florida. In September 1955 he became Senior Naval Member, Weapons Systems Evaluation Group, Office of the Assistant Secretary of Defense, Research and Development, Washington, D. C.

He was Commander Carrier Division SIXTEEN from November 1957 until December 1959, then had duty until March 1, 1960 in the Office of the Chief of Naval Operations, Navy Department. Following an assignment in command of the Anti-Submarine Defense Force, Pacific (redesignated Anti-Submarine Force, Pacific and later Anti-Submarine Warfare Force, Pacific) he reported on July 8, 1963 as Deputy Chief of Naval Operations (Air), Navy Department. On March 25, 1965 he became Commander in Chief, U. S. Naval Forces, Europe and served as such until relieved of active duty pending his retirement, effective May 1, 1967.

Admiral Thach and his wife, the former Madalyn Jones, have two sons, John Smith Thach, Jr. and William Leland Thach.

24 May 1967

(CITATIONS FOLLOW)

Adm. J. S. Thach, USN, Ret.   Page 4

Admiral Thach participated in twelve major engagements or campaigns. During World War II, he operated from the USS SARATOGA, USS LEXINGTON, USS YORKTOWN, USS ENTERPRISE, USS HORNET, USS WASP, and USS SHANGRI-LA. He has been awarded the following:

Distinguished Service Medal: "For exceptionally meritorious service in a duty of great responsibility as Commander of a Carrier Fighting Squadron, which he commanded for the first six months of the war. By his distinguished leadership and thorough training of his pilots in combat tactics and gunnery, he brought his squadron to the high state of efficiency which enabled it to play a major part in the destruction of nineteen out of twenty enemy bombers which attacked an aircraft carrier on February 20, 1942, and to contribute in great measure to the success of the air attack on Salamaua and Lae, New Guinea, on March 10, 1942. After analyzing the air combat reports of the Coral Sea Battle he evolved a system of fighting plane combat teams which he taught not only to his own pilots but to all fighting squadrons in the Hawaiian area. These tactics were used on June 4, 1942 by Lieutenant Commander Thach in leading an air combat against twenty Japanese "Zero" fighters with a four-plane division of fighter planes from his squadron during the successful attacks by carrier air groups against Japanese carriers north of Midway Island, resulting in the destruction of six of the enemy fighters and the driving off of the others, with the loss of only one of his four planes. This success was due entirely to the use of the fighter tactics developed by Lieutenant Commander Thach, and contributed greatly to the success of our forces in this battle."

Navy Cross: (Feb. 20, 1942) - Led his squadron against enemy bombers attempting to attack the LEXINGTON in the Coral Sea, resulting in the shoot-down of 19 out of the 20 enemy bombers in the attack.

Letter of Commendation from Admiral Nimitz: Led LEXINGTON Air Group attack on Japanese landing at Salamaua and Lae, New Guinea. Provided fighter escort and strafed enemy cruiser to draw antiaircraft fire away from dive bombers and personally causing many casualties among enemy gun crews.

Gold Star in lieu of second Navy Cross: Action in Battle of Midway. Led fighter escort in attack against enemy fleet. Engaged enemy fighter patrols, fought through defensive screen. Out numbered by at least 7 to 1, shot down six Zero fighters, drove others away and remained over enemy carriers as protection for torpedo planes and dive bombers during their attack and retirement.

Silver Star Medal: As Operations Officer, Fast Carrier Task Force off Formosa, planned successful attacks on enemy airfields and successfully directed defensive air operations against numerous large scale enemy air attacks when mobility was denied by the necessity to protect two crippled cruisers being towed at a speed of three knots until they were out of range of enemy air attacks.

Adm. J. S. Thach, USN, Ret. Page 5

Legion of Merit: As Air Operations Officer, Fast Carrier Task Force planned and directed 1,000 plane air attacks against over 100 enemy airfields in the Philippines. Designed method of "blanket attack" wherein enemy aircraft were pinned down continuously on all airfields and could not move against American transports and troops invading the Philippines.

Bronze Star Medal: Planned attacks on Japanese homeland from Okinawa to Hokkaido. Designed successful Task Force fighter defense against Japanese Kamikaze attack. Last two months of war not one carrier was hit.

Gold Star in lieu of a second Legion of Merit: "For exceptionally meritorious conduct...as Commanding Officer of the USS SICILY in operation against the enemy in Korea from August 3, 1950 to January 15, 1951. With outstanding ability, energy and high technical skill, he operated his ship and its embarked air group as a unit of the United Nations Naval Forces, furnishing invaluable support to our fighting forces in Korea by the destruction of enemy air opposition, troop concentrations and the interception of the enemy lines of communications, supplies and bases. During this period the ship maintained a superior performance in every phase of operations and the immediate and effective response to calls for extra effort reflect the highest caliber of leadership..."

In addition to the above, Admiral Thach has the Presidential Unit Citation; the Navy Unit Commendation with two stars; American Defense Service Medal; the Asiatic-Pacific Campaign Medal; the American Campaign Medal; World War II Victory Medal; Navy Occupation Service Medal; National Defense Service Medal with bronze star; the Korean Service Medal; the United Nations Service Medal; and the Philippine Liberation Ribbon. He also has the Korean Presidential Unit Citation Badge.

NAVY - Office of Information
Internal Relations Division (OI-430)
24 May 1967

DECLARATION OF TRUST

The undersigned does hereby appoint and designate as his (her) Trustee herein, the Secretary-Treasurer and Publisher of the United States Naval Institute to perform and discharge the following duties, powers, and privileges in connection with the possession and use of a certain taped interview between the undersigned and the Oral History Department of the United States Naval Institute.

1. Classification of Transcript.

( )a. If classified OPEN, the transcript(s) may be read or the recording(s) audited by the qualified personnel upon presentation of proper credentials, as determined by the Secretary-Treasurer of the U.S. Naval Institute.

(✓)b. If classified PERMISSION REQUIRED TO CITE OR QUOTE, the user will be required to obtain permission in writing from the interviewee prior to quoting or citing from either the transcript(s) or the recording(s).

( )c. If classified PERMISSION REQUIRED, permission must be obtained in writing from the interviewee before the transcribed interview(s) can be examined or the tape recording(s) audited.

( )d. If classified CLOSED, the transcribed interview(s) and the tape recording(s) will be sealed until a time specified by the interviewee. This may be until the death of the interviewee or for any specified number of years.

2. It is expressly understood that in giving this authorization, I am in no way precluded from placing such restrictions as I may desire upon use of the interview at any time during my lifetime, nor does this authorization in any way affect my rights to the copyright of my literary expressions that may be contained in the interview.

Witness my hand and seal this 19th day of April 19 76

Upon my death The Transcript is Classified OPEN.

John S. Thach

I hereby accept and consent to the foregoing Declaration of Trust and the powers therein conferred upon me as Trustee:

R.T.E. Bowler Jr.
23 June 1976

Interview No. 1 with Admiral John S. Thach, U.S. Navy (Retired)
Place: Admiral Thach's home in Coronado, 330 8th Street
Subject: Biography
Date: 28 June 1970
By: Etta-Belle Kitchen.

Q: Good morning, Admiral. This is your biography and sometimes I feel I'm like that man Edwards saying, "This is your life, Admiral," but it really is, and you've had such an illustrious and distinguished career in the Navy that I think we're awfully lucky to have you able to put these reminiscences of your life on tape for the Institute. I think we just might as well start at the beginning with your telling me some of your early days and might as well begin with when you were born and where.

Adm. T.: I was born on April the 19th, 1905 in Pine Bluff, Arkansas, and later moved to Fordyce, where I spent most of my youth. As far back as I can remember - I was two years old and we were visiting my grandfather in Tennessee on a farm - I think they called it a plantation in those days - and I took some poison. It wasn't my intention to commit suicide, but being at that age, they had little things that looked like cookies, rat poison, in the attic, someone left the door open and I crawled up there and saw these cookies and nibbled on one. It tasted sweet, so I sat down and started munching away and picking up the others. Well, that's where they found me, and it created quite a commotion in the house. I remember my grandfather saying,

"Get some mustard and some hot water," and they put this powdered mustard out of a can with hot water, stirred it up and made me drink it. It tasted so terrible, it made me throw up . . .

Q: That was the purpose of it!

Adm. T.: Of course, that was what they wanted. But they kept pouring this stuff down me and I said I didn't like it, it wasn't any good, and that didn't seem to worry them, so I desperately tried to think of something else more convincing, and I said, "I don't want a drink up all of grandmother's mustard. Leave some for somebody else."

Q: This is at age two?

Adm. T.: Yes, and I remember that.

Q: I'm sure it was a dramatic incident that you couldn't forget. But that really is remarkable to recall at the age of two, I think.

Adm. T.: I remember it very clearly, and the color the mustard was and just about how it tasted. I don't want to have to do that again.

Q: I hope you don't have to either!

Adm. T.: We used to spend a little time up there during the summer. I remember also people catching fish out of the pond (it was big enough to be called a lake today) with new bread that they could squeeze onto the hook. I've wondered since why they didn't use worms, but it seemed the fish liked that bread, so they'd catch them with bread.

I suppose the next thing that had some influence on my life was around the age of six, by this time we had moved to Fordyce, Arkansas, and my grandmother was living there then. She used to invite me to tea every afternoon at 5 o'clock, and I could bring any little playmate I wanted, so we would sit around and have tea and she would always bring out these tiny little goblets about as big around as the end of your finger, and put some wine or cordial in them and make us sip it. If anyone gulped it all at once, mind you, it was only as big as your little finger, then they had to have a lecture on how to sip wine. And this was at the age of six and seven years old. All the while she was telling us about Europe, and I remember her talking about the Bridge of Sighs at Venice, and how they moved in boats instead of carriages and horses and wagons. I realized later that what she was doing was teaching us the history of Europe and she was making it in very interesting story form. I'll never forget later when I began to study the history of Europe, I realized that I already knew some of it. She had been a school teacher. She'd lost her husband during the war between the states and she was left with three girls and one boy. In those days a lady couldn't do anything really in the way of work, except teach school. It wasn't decent for a lady to work anywhere else. So she taught school and put all of her children through school, and this, I thought, was a fine example of ability to do things in the fact of adversity. Later, I was talking to my mother . . .

Q: Excuse me, was she your maternal or your paternal grandmother?

Adm. T.: Maternal. Her name was Etta Bocage Smith.

Q: Oh, that must be where you get your middle name from!

Adm. T.: Yes, and her husband was a Captain John Smith, but not the original. Not the one whose life was saved by Pocahontas.

When I was about thirteen, jumping up a little, I became discouraged about what I could do and what I couldn't do. I mean my personal capability, not what I was permitted to do. And I remember worrying about this in front of my mother and she took me out on the back steps and sat me down and told me an awful lot about some people that she had known - she said, you can do anything you want to do, you can have anything you want to have, if you want it badly enough. She said, I know a man who wanted to marry a lady and he had to work and wait for 25 years, but he finally did it, and you can have any kind of job you want. You can do anything you want. You just have to want it badly enough. So I never forgot that, and it encouraged me. I think it makes people stop and think, when they believe they want something very much and they're disappointed they're not getting it or maybe they're not going to get it, how badly do they really want it? Maybe they don't want it badly enough, really, to go out and spend ten or twenty years getting there.

Q: Have you always been slender and tall, even as a young man?

Adm. T.: Yes. As a matter of fact, probably too much so, because I'll get to this a little later - but I almost didn't get into the Naval Academy because they thought I was sick, I was so skinny.

But in high school, and in my early days before high school - my father used to take me camping, hunting and fishing. Of course, this was aside from the annual vacation that my father and mother took with all the children to the river near Fordyce, Arkansas, about 20 miles from Fordyce - between Fordyce and Pine Bluff - called the Saline River. It was a beautiful little river, crystal clear most of the time, except after the spring rains, and I learned an awful lot from my father, not only how to catch fish, but I learned it without him ordering me to do this and do that, I learned that each person has to do his share and, as we say in the Navy, each person has to pull his own weight in the boat. When you're making a camp, if everyone doesn't do enough, why, it will get dark and it will be so late you'll be in a mess, and maybe made camp over a nest of moccasins, or something. He was a great fisherman, and it was a long time before I could come anywhere near doing as well with a fly rod as he could.

But he taught me a lot of things about how to survive. We would go for two weeks at a time in a very light boat, almost like a canoe, except it was flat-bottomed, on this river and never see any sign of a human being in two weeks, not even a foot track or a horse track or anything.

Q: Just you and your father?

Adm. T.: Just my father and I. We would take just the bare essentials to survive in case we didn't catch any fish or get any game, but we almost always did. And this was quite an experience. I learned from the game and the fishing and everything a little bit about nature, and how it sort of relates to people. Without my realizing it, he was teaching me some important things. Of course, he was a school teacher.

Q: Oh, your father was a school teacher?

Adm. T.: My father was a school teacher, and my mother was a school teacher. My father taught school for 18 years and my mother taught school for 16. They met in the school room. She was a fairly new teacher in grade school, and he was principal of the school, and he used to come and visit the various classrooms and he seemed to be spending more time in her classroom and it worried her because she thought she wasn't doing very well. But that wasn't the reason he was coming around so often.

Q: Haven't you often thought how fortunate you were to have selected the right parents?

Adm. T.: Oh, yes. I was very wise to do that.

Q: Your whole career, your personality, characteristics, and everything, you can even feel in the short comments were related to what your parents taught you and . . .

Adm. T.: Oh, there's no question about it. Our family, mother, father, and children, were all very close. Of course, we had the usual kid squabbles, but we never drew apart, even now.

Q: How many children were there?

Adm. T.: There were four of us, Harmon, Josephine, Jack and Frances, two girls and two boys, and they seemed to know how to do that, just properly balanced, didn't they?

I was very determined to do something in athletics, although I was fairly small, but I had this advantage that there weren't many people in that small town high school at Fordyce, and my second year in high school I made the football team. But I had some discouragement there because I was playing end, and I was all right on offense, I could run pretty fast and catch the ball, but on defense, when they threw those two backs at me and knocked me down - I was not very good on defense and that worried me because we didn't have an offensive team and a defensive team.

Q: You were there for the whole game!

Adm. T.: We were there for the whole game, offense and defense. So we had to have someone who could keep them from doing that end run on you, and I wasn't too successful at doing that. My senior year they shifted me to quarterback and I was calling signals, doing all the passing and kicking for that team. We were quite successful. We came very close to winning the State championship although this was a little town of about 3,000 people. The following year, my brother-in-law, Bill Walton, who had in the meantime married my sister, Josephine, became coach at Fordyce and he did win the State Championship.

Q: That's remarkable for a town that small, isn't it?

Adm. T.: Yes. We had to fight Pine Bluff and Little Rock and all those people in the big schools that had several teams and, incidentally, we didn't have enough to scrimmage against each other. We had to take the left side of the line and shift it around to be defense against the right side of the line and only run plays one way to get a scrimmage. There just weren't any good substitutes. We only had two or three, so we had to last the whole game. In my senior year I played 60 minutes of every game of an 8-game series. I never was out at all. I played safety on defense, quarterback on offense, and I remember we were playing Hot Springs, Arkansas, and this big burly full back got through the line and I was the last one so I had to hit him, and he knocked me flat and I had the wind knocked out of me, and the coach came on the field and I thought he was going to help me. All he did was lean over and say, "Get up, get up!" Couldn't afford to lose one player.

Q: What were the events that led up to your going to the Academy, Admiral?

Adm. T.: Well, primarily, my parents couldn't afford to send me to a college, and this is the same thing that happened to my brother. My brother being four years older than I. So he decided maybe he could go to West Point, and so he applied for an appointment to West Point from one of our congressmen and they told him that, well, they didn't have any more appointments to West Point but they could get him one to Annapolis. He said, "What's that?" and they said, "Well, that's the Naval Academy. It's for the Navy the same thing that West Point is for the Army." He said, "That may be all right." So he went. Then the fact that he was there influenced me to want to go. So I remember - well, in the first place, by this time my little high school had become qualified to be on what they called the "accredited list" of high schools, so that without taking a mental examination you could go directly from that high school into the Naval Academy, if your grades were good enough.

Q: Without taking an entrance exam?

Adm. T.: I never took an entrance exam to the Naval Academy. But I had to have an appointment from a congressman or a senator, and this famous old Joe T. Robinson finally gave me an appointment. I remember he visited Fordyce, Arkansas and all the city fathers knew I wanted to go to the Naval Academy and I needed an appointment and they twisted his arm and I wondered why I was suddenly called to go and talk to him. They said, now you tell him what you want. So I did. He asked me a few questions, and he was noncommittal. He left and then in a few days he wrote and said he would give me the appointment. But my grades in high school had to be fairly high in order to get in, and this was - may have been - a most unfortunate thing because the principal of the high school was the football coach and the history teacher and science teacher was the basketball and track coach, and I was out on the teams of each one of these and I discovered later that they must have been giving me grades that I didn't deserve. I remember going to the principal after he'd given me a final mark in math, which was something like 96 per cent, and I said, "Don't you think that ought to be a 98?" I don't remember whether it was 94 or 96. I said, "Don't you think that ought to be 98? I want to be sure to get into the Naval Academy." And he said, "Yes, I guess so," and he changed it right there.

Q: Not really!

Adm. T.: Yes. This should have given me a hint that I wasn't that good, and it didn't take me long when I got into the Naval Academy to discover that, sure enough, they'd been giving me trades that I didn't deserve.

When I went to the Naval Academy I, of course, had to take a physical exam. I arrived there and went through the physical exam and after it was over, the doctor called me in and said, "You don't look very well. Have you ever had tuberculosis?" And I said, no. He said, "Well, we're going to have to get a special x-ray of your lungs because you haven't passed the physical."

Q: How tall were you then?

Adm. T.: I was almost six feet then and weighed 135. But I was trained down to a very fine point from continuously being in training for football, basketball, and track.

Q: How tall are you now?

Adm. T.: I'm exactly six feet, but I was around 5 feet 11 then. So I had to sit around Annapolis biting my nails for a couple of days while they evaluated my x-rays. I went back in at the appointed time and the doctor said, "Well, we can't find anything wrong with you. We're going to let you in, but you've got to build yourself up. Have you ever done any sports or athletics? Maybe we can put some beef on you by - if you go out for some sort of sport. Have you ever done any sports?"

Well, of course, this insulted me, but I kept my head and I said, "Yes," and I told him what I'd done. He said, "Well, you've just got to eat more." So, I was in.

Plebe summer we were out drilling with rifles and there was a Lieutenant Gerald Bogan, who was the officer in charge of us, and about our second day of drill a classmate of mine by the name of John Madison from Louisiana - from Baton Rouge, Louisiana - Gerry said, - excuse me, Lieutenant Bogan said, "Column right," and sure enough, Madison did column left, and Bogan yelled at him, "Hey, you dummy, come back here," and he dropped his gun. You know, this only happens in movies, and I had to laugh. I thought it was funny, and I busted out laughing. Well, Bogan came right down the line and he said, "Who laughed? Who laughed?" He got to me, and I said, I did. Didn't you think it was funny?" I didn't know anything about the discipline of the drill then, and I thought it was funny, and didn't know why he didn't laugh. Well, he called Madison a dummy - that's where he got his nickname "Dummy" Madison. He has since become a very successful lawyer and he's a very smart man. But that was my first introduction to Gerald Bogan.

Q: Did he punish you?

Adm. T.: Oh, he ran us up and down the field till _he_ became completely out of breath, and that was our punishment for somebody laughing in ranks. I guess I wasn't the only one,

Thach #1 - 12

but I laughed the loudest. But this didn't bother us. We were in pretty good training.

Later, I ran into him several more times which I'll relate when the time comes.

Q: You say you liked the Naval Academy?

Adm. T.: I just loved it. A lot of people, you know - oh, some of them Frenched out, just to be out for a little while, go over the wall and come back in in the middle of the night. I never wanted to do this.

Q: Did you have any problems with your academic program?

Adm. T.: That's what I'd like to talk about. Yes, plenty. When I went to the Naval Academy I was fascinated and very impressed - of course, it's a beautiful place - but one of the things I was impressed with more than anything else was the facilities for athletics and so forth. In my little high school, they had been talking about building a manual arts building, so you could learn how to do carpentry and things and I wanted that course so bad, but they didn't have the building finished and when I graduated they hadn't instituted the course. And I thought, gee, I was born too soon. If I'd only come through later, I could have got in there and learned how to build things. Maybe I could build a boat. So this is one of the reasons I was impressed with the Naval Academy because they had everything - wonderful gymnasiums and swimming pools, all sorts of equipment for training and so forth. This was just fabulous, and I felt like I was on a vacation until I ran into the problem of the academic studies. I found myself, after the first two weeks, failing in every subject.

Q: Not really!

Adm. T.: Yes. On the tree, they called it. Well, I learned then that I didn't know how to study. I had not learned in high school, so I had to really buckle down and learn how to study. One of the reasons, I think, that I didn't do too well was because I was so interested in football. My plebe year I was on the B squad. B squad scrimmages against A squad and has to run the plays from Princeton, Notre Dame, Army, Pennsylvania, each week had to learn a new set of plays and signals, and that was the job of the B squad to give the A squad a chance to see these plays running at them and to work against them, so that they'd be a little bit better ready for the game when it came up.

Q: That must have taken an awful lot of time.

Adm. T.: It did and I was a quarterback of this B squad team and I had to know where everybody went and I had to learn these plays. Well, of course, I studied real hard on that and I was quite successful, but I was neglecting my academic studies. Sometimes, we'd make a touchdown against the No. 1 A squad, and that gave us a little boost in morale because we thought we were showing them something, and we were. But fortunately - or I felt at the time, very fortunately - I knocked my shoulder out of place making a tackle and they couldn't get it back in and had to take me to the hospital and they reduced it there, and I had it in a sling for a while. Finally got back out to football near the end of the season, and I still had my place on the B squad, running that team, and I knocked it out again, and the doctor said, You've had it, you can't play football any more. This really hurt my pride because then I had the egotistical idea I could be an all American if given the chance. I could carry the ball and evade tacklers as well as hit a receiver on the finger tips in a dead run. That same team went up to the A squad the next year intact. This whole thing was perhaps a blessing in disguise because maybe it saved me academically. I asked the doctor what I could do in the way of athletics. I said, "I can't just sit around here and do nothing." He was being facetious and he said, "Why don't you try wrestling?" I took him seriously and I did. I got on the class wrestling team and learned quite a bit there.

My class was a large one. We started out with 1,006, and finally graduated only 500. So although I stood near the bottom of the class, I feel that I really stood in the middle, because when you think of the universities today with so little if any attrition. Everybody seems to graduate. I don't hear of anyone flunking out of a university any more.

Q: Attrition's pretty high in the freshmen's class in the universities.

Adm. T.: Is it? Well, it was 50 percent at the Naval Academy then. But I think this may have been intentional because they were graduating at that time more than the Navy needed, or more than the appropriation called for in personnel, and they had to cut down somewhere, and they did it the best way by - they increased the math course, and they changed raincoats on us and that discouraged some people. Had to buy a new raincoat.

Q: Really!

Adm. T.: They were doing everything to try to get us out, but some of us wouldn't. By the time I got to the first class year I felt that I had it made, and I wasn't too concerned then about academics. I was still having a wonderful time at the Naval Academy. I liked the place. I was enjoying all this so much and I wasn't too concerned about where I stood in my class, just so I got through.

Q: You were having the best of both worlds, really!

Adm. T.: Apparently. Of course, I didn't realize then that class standing at the Naval Academy was so far reaching. I would have to live with it the rest of my life, which I did. There were times when, for instance, I wouldn't be assigned quarters because somebody two or three numbers senior to me, who graduated from the Naval Academy two or three numbers ahead of me would get them and I didn't. That, of course, later didn't make any difference. But I did enjoy the Naval Academy.

You know, we made three midshipmen cruises. The first one was after plebe year, it was called the youngster cruise, and I had the bad fortune of making the last three coal-burning midshipmen cruises. The year after that they changed the last coal-burning battleship to an oil-burner. I remember one time when we'd been coaling ship in Philadelphia and this fine coal dust just gets in everything, it even gets in your eyelids. Some of my friends were in such a hurry to get ashore, they took a good shower but they didn't soak the coal dust out of their eyelids, and that night we were at this dance and all the girls thought they were so handsome with those beautiful eyelashes. In effect they had mascara on, and we kidded them about that. But this coal-burning business is something that a lot of people don't realize is a difficult thing, especially when you have Welsh coal which is nothing but mostly powder. This was my last year - my last cruise, called first class cruise - the classes just junior to my class were very small. In fact, you could hardly find somebody to do anything, so, in effect, we used to say we made three youngster cruises. Instead of supervising the labor of a squad of youngsters, we had to do all the work, scrub the decks, and stoke red-hot doors in the boiler rooms, for three different cruises. In each boiler room there are four doors leading to the coal fire on the gratings. These doors are about two feet square and under forced draft they usually become red hot. You are supposed to open the doors with the shovel, pitch a shovel full of coal in on the fire in such a way that it will spread evenly. The distance from the door to the back of the fire box under each boiler was at least ten feet and it took some skill as well as energy to swing a full shovel through that little door and get some coal all the way back to keep a level fire.

This was my 30th day of firing the boilers along with a classmate of mine, a man by the name of Eddie Van Sickle - he was an old cowboy from Montana and a wonderful person. We were going through the Panama Canal and so they had to have a lot of extra steam up, all the boilers on, in case of an emergency. If they ran on to a mudbank they'd have enough power to back off, etc., so we were under forced draft and they sent two youngsters down to pass the coal out of the bunkers on the steel floor boards right in front of the four boiler doors, and it was so hot that these youngsters got sick and passed out and we had to haul them up by the heels, and we expected some one to send two more fresh ones down, but they didn't. And, of course, we were always very gung-ho, as the Marines say, about keeping the steam pressure up because there were enlisted men manning a boiler room just across the way, and if we let our steam drop when we were training to be officers, and their steam did not drop, this was very bad.

Q: You lost face!

Adm. T.: We lost face, exactly. So we were very much imbued with this and Eddie said, "Well, let's take turns getting in the bunkers and getting the coal out, and the other one will fire these four doors." This was a pretty rough deal, especially as the temperature was 140° and we were drinking oatmeal water to keep from getting too dehydrated-with oatmeal in the water you can drink more of it without throwing up. Well, the four hours were up and nobody came down. We got the water tender to call and tell them that we hadn't been relieved. What we should have done was thrown our shovels down and walked on up and said, "We've had our four hours and this is our thirtieth day, we're supposed to go to the deck force," but we didn't. We kept the steam up, and worked for eight hours.

Q: How could you possibly physically endure it?

Adm. T.: He lost 15 pounds and I lost ten.

Q: In one day!

Adm. T.: In one eight-hour period. But we kept the steam pressure up and that was the thing we had to do. There was a mix-up on the watch list. The people who made it out thought that we were - that our company would go to the deck force four hours later than we were actually supposed to, so they didn't provide for any relief for the next four hours for Eddie van Sickle and me without even any youngsters. We just couldn't get the word to the right people, so we stuck it out. And that was quite an experience.

The water tender during the second four hours of this long watch was an enlisted petty officer second class. His name was Murphy but he looked a bit more Polish than Irish. He was tall, well muscled but gave the appearance of being slender. We had stood other watches in the "black gang" with Murphy and had gotten to know him pretty well. He had a deliberate manner of speaking with considerable poise -- never talked very much, but when he did we listened. He was an experienced old man about twenty seven years old.

The water tender's primary job on watch is to keep the water in each boiler at the right level, otherwise there could be an explosion or burned out boiler tubes. He also had the responsibility of seeing that the plant was operating under safe limits. "Murph" knew exactly how to adjust the draft when a firebox was "panting" to stop it and still let enough air in. This surging of draft air back and forth through the fire could cause a dangerous flare-back if it continued. He never helped us unless he thought we needed it and we had a great respect for him.

The first time we stood a coal shoveling watch which coincided with his water-tender watch he said he needed a little exercise, picked up a shovel, scraped the coal into mounds just to the right of each fire box door. With a quick twist of the shovel he flipped the door open, scooped up the coal, took a long smooth back swing and with an unhurried pitch spread the coal evenly clear to the back of the fire box -- all of this with no lost motion and the grace of a ballet dancer. We realized we were watching a real pro with a shovel and it was a thing of beauty. After he was satisfied the fire was well stoked, he strolled around to the side of the boilers to take a good look at his gauges, gently tapped one and gave a small twist to one of the many control valves in his domain before he returned to open another door. "Murph" didn't need the exercise - he was simply showing us in his own way how to handle the shovel. And we were just sitting there enjoying the rest. Finally he put down the shovel, looked at us and said, "Thanks." Eddie and I both said, "Oh, you're welcome, anytime." We looked at each other and giggled. He gave us a fatherly, solemn look and went back to fiddle with his valves.

We discovered, much to our delight, that "Murph" could do other things with a shovel. Sometimes, especially on the mid-watch, if the steaming was light as it was with low cruising speed, he would polish a shovel with a clean rag until it was shiny bright. Then he miraculously produced from a rag locker three big onions, some canned meat and three forks. After chopping the onions and mixing them with the meat on the shovel, he sprinkled on some kind of sauce from a small unlabeled bottle and held the shovel in over the hot coals. In a very few minutes it was getting brown and sizzling. He carried the shovel to the middle of the steel boiler room floor boards. We sat around in a circle and ate. It was absolutely delicious!

After the youngsters who got sick in the coal bunker were taken away Eddie Van Sickle and I had to work fast whether in the bunker or stoking fires. One reason for this was the forced draft which burns the coal faster but the main reason was the Welch coal. I stuck my head in the bunker and asked Eddie to see if he could find some lumps. He said, "In the first place I can't see very well in here and it's mostly dust anyway." It was pretty discouraging to pitch in a shovel full only to see most of it go "Whoosh" - right up the stack - knowing you'd better hurry and feed the other doors before the fires died down. "Murph" in his usual philosophical approach, said, "That Welsh coal is a real character builder alright." I had the feeling he was trying to tell me something.

When my turn came to go in the bunker again for an hour, I was struck by the amount of coal we had used up. At first it could be reached from just inside the bunker door. But by this time I had to walk toward the back pushing the shovel in front of me to find where the coal started. There was no ventilation -- that coal dust just hung in the dead air and got in my nose, mouth and throat. I tried to avoid breathing until I got to the door with a shovel full - but it was a losing battle. In today's clean air campaign that bunker would get a low mark.

During my next turn at stoking the four red hot doors, I had clinker trouble. If you don't break up the clinkers when they form in the fire, there is a slice-bar of solid steel about two inches in diameter and fifteen feet long. I was punching away at these nasty clinkers which make the fire inefficient, when I ran the slice-bar into a big one. I tried to pry it up hoping it would turn over but that didn't work and when I tried to pull the slice-bar out to give another lunge at it, I couldn't. It was stuck! I heaved on it sideways, up and down and finally with one more pulling effort it came out suddenly like a big red snake with humps on it. As one of the humps passed my stomach I heard a sound like "ssst" and didn't want to look. It wasn't a severe burn - just a four inch streak of blister. But what a pickle I was in! I had spent too much time with that slice-bar and the other fires must be dying down.

At this point I considered asking "Murph" for some help but I was too embarrassed to let him know what had happened. I was glad he had been spending most of the time around the corner with his indicators and probably hadn't seen my amateurish performance with the slice-bar. I decided I had to catch up alone and not tell him or Eddie.

At the end of the cruise the day before leaving the ship, I saw "Murph" again and told him I had come close to asking for his help at one point during that last fireroom watch. He said, "Well, you don't know how close I came to picking up a shovel after you had curled the slice-bar and burned your stomach." So -- he had seen it all! I said, "Thanks "Murph", for not picking up that shovel." He didn't say any more, just shook my hand, nodding his head slowly.

On graduation, my brother's ship happened to be anchored in the roads near the Naval Academy. The commanding officer's name was Captain Snyder. Before we graduated I had been introduced to my brother's skipper and I was very impressed. He was a fine looking man with four gold stripes on his sleeve and scrambled eggs on his cap. Well, as a coincidence, just after graduation and after having had my commissioned officer's ensign stripes pinned on by my sister, I saw my brother at some distance, and I waved at him. I said, "Hey, . . . " I said something, maybe something facetious. Captain Snyder was in between us and he thought I was talking to him and he came over and said, "Congratulations, young man." And I said, "Oh, Sir, I wasn't calling you. I was trying to get my brother's attention." He said, "That's all right. I wanted to congratulate you, anyway." My first act after getting ensign's stripes was to almost get fresh with a four-striper.

Q: What is your brother's name?

Adm. T.: James Harmon Thach, Jr.

Q: How did you get your nickname?

Adm. T.: I got it, of course, from my brother. My brother's name was Harmon and my name was Jack. There was no Jimmy Thach at home. But he went to the Naval Academy and one of his roommates was Vin Conroy and another one was Bob Bell. Vin Conroy was quite a famous football player - captain of the football team. My brother had also busted his shoulder so he became manager of the team. So he was well known to the football squad as Jimmy Thach, because "Ding Dong" Bell, when he asked him what his name was when they first started rooming together, and he said, "My name is Harmon," he said, "I can't say that. Don't you have another name? That sounds pretty awful." He said, "Well, my first name is James," so Bob says, "Okay, Jim, you're Jimmy," and so all his classmates picked up Jimmy. I went to the Naval Academy three weeks after he graduated and went out for the football squad in the fall and made the training table because I knew something about football even though I didn't have enough weight. I went to the training table and they said, "Well, hello, who are you?" Of course, they didn't treat plebes like plebes because we could "carry on" at the training table - that was one of the wonderful features about making the training table in any sport, and I said, "My name is Thach," and they said, "By the way, are you any relation to Jimmy Thach who just graduated?" I said, "Yes, Sir." They said, "Well, what was he? Your grandfather or your uncle?" And I said, "He's my brother." So then they said, "Hey, come here, everybody look, here's a little Jimmy Thach." And I said, "Oh, no, my name is Jack."

Q: It's really John.

Adm. T.: Yes. I'm John Smith but my parents called me Jack. And they said, "Oh, Okay, little Jimmy." And I protested too much with all my classmates. I kept telling them my name was Jack and I said, "Wouldn't it be terrible if I was fortunate enough to get through the Naval Academy and graduate and then we'd have two Jimmy Thachs as officers in the Navy." And they'd say, "Yeah, wouldn't that be funny, Jimmy." So my wife never knew my name was Jack until after we were married. We were Jack and Harmon at home, and both Jimmy Thach in the Navy. That's how it happened.

Q: So there were two Jimmy Thachs! How did they distinguish between you?

Adm. T.: Sometimes they didn't.

Q: So we have you graduated.

Adm. T.: I was assigned to the USS Mississippi.

Q: I have a note that you went to a short course in aviation that summer.

Adm. T.: Oh, yes. I did.

Thach #1 - 26

Q: How did that happen?

Adm. T.: At that time they had instituted a plan to introduce all of the young new ensigns to aviation and give them a flight and let them sit in various positions in the airplane. We were given a number of flights in patrol types - seaplanes - a flying boat. It was the H-16 at the time, multi-engine, large thing and it carried a number of crew, forward gunner and an after gunner, a bombardier, and so forth. So the aviators put three or four of us at a time in one of these planes and took us off and demonstrated a few things about navigation and taxiing the airplane and so forth. Just to introduce us to aviation and that's about all that was. I enjoyed it. I always liked to get up in the bow where you could stick your head out of the cockpit and see where you're going.

Q: Did you particularly like it and think this is what I want to do, or did you just find it interesting?

Adm. T.: I just found it interesting.

Q: No dedication to, now I'm going to be an aviator?

Adm. T.: No, not at that time.

Q: And then you had your first assignment as a naval officer on a couple of big battleships?

Adm. T.: Yes. The first one was the <u>Mississippi</u>, and I was assigned to communications duty as one of the assistant radio officers, and learned quite a bit about the system of communications in the Navy. I think at that time the Navy was further advanced in communications and communications procedures than any other service. Since then, at various times, the Army has overtaken both the Navy and the Air Force, and the Air Force has overtaken us. We're all pretty sophisticated now in communications, but at that time I was appalled to learn that the Army couldn't send a message to more than one person. They couldn't make a multiple address in a dispatch. They'd have to put all the instructions about who else to send it to in the body of the message - this sort of thing. And, of course, I had the job of carrying these dispatches around to be sure that somebody took action on them within a certain time. I was very impressed with the fact that there was such a thing as a priority message. That meant that you didn't walk when you took the message in your hand, you ran, and the person who was supposed to take action on it didn't do anything else - you didn't eat lunch or dinner or whatever it was - he didn't do anything until he got the action completed. This was what the communications manual said, but that wasn't always exactly what the commanding officer did when I took him a message. He'd say, "All right, put it over there. I'll get to it when I have time." But he had other things more important to do, at that moment.

We had a wonderful group of junior officers aboard the

Mississippi with a very fine junior officers' mess, and I'll never forget some of the good friends, mostly classmates, that I made there. One of them, Walter Price, is living right here. He was a good old Mississippi shipmate. While I was aboard the Mississippi the Navy decided that they should have what we called an elimination course in aviation. This was in 1927. The people on the West Coast they sent to San Diego to have a course to see whether - what percentage of Naval Academy graduates - could learn how to fly, whether you wanted to or not. So they gave you about six hours of dual instruction in a training plane, and if the instructor found you safe for solo he would let you solo the airplane, one flight.

Q: Where were you then?

Adm. T.: Right here at San Diego. We were flying from North Island. We were living in BOQ at the air station. At the most, they would give you eight hours, some people got eight hours, and some of them got eight hours and never did solo. I have five and a half and my instructor was a fellow by the name of Bubbles Fisher, and what a character he was. His appearance resembled somewhat a gorilla. He was real tough looking and he *was* tough. He would frequently get in fights but he always won -- that is in off-duty fracases. I was pretty frightened of this fellow because he was very rough-speaking and acting, but he did teach me how to fly, and I was never so surprised in my life because I didn't think I was doing very well on the take-offs and landings, and then we were practicing landing and take-off down at Ream Field, near the Mexican border. He taxied over by the trees and got out of the airplane and he said, "Okay, take it up, take it 'round the field and land it." I almost said, "I don't think I know how."

Q: Let me understand, had you just been up one time then?

Adm. T.: No, five times. He never told me how I was doing, he just wasn't very communicative, but he told me what to do and he was teaching me what to do, but he never told me whether I was good, maybe good, or maybe some hope for me - I didn't know. But when he got out of the plane and left me with it all alone and said, "Taxi out and take off and fly around the field and land. Taxi back over here and pick me up." So I took off and I've never had such a lonesome feeling. I was flying from the rear seat and there was nobody up there in front where the instructor usually sits. So I finally came around and landed and bounced the airplane. I thought I was going to crash. I thought it was a pretty bad bounce, but apparently it wasn't so bad, it didn't hurt anything, and I taxied over and he said, "Okay, that's fine. You've solo'd, you've finished - finished the course."

Later I got to know him very well when we were both in a _Saratoga_ squadron and I can relate about that later.

Q: Did you know then that you were going to go on and be an aviator, or did you just say, "Thanks very much?"

Adm. T.: They had a little form among a lot of other forms you fill out. "Do you desire further flight training?" And I put down, yes. But I never did make a formal request to go to flight training, as most people did. They just sent me later when I was aboard the California, and by that time I'd become very interested in cryptanalysis and in the communications field. I'd taken a short course in cryptanalysis - code-breaking - and I thought, when I got these orders to go to Pensacola, I thought, well, maybe, I can postpone this a little bit, so I went to see George Murray. He was the aviation officer on Admiral Pratt's staff - and asked about it, and he said, "Look, if you don't go now you never will. You'd better go now or they won't take you later." I said, "Oh, they won't? All right, I'll go. I'll go quietly."

Q: You said you had another item about the Mississippi.

Adm. T.: I was transferred to the California because they needed some more communication junior officers to be on Admiral Pratt's staff, and I'd been there about two or three months - and my brother was ordered to the staff as assistant operations officer - so this is the first time that I'd ever had duty in the same unit as my brother, and it was the last time, too. They kept us in different oceans after that.

Q: You were an ensign and he was a . . . ?

Adm. T.: He was a lieutenant JG. We were exactly the same

height and very nearly the same build, and our voices were precisely alike. Actually, my mother couldn't tell us apart when we were talking to her in the next room. We used to play tricks on her by - she would say something to him and I would answer, and vice versa. So we were sometimes mistaken for each other, unless you saw us together it was a little difficult to tell. I thought we never looked very much alike. He had a very regular handsome face, and mine was sort of screwed up. Anyway, one thing happened, I remember. We were anchored in San Pedro Bay and we were both bachelors at that time, and he had somehow acquired two dates for a Saturday night, so he came to me and said, "I've got a little problem you can help me with. I made a date with two very nice girls, and I don't want to drop either one of them. I don't want to insult either one of them, and I can't take them out together. Why don't you just pretend you're me and take this one out." And I said, "Oh-ho, this won't work." He said, "Oh, yes, it will. I've only had one or two dates with her. She won't know the difference." So I said, "Well, I went ashore last weekend and I'm a little low on money, and my best suit is at the cleaner's, so if you'll just lend me a little bit and let me wear this good dark charcoal gray suit." It fit me perfectly. I could wear his hats, shoes, trousers, waistline, shoulders, everything. So he had to do that, reluctantly. I kept the date and the girl doesn't know the difference to this day.

Q: Isn't that interesting! Did he ever pull rank on you?

Adm. T.: No. He was a very wonderful person. If I ever had an ideal, it was my older brother.

Q: That's a nice thing to be able to say about your brother.

Adm. T.: I think so. Some brothers really honestly don't get along very well, and some families don't get along well. We always did and whenever it was possible to get together, which wasn't very often, we always did and had a wonderful time. And when we could arrange it, which again was not very often, we would try to arrange leave at the same time, so we could both go home together, and when that happened, why, we kept the neighbors awake all night because the Thachs were known as the "shouting Thachs" in Fordyce, Arkansas. An endearing sort of term, but we had so much to talk about and had so much fun, (There were four children then and my mother and father) that we just never knew what time it was, didn't worry about whether we went to bed or not.

Q: Isn't that a beautiful background to think about?

Adm. T.: Oh, it is. And it's still the same way, when my two sisters get together. So the fact that I had the same nickname, if anybody said, Jimmy, I would answer.

But I went to Pensacola in March of 1929. En route I had some leave and I went to New York. I had a acute attack of appendicitis and I was taken to a civilian hospital in New York

City. My blood count was very high and they wanted to operate, and I said, "No, wait a minute. I'm on my way to Pensacola, you can't operate on me." And they said, "We may have to." And I said, "Well, if there's going to be an operation to be done, I'm going to get an ambulance and go to the Navy hospital, because this is a civilian hospital and I can't afford an operation here." So they said, "Well, we'll put on an ice pack and we'll watch you during the night and check your blood count again tomorrow." The next day the blood count was a lot better, and I felt pretty good, so I kept a little rubber ice bottle under my belt and went on, went to some parties and danced, and the girls thought I was a pretty cool customer, with an ice pack on me. Anyway, I went on to Pensacola and I wanted to get into that place by that time so bad, I thought I'd better not mention this appendix. It was still bothering me a little bit. I'd had some trouble with it before - kind of a chronic thing. Every now and then I'd have these flare-ups, and, as luck would have it, the day I got to Pensacola I had one of my worst pains right when I was taking the entrance physical exam in Pensacola, which is a pretty tough physical. I didn't say anything about it.

Q: This was immediately after the New York attack?

Adm. T.: Yes, I just went right on down. I was in New York for only a few days, and had another flare-up while I was taking the physical, but I thought I'd better not say anything about it because maybe they wouldn't pass me, so I went ahead with the physical and I passed it. Then I went to the sick bay and turned in, and said, "I've got an appendix attack." The doctor said, "Well, it's not too bad, I guess. Your blood count's not too high. Stay here overnight." Which I did and I got up the next day and it seemed to be all right, so I went ahead and got through Pensacola.

I had a wonderful instructor, my first instructor. We started out in seaplanes, at that time. His name was Lamson-Scrivener. He was a Marine, and he really knew how to teach, so I was very happy to have him. On my first check the check instructor didn't seem to be too happy with the way I could pick out the wind and land right into it. I put it on a little too hot, not with the nose way up and let it drop in, but I squeaked by that check, and I still didn't think I was doing too well, and lo and behold, I got to my final check, and so the squadron commander walked out, and who was he? Gerry Bogan. That almost scared me out of my skin. I thought, my last encounter with that fellow was when I laughed and he thought I was laughing at him, I guess. But he came out and he said, "Take off," so I took off and did some pylon turns, and he took me up and had me do wing-overs, and I thought the test was just beginning, and then he knocked the stick out of my hand, and dove down, and came in and landed, got out of the plane and he said, "Well, you can fly." I thought he was going to say, "Down, you're no good." He said, "I can tell by the way you do wing-overs. No problem." But I don't know whether he knew - I don't think he knew who

I was, that I was the plebe who had laughed so loud and had made him so mad.

Q: You didn't remind him, I'm sure.

Adm. T.: I didn't remind him, I'm sure. Well, that was interesting. Then we went on through to land planes, and on my first check in land planes, Lieutenant Lobaugh gave me the check, and gave me a down.

Q: He did!

Adm. T.: Yes.

Q: What was the matter with him?

Adm. T.: Well, with me, I guess. He said when he cut the engine I didn't push the stick over fast enough. I'll admit I didn't bounce him out of his seat, but apparently that's what he wanted. He was very concerned about students that would have an engine failure and wouldn't soon enough stick the nose over and keep flying speed. That was a thing that he was hepped on. But I felt that I'd stuck the nose over fast enough. I didn't want to just spoil all the lift on the airplane, and why stick the nose straight down when you want to look around and find a field to land on, and I didn't think that I was going to spin in anyway. I would keep gliding speed.

But he bilged me on that, and, of course, that really worried me. By that time, I felt if I didn't get through Pensacola I'd go out and shoot myself. I really believed it. I wanted it more than anything I'd ever wanted. And I was playing tennis - I grew up playing tennis - and I enjoyed the game very much and I was pretty good. But the next day after I'd gotten that down, I was out playing, I think it was a weekend, and I was playing tennis and sprained my ankle, stepped off the edge of the court trying to go after a ball and had a bad ankle sprain. So I had to be off of it for some time and all this time, here, this down was shaking me. I had to get two ups then by two other instructors, otherwise I was out. And they were throwing people out right and left. I've forgotten the percentage, but I think we graduated about 35 percent of the students we started with. Of course, some of them got killed, but others failed flight training and ground school.

Anyway, that worried about ten pounds off of me. Then I managed to fly two ups and finally wound up standing 1 in my class both in ground school and in flying, which was something of a surprise to me since I'd done so poorly at the Naval Academy. They usually sent people where they wanted to go when they stood 1, and I had requested a fighter squadron, and I was ordered to VF-1, which was the famous high hat squadron.

Q: You requested it?

Adm. T.: Yes, and they gave it to me.

Well, I arrived at VF-1 and who should be the skipper?

Gerry Bogan!

Q: Where was this?

Adm. T.: Right here, at North Island, on West Beach. But by that time I wasn't quite as afraid of him as I used to be, and he was a fine gentleman and we had a good squadron.

When I became engaged to be married, I was in that squadron and Gerry was the skipper, and I told him I was planning to get married at such-and-such a time, and he said, "No, you can't do that. I've got other plans for you. We're going on a cruise." I didn't know about the cruise. So we just got married a little earlier.

Q: Tell me your wife's maiden name.

Adm. T.: Madalyn Jones, who is the daughter of Dr. Leland D. Jones. She was born right here in San Diego and at the time we met, she was a senior at San Diego State College majoring in music and education.

Q: Before you start on your cruise, I'd like to have you tell me about the kind of training that you did with this high hat squadron and why it was called the "high hat", the people in it, and . . .

Adm. T.: Long before I got to this squadron, I understand that one of the commanding officers, way back, and I don't know which one, flew out to land aboard a carrier to go on a cruise, and he'd landed aboard in a high hat, and from then on it was always the High Hat Squadron. This is second-hand information.

Q: It was called that when you went there?

Adm. T.: Oh, yes, each plane had a high hat on it. That was the official squadron insignia.

Well, this squadron was quite famous for flying in a nine-plane formation with all the planes tied together by 21-thread manila line and taking off with all the nine planes tied together, and going up and doing maneuvers, and landing without any lines broken. This wasn't as difficult as it might seem. Landing and take off was the most difficult because you had to all start at just the same time. If somebody would get behind and couldn't catch up we'd either pull him into somebody else or break the manila.

Q: How did you do training for that?

Adm. T.: You just took off in close formation and stayed in close formation, doing loops and everything else, and come back and don't ever get out too far. This was normal anyway. Then we decided - well, we always fly close and nobody ever gets out too far, why don't we tie them together and make a little interesting show out of it to demonstrate the proficiency of formation flying in air shows, Cleveland air races, and things like that. This was one of the things that VF-1 did at the national air shows.

Q: That's what I was going to ask you because I know you were in many shows.

Adm. T.: Sometimes they would have two different squadrons and sometimes one - usually just one, and they would do various things, and in some cases would demonstrate the dive bombing technique with these little practice bombs with a shotgun shell in them to make a flash when they hit the ground. Of course, one of the most famous were the Three Sea Hawks, but I was never a member of the Three Sea Hawks. Tomlinson, Davis, and Storrs were the three sea hawks, and they did fantastic things, like flying on their backs right down low over the ground in front of the stands, but they had their carburetors fixed so they could do this, which was nice.

Q: Did you make a movie?

Adm. T.: When I was in VF-1, MGM wanted to make a movie and they received Navy cooperation. Lieutenant Commander Spig Wead, who had been a commanding officer of a fighter squadron, perhaps VF-1, I think it was - he wrote the story. He was at that time paralyzed due to a fall down some stairs going to work one morning, right here in Coronado.

Q: Not in an airplane crash!

Adm. T.: Not in an airplane crash - ever, but he remained paralyzed for the rest of his life, but he became a writer. He wrote a lot of good stories. Some were published in the Saturday Evening Post, and he wrote Hell Divers, which is a story about a fighter squadron - this was a two-seater fighter squadron, it had guns in front and a rear gunner in the cockpit. Wallace Beery played the part of a chief petty officer, rear gunner, and Clark Gable was another chief petty officer in the squadron, and John Milljohn was the commanding officer. We did quite a bit of flying in this movie and it was one of the first movies of a military squadron where they showed this tight formation flying and the peel-off dive bombing and all those various gunnery practices that we did, firing at a sleeve towed by another airplane. It showed all of this. There was one three-plane section in VF-1 led by Lieutenant Herbert S. Duckworth that was selected to do most of the flying and the difficult maneuvers. Southwick was one of his wing men - Bud Southwick, Edward Page Southwick - and John S. Thach was the other wing man. We flew together for two years and it became so second nature it was just like walking, flying in the same formation. Duckworth didn't have to give any signals. We could tell by looking at the back of his neck what he was thinking about and what he was going to do. So he never worried about it. We just did them because we were right with him, just like I was his left arm and Bud was his right arm. It was as simple as that. But I did 75 hours flying in that movie, and of course we didn't get paid for it, because the Navy was cooperating and that was part of the Navy's cooperation.

George Hill was the director and a very fine person. He was sort of a perfectionist. He would do scenes over and over again and get them just right, except one scene where I was supposed to depict a landing on a sandy beach on an island and then ground loop the plane at the end, and it would almost crash but not quite. It was ground looping, so the tail would rise up and the plane would spin around facing the other way, and they had all these cameras set up. They didn't require an actual landing but I pushed full throttle and got my tail up and came into the camera, just going at about the speed that you would have if you landed on the sand like that, and then kicked on one brake. I knew this airplane very well, I knew just how hard to brake to make the tail rise (without flipping over on my back), then spin around. He only took that shot that once. He said, "I can't let you do it again."

Q: Aren't you glad?

Adm. T.: No, I could do it again. I mean, I wasn't doing anything dangerous, but it looked dangerous. The most dangerous thing - I really almost killed myself - was because they had to have process shots so you'd take the background of a picture and then on a stage sound screen, they would have the characters that they wanted to show in the foreground, then project the film with the sky and hangars and horizon and everything, taken from an airplane with a camera on it, (with the camera on the wing pointing forward, for example). In the studio they would put the movie actors in a fake cockpit right in front of that screen and shoot it all over again, so it would look like the actors were in the air, and that was known as a process shot. So they put this 80-pound camera on the wing of my plane out near the wing tip and I was supposed to come down and do a slow roll right in front of the hangar and almost hit it. I went up to altitude and did a slow roll to the right. The camera was heavy and I had to carry a lot of left aileron, but the roll worked out all right. But I was pretty stupid because when I came down to make the run, I was in such a position that I rolled to the left - (it looked at the moment like it might be better). When I tried to roll to the left, I got halfway around on my back and that 80-pound camera wouldn't come on over and I was on my back headed for the hangar. So I had to roll back the other way. This process shot turned out to be a pretty good thriller, but I wouldn't do that again for any amount of money. Hell Divers was shown in various theaters for 15 or 20 years. I haven't seen it on TV yet.

We had a wonderful publication, manual, in those days, and I might, just for the moment, go back about 100 years in the U.S. Navy. The ships one hundred years ago had guns to shoot, so the Navy Department devised a training manual called <u>Orders</u>

for Gunnery Exercises, with the short title "OGE", and it prescribed certain rules to make the firing realistic as close to battle conditions as possible. Well, about 1925 or 1927, a couple of years before I went into aviation, the aviators in the Navy decided that's a good thing, we'll have an OGE for our aviation squadrons, too, which they did. I had the good fortune to assist in revising the OGE from time to time, the first time was in VF-1. The reason it had to be revised - and this was one of the good things about it, it wasn't a dead book written too many years ago. Every year it had to be revised by a board - for the fighter plane part, composed of fighter pilots from the fleet, and the torpedo plane part of it, by pilots, from a torpedo squadron, and so forth - all with the set goal and objective of making it more and more realistic. Now, of course, in every outfit you'll find one or two real good sea lawyers, and if there was any loophole in one of the rules to permit them to get a better score by slipping through that loophole, they would do it. So eliminating the loopholes kept everybody as honest as possible.

In fighter type aircraft, aeriel gunnery exercises were conducted by shooting at a cloth sleeve towed by another aircraft. The firing runs were made by approaching the target sleeve from various angles, each run from a different angle specifically prescribed in the OGE.

There was one little attack, firing at a sleeve, called a humming bird. You were supposed to be depicting the idea that you're sneaking up underneath a big bomber, and supposedly, the crew of the bomber wouldn't be able to see you, and you'd sneak up under him and fire. Well, you were supposed to come up and shoot and then fly away. What did people do? They came up and skidded and hung there until finally they got the end of the gun almost on the sleeve and then let go and all the bullet holes were in a space the size of the palm of your hand. Well, that wasn't very realistic. So we had to change that rule, and say, now, you've got to continuously close the range. If you hesitate and drop back a little bit, the referee would call you out, and you were disqualified for that record practice, and you couldn't have another chance to get an E on your airplane. An E was very difficult to get. You had to train a little harder and be pretty good at it.

Q: I wish that on the tape it would show the picture of how you demonstrate, but unfortunately, fighter pilots talk with their hands.

Adm. T.: I mentioned Bubbles Fisher before and he was in a Saratoga squadron, not VF-1, it was another fighter squadron, VF-6, and he was a terrific fighter pilot. Given equal altitude nobody could beat him, and he was physically a tremendous person. One time, he had a forced landing at sea and he swam some phenomenal distance - I don't know whether it was 75 or 100 miles, but finally, having gotten rid of his clothes, one afternoon he came out of the sea on a beach up here between San Diego and Los Angeles and, it frightened all the people on the beach. They thought he was some sea monster, so they called the police and got him arrested, and he had a hard time convincing them that he had been forced down quite a distance at sea and just swam in. He finally did by getting on the telephone. So they brought him some clothes, and let him go.

Other people in VF-1, the High Hat Squadron - the executive officer under Gerry Bogan, Alan Flagg, who was a very fine gentleman, Strangler Lewis, who was a wrestler at the Naval Academy and looked it. He was a good fighter pilot, too, one of the best. Apollo Soucek, who held the worlds altitude record at that time. Then there was Bill Hamilton, as well as Herbert S. Duckworth, who led my section. We had a wonderful thing called a camera gun, and this camera was synchoronized with a firing trigger so that you could go up and fight each other with a camera gun, and it had a little stop-watch in it. That showed up in the corner of every frame of the film. Before you left the ground all the watches in the camera guns were synchoronized, and you could go up and practice fighting and then come back and look at the film and you could tell exactly, there was no argument about who shot who first. This was something that was unique in the U.S. Navy. No other aviation squadrons had it.

Q: Wonderful training technique!

Adm. T.: Oh, it was a tremendous trainer. It solved all arguments, and it would show on the film just how much you missed and you could figure out why.

Jack Tate was another section leader, and he was a fabulous character. He was full of stories of his experiences that he told plainly as if they were true stories, but they were so fantastic that they were unbelievable, so we didn't believe most of them. He became noted for telling tall tales. Later, I ran into him again. It was as a test pilot and so I have a little follow-on for that.

Bubbles Fisher was out doing some dive bombing training. Sometimes we had a destroyer that could tow a target for us. This day there was one small cloud out there and the destroyer was steaming down wind and the cloud stayed right over the target, and it made Bubbles mad. He flew down alongside the destroyer to try to get him to change course. He didn't so Bubbles thought, well, I'll just dive on him and scare him and make him do it. So he dove down and he waited too late to pull out and he pulled his wings off, and that's how he was killed. He was quite a gent while he lasted.

Q: I'd like to have you tell me, if you can, evaluate common characteristics of these people, that made them fine fighter pilots.

Adm. T.: I think probably the most common characteristic was their love of competition. We had a soft ball team, and you could see it there. The good fighter pilots worked real hard at soft ball, and when they went to steal second base they weren't kidding. They wanted to get there. They had to have a certain amount of aggressiveness, and then, of course, being able to capitalize on one's experience and get better each day and each year. Those are the things that I think were common characteristics of good fighter pilots, and I can talk a little more about that when I get to the point where I had command of a squadron.

Q: They certainly had to be fearless!

Adm. T.: Well, they liked doing what they were doing. The first time I ever flew in an airplane, on the take-off, it was frightening. I tried to hang on to something, you know, just like suddenly going on a roller coaster start, it makes you catch your breath. But it wasn't long before we lost all that feeling, and I really felt more at home with this little frame and canvas, fabric around me, in the air and didn't feel any fear of it being high, like high places, but I've always had a fear of standing on the edge of a tall building. I don't like high places. When I'm in an airplane I don't feel like I'm in a high place. It's just a different medium and I'm at home in it.

Q: Do you feel in a plane that you're the master of your own destiny?

Adm. T.: Yes, that you know what to do, and you never think

you're going to get killed. Just flying. Now, fighting in the war, that's a little different thing.

Q: But there would have to be a certain, not reckless, because if you were reckless, you didn't live long, but a certain lack of worry of death.

Adm. T.: Yes, that's right. You had to be able to face an emergency, such as a forced landing, when you didn't know where you were going to land, or how. You had to have a feeling that you could handle the situation. Or if your plane caught on fire. I've never had to jump, I never particularly wanted to jump, but wouldn't hesitate if the airplane was on fire and burning up. No use in going down in flames. Those things - it's your routine, daily. Fear, I think, has much to do with the unknown. We all fear the unknown. We can imagine something pretty horrible, if we don't know what it is. But if you know about it and you live with it every day, you lose a lot of the normal fear that's in a human being.

Q: You're saying, too, I think, that the more finely you're trained, when you know and you lose the fear because of the training.

Adm. T.: Speaking of Ducky Duckworth - his name was Herbert S. but we called him Ducky - we would frequently, Bud Southwick and I, fly along close with our wings stuck in between his wings and the tail, and we used to claim that every now and then he would go to sleep. He didn't, but we used to accuse him of this. He'd be flying along and we would decide he was asleep. We used this excuse to play a little trick on him. One of us would slide up and, if on the righthand side, put the left wing right over his horizontal stabilizer, his flipper, that controlled his up and down - nose up and nose down - movement. Just slide it right over there and touch it and push it down so it would jump him up in the seat and bump him down.

One time we came back from a flight, having done this, and Gerry Bogan had noted in Saturday morning inspections red paint on the silver left wing of my plane and Bud Southwick's plane. Now the line chief knew what was going on and Gerry said, "How did that red paint get on there? We've got red tails. What have you guys been doing?" The line chief said, "Oh, captain, these young kids when they move these planes around in the hangar sometimes brush the wing against a tail. I'm going to have to have a training program for them to show them how to be careful moving airplanes around." Then he looked around at Bud Southwick and Bud is standing there perfectly straight-faced.

But we could do this, we felt, with perfect safety, and as it turned out it was. We knew what we were doing. We didn't put the wing underneath the tail and make it fly up right into us. This would be risking destruction of government property. This was 1930 and 1931.

The skipper designated me as squadron navigator and I had

to calibrate all the compasses and also keep track of the navigation when we were flying from the carrier and so forth. Sometimes I would fly in a scouting type airplane that had radio with a radioman in the rear seat. One time a new airplane came for the skipper and I had to calibrate the compass. It was very difficult to calibrate, one of the tough ones, for some reason, but I thought I had it all right. We were flying out on one of the exercises from the carrier and as Gerry Bogan started to head for home after attacking something, he was going about 40° off course according to my navigation, so I called him and told him that. And he said, "I'm heading 350," and I said, "No, you're not. I'm heading 350 and it's about 40° off." So somebody else spoke up and said, that's right, they backed me up and so we came on in and he said, "Well, recalibrate that thing again. We would have been led off and gotten lost." I worked on it and finally took a small compass and started moving it all around, and discovered there was some magnetism in the wing of this airplane, and we cut it open and found a little magnet that had nothing to do with the airplane, it was left in there apparently when the wing was produced.

Q: Did you ever know what caused the magnet to be in there?

Adm. T.: No. Apparently, it was either inadvertent or deliberate sabotage. It was placed in a place where it would certainly pull the compass off a certain heading, but not on others.

Thach #1 - 51

I doubt if it was done by anybody in the squadron because the wing had not been cut, so it would have to have gotten in there when the wing was manufactured.

Q: Who manufactured these airplanes?

Adm. T.: This was an F8C-4, Curtiss. It was manufactured in Buffalo, New York.

Q: When you're speaking of VF-1, you're speaking of being on the Saratoga?

Adm. T.: That's right. It was a Saratoga squadron.

Q: And you spoke of a cruise being delayed - I mean your marriage was accelerated because you were going on a cruise. Where did you go on your cruise?

Adm. T.: It was a cruise that involved the big fleet problem, fleet exercise, simulation of combat operations, including search problems, one side against the other, and it wound up finally with the problem of attacking and defending the Panama Canal. So it covered a good bit of the eastern Pacific. It was always interesting to me that after landing aboard a carrier for three or four months at a time, and not landing anywhere else, when you brought your airplanes back and came in, say, to North Island and landed, it seemed much more difficult to land on a field than on a carrier, because on a carrier once the hook had you, the landing is over - you're in.

Q: But that carrier must look like an awfully tiny spot to hit when you're in the air, doesn't it?

Adm. T.: It does when you're at any altitude, but it just seems like home. I remember one cruise. Ducky Duckworth was trying to help lower the interval between aircraft landings. This is important because you don't want the carrier to have to run into the wind any longer than it needs to, so there's always competition between squadrons and between carriers, especially, for example, if the Saratoga and the Lexington were operating jointly in the same formation, and they'd give the signal to land, we'd always try to get in and get our planes on board before the Lexington and vice versa. Well, Duckworth decided that if normally the best wire to catch for a safe landing was wire No. 2 or 3 . . .

Q: Is that from the front or the back?

Adm. T.: From the ramp, the stern, counting No. 1 wire the first one you would get to. This brings you in so there's little danger, from a pitching deck, of hitting the ramp instead of being high enough to catch the wire and still down soon enough so you don't hit the barrier. Steel cables are strung across the deck up to eight feet high attached to supports to form several barriers. The barriers can be raised when a plane is landing and quickly lowered to allow a plane to taxi over them. Ducky said that, now, if we all just not catch No. 1 or 2 wire - there are nine wires, incidentally - let's all catch 7 or 8, and then we can get out of the gear in a hurry and the next guy right behind you, he can come in, and they'll be quicker. Somebody said, "Wait a minute. You might miss 8 and also 9, and then you're in the barrier." And Ducky said, "I don't think so, I can prove it. Next time I'm out I'm going to catch No. 1 wire. The time after that No. 2. The time after that No. 3, and so on, and then I'll catch No. 9 wire. And I'll show you that it can be done." And he was plenty good. If anybody could do it, I thought he could. So we were all watching every time he came in, and sure enough, he caught No. 1, 2, and so on. Each time he caught a different one, No. 5, 6, 7, he caught No. 8, and he almost caught No. 9 the next time, but he missed it by about an inch with his hook and went into the barrier.

Q: Ruined the airplane!

Adm. T.: Yes. Well, to a degree. Not a complete washout.

Q: Did it hurt him?

Adm. T.: No. The barriers are made to take up the kinetic energies slowly enough so that it is not exactly like a collision with a stone wall.

Q: What did you do? Did you follow his suggestion?

Adm. T.: Everybody gave him a bad time about that. To a degree, we tried to, but we didn't want to try to catch No. 8 or 9.

Q: You didn't want to press your luck too much?

Adm. T.: No. Neither did he after that.

Q: Admiral, I have a note that says that you were recognized as one of the Navy's aerial gunnery experts and that you repeatedly got E scores in every type of combat aircraft that you flew. Could you amplify that or explain it? Perhaps tell me what's involved in getting an E score?

Adm. T.: An E score in any official gunnery practice means that you get a prescribed high percentage of hits, for example, if you're shooting a fixed machine gun, you've got to get a pretty high percentage of all the rounds that you fire into the target. In my case, I think that I can reflect back to my father, who, long before I was in high school, taught me how to shoot and I'll never forget some of his instructions. He said, "When you're shooting at a bird on the wing, such as a quail, (we had wonderful quail country there), shoot where the bird is going to be when the bullets get there, not where he is now, and remember at the ranges which you have to shoot a bird that he can travel two, three, sometimes five, feet while your bullets are going from the end of the gun to the bird." I learned that basically as a very young boy. As a matter of fact, the very first quail he ever let me shoot at came after I had watched him and he was teaching me all the time when he was shooting when I was barely old enough to even think of it, and finally he gave me his big heavy 12-gauge mule kicker, and we had this beautiful English setter, which I could talk about for a long time but I won't, just suffice it to say this dog never missed a single - I have seen him start to clear a rail fence, having no scent on this side, he thought maybe there was something over on the other side, and he got a scent of a covey of quail just when he was in the air, after he'd left the ground. He reached down with all four feet and grabbed the top rail and froze there, because the covey was right down over the fence, and he didn't move a muscle - he didn't flush the covey until we got up there. So I was steeped in all this wonderful life of outdoors, and I learned how to handle a gun. The first time, as I said, he gave me this heavy gun, and he knew there was a single nearby and the dog pinned it down, and he got me just in the right position and gave me the gun and he said, "Now, remember what I've told you." Then he flushed the quail. Well, I was so intent on aiming at the right place and I squeezed the trigger off, just like he said, and that gun kicked me flat on my back.

When I got up he said, "Well, you got the bird but you didn't keep your feet very well."

Shooting at a moving target in the air is a very similar thing. In other words, this was a case where my work was my hobby that I grew up on. I think I had a head start on most of the youngsters who hadn't had similar experience. I could sort of sense how much lead to take, if any, on the angle off the target. And one of the wonderful things about the orders for gunnery exercises was the fact that they required you to make these angle-off deflection shots, we used to call them, where your target is going across in front of you instead of straight astern of it for a no-deflection shot. I'll talk some more about that when I get into wartime duties.

Of course, everything depends on not only opportunity to train but how one trained. You may learn more if you can train with just 2 or 3 rounds per burst, where in record practice you may be firing a burst of twelve or more on each approach. Be sure that you study the target when you get it back and see where those two or three rounds went and realize just where in your approach you squeezed the trigger, you get an idea of how close you are to making a mistake and missing, and you learn from this, by doing it over and over again.

Q: And you had an E score in every type of craft that you flew?

Adm. T.: Yes, that's true. It just seemed to come almost second nature, and I loved to train. So I was doing something that I just wanted to do all my life.

Q: You fit into your environment!

Adm. T.: Yes, I guess in my early days in the Navy I was far better fitted for this sort of thing than I realized. And, of course, I guess every young man likes competition, and there was always terrific competition between not only individuals but between squadrons to see how well you could do. Just like any other contest.

When my tour of duty was up in fighter squadron 1, (the High Hat Squadron based aboard the Saratoga,) I was ordered to duty in the experimental division at the Naval Air Base, Norfolk, Hampton Roads, Virginia. This served at that time, similar to the test center at Patuxent River, although Patuxent River combines the test work that we used to do at Norfolk and the work that used to be done at Anacostia in Washington, D.C. together in one test center. In Norfolk we had the job of conducting all roughwater tests of experimental seaplanes, testing the aircraft that were proposed by various manufacturers, experimental aircraft, the new carrier-based types we tested by landing on a deck that was built into the field at Norfolk. We also conducted certain gunnery trials, evaluations day and night, of various types. So this was a wonderful opportunity to fly all different kinds of naval aircraft. Of course, we had some test-bed types there continuously for the purpose of testing certain equipment. We received the first experimental

type from each manufacturer when there was a competition to
see which aircraft if any, should be considered for a production
contract. And, believe me, they sent some strange looking airplanes to the test section. In those days, it wasn't necessary that the contractor demonstrate the aircraft. All he had
to do was get it to the Navy, somehow. And we often wondered
whether he brought it on a flat car or really dared to fly it.
We had nicknames for them - one of them we called "The Pleasant
Surprise," this was sarcasm because it had the gliding angle
of a brick, and as soon as you reduced the throttle, why, the
nose would drop straight down and you could do a very good job
of landing, if you didn't put it back on in a hurry. Another
one was an amphibian type we called "The Tower of Jewels"
because it just seemed to go straight up for ever and finally
you got to the cockpit and it looked very topheavy to me, and
it also had other problems and could not be accepted for production.

Q: Did you ever find any that you refused to fly?

Adm. T.: No, because we didn't know whether they were any good
or not until we tried to fly them. We found some we refused
to fly a second time. Once was enough. Not often, but usually
it was when you got into testing certain things like a carrier
approach where you have to have a controlled slow speed tight
turn, and then suddenly, when you got the cut from the landing
signal officer, chop everything off and catch a wire.

I remember that Boeing Aircraft Company for a long time really had a corner on the fighter type market. They produced fighters for the Navy and the Army Air Corps. For example, the Boeing F4B was also the P12E in the Army Air Corps, a pursuit type. So it got to the point where no one else thought of building a fighter, but then about this time the Navy had a competition and several other manufacturers entered it. The Boeing aircraft was a low-wing aircraft, the XF6B. Then there was a little company that sent down an aircraft that - a little company by the name of Grumman that nobody'd ever heard of - and they went down an airplane that looked like it had - well, a little fat-chested thing like a dove. I remember I was on the project of the Grumman and Doc Purvis, who was another member of the experimental division, had the Boeing, and one of our tests was to line the aircraft up on the runways - on the field, (we really didn't have runways inthose days), it was a grass field - and at the word "Go," see who could - which plane would get in the air first, and the Grumman got in the air and I was able to make a diving pass at the Boeing before it got off the ground. And the representatives of the Boeing Company were mad as hops at me. They said, you were just showing off, and I said, "Well, let me get in the Boeing and put Doc Purvis in this airplane and see how we do. I'll do my best to show off there, too." And the same thing happened to me. I couldn't get it off the ground until he had his in the air and turned and made a pass. But the worst thing about it was that on a carrier approach, when you got down slow in a turn, it did a stall whip-off on the high wing and dropped into the ground and this wasn't a very good characteristic for a carrier landing.

I remember when Admiral Ernie King was Chief of the Bureau of Aeronautics, we had just about completed these tests and he wanted to come down and see the aircraft and see how they were doing. So Doc said, "I'm pretty familiar with the XF6B. I think I can make a good tight carrier-based turn and maybe it won't fall off. Let me demonstrate it." He did and the wing actually hit the ground before the wheels did, and he cartwheeled a little bit, but Admiral King said, "That's all I wanted to see," got in his airplane and flew back to Washington.

For a moment, I'd like to go back to VF-1, High Hat Squadron. When Lieutenant Commander Arthur W. Radford relieved Lieutenant Commander Gerald Bogan, and then Radford had the squadron, and I was his wing man. One of the things I remember - at that time we were having some trouble with fabric on the tail of the aircraft. You know, the tails of those aircraft, the F8C4 type, two-seater fighter with the wing and tail surfaces were framed with fabric cover, and we were diving these aircraft at terminal velocity, and sometimes we'd come back with part of the fabric shredded off of the tail. The fabric was getting weak and old before it was due for major overhaul, and we were quite concerned about this and Lieutenant Commander Radford made it a point when the commanding officer of the Saratoga came to inspect the squadron, to tell him about this. The commanding officer was Captain Douglas, and I felt at that time, right or wrong, that he wasn't very close to the problems of the squadrons aboard his ship, that he paid more attention to other things, running the ship and so forth, and that he just didn't seem too interested in our problems, which of course, was part of his ship. So Radford explained about the fabric becoming weaker before it should and this was a trouble that we thought ought to be corrected and that maybe the aircraft should be taken to overhaul for this purpose a little earlier. Douglas was a big, raw-boned individual, and he said, "Well, let me see the tails of some of these airplanes." So he came down the line of aircraft and the first one he got to, he said, "This looks all right," and he took his two fingers and kind of punched on it and his whole hand went right through the fabric of the tail. So that was one way that Radford proved the point, and later, of course, he became chairman of the Joint Chiefs of Staff. He was a very fine fighter squadron commander. He always looked at the large picture of why are we here, what are we doing, and what are we trying to accomplish, in the sense of using the whole strategic problem of the Pacific Ocean and her relationship with other countries, and he used to talk to us frequently about what Japan was doing, what they might do, and how we had to be ready and why we should be ready because we had to maintain control of the sea and keep our merchant fleet plying the oceans without being interfered with.

Q: You were telling me that you had an unusual recollection relating to Admiral Radford.

Adm. T.: Yes, this may be a strange way to remember the man who later became chairman of the Joint Chief of Staff, but I also remember him for many other good reasons. But I was assigned as his wing man one time during a large fleet exercise when flight quarters suddenly sounded. I knew that we were scheduled as soon as a certain target was discovered to go over and hit it and then come back and land aboard. So, when flight quarters sounded, I had to go to the bathroom, but I just felt, well, I can wait, we'll be back pretty soon, and I went ahead and manned the plane on time and we got in the air and we did hit this target and had a little simulated fight with another squadron that was defending it, and then we climbed back up to altitude and Radford got word that supply ships of the opposing side had been discovered, but they were quite some distance away, so we flew on and found them and attacked them, and then finally got back over the carrier, but they didn't land us, they just kept us wheeling around there because they wanted to wait to get another squadron in the air. So about four and a half to five hours had passed, and my bladder was about to pop . . .

Q: I gather there were no relief tubes in the planes in those days?

Adm. T.: Not in those days. Some people carried a little pint milk bottle, but I didn't have one at that time in my plane and I had a rear seat passenger, and I thought maybe I can climb out on the wing without getting any splattered on him. This was a new rear seat man and I didn't know whether he knew how to fly her very well or not, so I tried him out and he held the wings pretty steady, but when he realized what I was going to do, I was going to climb out on the wing and relieve myself, he had a horrified look on his face. I don't know whether he thought maybe I might get some on him or whether he was afraid I'd fall off the wing. I'd get my foot out on the wing and start to get out and he'd let the wing fall off and I'd have to scramble back in. I realized this was probably the first time this young man had ever tried to fly.

Q: What would you hold on to?

Adm. T.: The struts. You see this was a biplane, so I'd hold on to the struts leading between the fuselage and the upper wing. I'd climbed out on the wing before, so I knew I could do it, but an experienced pilot would be flying the airplane, and this fellow was anything but experienced. I discovered later this was the first time he'd ever been asked to fly, although he'd flown as a passenger quite a bit. I tried this two or three times, having pulled away from the formation a certain distance so I'd have a little room in case he wasn't flying very straight - I wouldn't trust him to try and fly in formation. Well, about that time I looked over and Radford was zooming up and down, which means "join me, join up." I suppose he wondered what I was - what kind of shenanigans I was trying to pull. So I reluctantly went back into formation, having tried to get out on the wing two or three times. Finally we landed aboard after five and a half hours, and I could hardly get out of the airplane I was in such misery, but that taught me a lesson that whenever you have a chance to go you'd better go.

Q: I'm sure that Admiral Radford would be surprised to know what incident calls him to your mind!

Adm. T.: I think he probably would, although he's a very good friend.

Q: I gathered from your previous comments that he would have been an effective influence in your Navy career, too.

Adm. T.: He definitely was. This man at a very young age understood the whole strategic situation in the world, and he used to talk to us about it.

Q: I would think putting yourself in the picture at the proper place would have been helpful in doing your job better.

Adm. T.: Oh, no question about it. He taught me by his example in what he did that no matter what job you have, try to relate it to the objective, not only of the whole Navy, but the whole country. What do we want the United States to be.

We want to be sure that certain things do not happen to this country, such as being squeezed back on two percent of the earth's surface, which is the United States. We could feel free on two percent of the earth's surface and that's all. If we're surrounded by people who want to do away with us and 98% of the world is controlled by them, that's the beginning of the end. In fact, it's very near the end, because we would have no commerce without being under the control of another country and we would have no place to go.

Q: That's remarkable, isn't it?

Adm. T.: I think so, especially as a lieutenant commander. Now, he was a very young man, yet he saw this whole picture, and he always related what we were doing individually to accomplishing the mission of the whole Navy and the best interests of the United States. He used to say often to us, "Now, when you're deciding whether or not to do something, start with your country. If it's not good for your country, it's probably not good for your Navy. If it's not good for the Navy, it's not good for your squadron. If it's not good for your squadron, it certainly isn't good for you, so let it alone. Don't push it."

Q: Wonderful advice! Did you try to follow that when you became commanding officer?

Adm. T.: I did, yes. There were other people that influenced me as well, as far as leadership is concerned. But I think Radford is one of the most prominent. When I reported to the Joint Chief of Staff as a member of the Weapon System Evaluation Group in Washington, he was chairman of the Joint Chiefs, and I, of course, saw him a few times interveningly. He was commander-in-chief, Pacific, during the Korean War.

Q: To return now . . .

Adm. T.: Back at Hampton Roads and the experimental division. I mentioned that one of the section leaders in VF-1 under Bogan was a character by the name of Jack Tate who always told tall stories. The day I reported for duty as a test pilot, Jack Tate and "Country" Moore - Edward Peerman Moore, who was on the Olympic crew in 1922 that won the Olympic crew championship, I think it was in England - anyway he was called "Country" Moore because he, I suppose like many of us, came from either a small town or a farm, but he had actions and speech such that the nickname seemed to fit him, although he was a very smart man in many ways. He had the rough surface and seeming basic good sense of many American farmers. Well, Jack Tate, "Country" Moore, and - I believe Doc Purvis were already there - anyway, they met me and said, "There's a very important test we're just completing. We want to finish it today, although you just reported and you still have on your blue service dress uniform, you can just put on a pair of goggles and come out and fly this airplane." Well, I had just walked in 30 minutes before then and reported to the skipper of the division who was Jimmy Dyer, and I left him and walked out and they grabbed me and said, "We got to finish this test. We have flown it and we want you to fly it to get another opinion." I said, "What is it and where is it?" They pointed it out and said, "Country" Moore's flying it now, and it was a torpedo plane, a TG, and they said, "The problem with this plane is that it has a difficult horizontal stabilizer control. It gets nose-heavy and it's hard to hold the nose up and it needed some kind of a fix on it, so we put these paddle-type balances - manufactured these paddle-type balances and put them on, so that when you do move the flipper (we called it, that's the horizontal stabilizer) up, it helped you to move it up further, and likewise, nose-down and nose-up. It helped." I went out and I saw "Country" flying this thing and he was going along kind of like a roller coaster, that's the way he was flying, and I said, "What's he doing that for?" And they said, "Oh, he's just sort of testing it out." And I said, "All right." So when he landed I got in the thing and they said, "Now, what we want you to do is to make a landing on this deck. There's one wire across there and you can catch that, first make a three-point landing, and just catch the wire normally with the hook, and then come 'round the next time and make a two-point landing. Keep your tail up. Sometimes you have to come in a little fast and have good control and just roll it on the deck and catch the wire. And then on the third one we want you to come in but not let your wheels touch the deck. Keep your wheels off the deck and just hook it in free flight, and see how the plane does." So, I said, "Well, I'll try. I'll see what I can do." "Country" Moore came in, landed, and taxied up, and they went over and talked to him and he looked up at me and waved, and he gleefully got out of the plane, I thought a little too happily. Anyway, I took it off and pulled the nose up off the runway and it seemed to keep on coming up! I had to push it back. And then the nose went down. I pulled it up and I discovered why "Country" was flying like a roller coaster. I flew around a little bit then decided, well, I'd better get this over with, and flew in and in my up-and-down gyrations I finally got it at the right place and cut the gun, got on three points and caught the wire. They said, "That's fine. Take it away and do the second one, roll it on, and then free flight." I came down and tried to roll it on, but I missed the wire, so I went around again, and I said, "I'm going to do it right this time, and I got it on and the wire caught and stopped it. Then I went to try to do the catching of the wire in free flight without letting the wheels touch. I came in and apparently I was just a little bit too high, but since the plane was gyrating up and down, I thought, well, maybe I can try to keep the wheels off, and as I did I caught the wire, but I was pulling back on the stick - here I was in free flight, and the thing kept coming right back in my lap, and I tried to push it forward but it was too late. So it caught the wire and tried to fly on away but couldn't and, wham, right on the deck, and I remember two wheels going up, up past my right hand and one past my left, and it just busted the landing gear and everything all up.

I looked out and there those people were rolling in the grass, just laughing, saying, "The test is over, the test is finished." And they came over and I was mad as heck, and I said, "What did you do to me? Here, the first airplane I get in I crash it. I've never crashed an airplane before in my life." Well, they said, that's what we wanted. Somebody had to do it.

Q: That was a mean trick!

Adm. T.: Oh, yes. Typical of Jack Tate and "Country" Moore. Although they were very good friends for many years.

Q: Apparently it proved the point that the airplane was no good.

Adm. T.: Yes, the airplane was no good.

Q: But they knew that without you having to . . .

Adm. T.: Oh, sure! But they wanted somebody to finish the test, and they caught me just as I arrived. That was an interesting beginning.

Speaking of "Country" Moore, he and I were assigned to

rough-water tests of patrol seaplanes, the boat type, and he being senior to me, he was the pilot and I was the co-pilot. In the rough-water tests, we were required to make ten landings and ten take-offs in waves that were at least six feet high. Now, a six-foot wave doesn't seem very high. When you think you see a six-foot wave, you're seeing about a three-foot wave. A six-foot wave looks very high, especially when you're sitting on it in a little seaplane. But we had made several of the take-offs and landings in the thing (the XP2Y) and it was taking a beating . . .

Q: Who measures it so that you know that it's a six-foot wave?

Adm. T.: We had a barge out there and boats standing by, crash boats to pick us up in the water when we crashed the airplane, and often this happened, because the airplane was being tested and it didn't pass the test. That means you get wet.

Q: And they did have a device for knowing when it was . . .

Adm. T.: For knowing when it was six feet, yes. Often we'd wait for days for the wind - a storm or something to build the waves up so you could get six-foot seas. They had a way of measuring it alongside this barge, which was anchored out in outer Hampton Roads area, out in the channel where you get a full sweep of the wind clear across Chesapeake Bay, and it could get pretty rough out there.

So, we had made a few landings in the thing, and I kept thinking, how in the world do those engines stay in this airplane, because there is a big shock when you hit the front of a wave, why they didn't just fall out because they're heavy, you know, and it would feel like, almost like, running into a brick wall at about 60 miles an hour. The mechanic came up and he said, "I think we've got a little leak starting back aft," which was sort of normal, a few rivets popped, from the beating it was taking. So "Country" Moore said, "Well, I'll crawl back there and watch it. I want to watch how these beams and stringers bend anyway on the take-offs and landings, so you go ahead and take it around and I'll stay back there for the next two landings and take-offs." So, he did, and we had the same kind of a rough banging. He came up kind of groaning, and he said, "Oh, boy, it feels even worse back there than it does up here.

And the next day he claimed that his feet hurt, and he stood around there working and flying for about a week and he says, "Gee, my feet hurt." Finally, we said, "Why don't you go to the doctor if your feet hurt so much." He went to the doctor and found he had two bones broken in one foot and one bone in the other from this rough-water test because he'd been down there sitting on his heels when we hit these waves, and he didn't even know it. But this was a pretty tough guy and he didn't want to be bothered with his feet hurting if it wasn't anything serious. Only a few broken bones.

Well, I remember on one day I flew a dive bomber in the morning for carrier landing tests, a seaplane in the afternoon for rough-water tests, and then an experimental fighter at night for night gunnery tests -- all in one day. This sounds a little strange, but - because today before a pilot even flies an airplane, much less does a test pilot job on it, he does a lot of familiarization and a great deal of just normal flying and getting quite a few hours in the airplane before he does any real tests.

Q: And you'd never seen either of these three before?

Adm. T.: No. But we used to have a joke about that. When somebody said, "Well, look, I don't know whether I want to go into this sort of test. I'd better have a few familiarization flights - we'd usually have one or two before we did a rough-water test. But the usual question from one pilot to another, one getting in the airplane and the other getting out, if he hadn't flown it before, he'd say, "Well, now, tell me, if you push the throttle forward, does it go that way, and if you pull the stick back, does the nose come up, and if you push it forward, does the nose go down?" "Yes." "Okay, I know how to fly it." And so you get familiar with it.

Q: That way!

Adm. T.: Yes, but there weren't very many instruments, anyway.

There wasn't too much to become familiar with. If it was a good airplane, it flew all right. If it wasn't you had trouble with it. I remember we'd finally have to make these landings with a full load, sometimes with 1,000-pound bomb aboard, or something like that - not a fused bomb, but the same weight.

Q: But this one day you did three different ones?

Adm. T.: Yes, all different types.

Q: Are you going to expand more on that?

Adm. T.: Well, I might mention that the seaplane was a little amphibian where you sat in the hull. This was a single-engine type. You'd sit down in the hull with your shoulder about at the top of the hull and obviously your face very close to the water. And then you stuck your legs up in front to the rudder, up in the forward part of the hull, and the engine was right over your head, and the propeller was missing the hull by a few inches right over your knees, and I was a little squeamish about giving this rough-water test, but I thought, well, we have to try it. But what I wasn't worried about, happened. The fact that when I first started my take-off in the rough water, the water splashing over, the propeller picked it up and completely obliterated the windshield, right under the engine and close to the water, there was just a stream of . . .

Q: Blinding!

Adm. T.: Completely. I didn't realize this until I got in the air and found that I was flying 90° to the right of the place I tried to - of the direction I tried to take off. So this was a problem and one of the reasons we had to turn that plane down.

Q: That seems like a good reason.

Adm. T.: Yes, I didn't want to fly it any more, and I didn't. I was really afraid that if the hull buckled a little bit, it would push the fore end of the hull right against the propeller, and then it might cut my knees.

Q: And what happened on the one that you flew at night?

Adm. T.: This was all right, except the lights went out, the instrument panel light, and I couldn't see the air speed meter of any instruments and had to come in and land. But the field was lighted all right.

Q: Didn't you sometimes feel you were lucky to escape with your life? After those jobs?

Adm. T.: Well, flying was considered an extra hazardous occupation and being a test pilot was even more so. We felt we should have an adequate amount of life insurance but the insurance premium rates were high for military flying and I used up most of my flight pay on life insurance.

However, we felt we were lucky to be able to fly all these different types, because it was giving us some training that no other - that the average naval aviator or pilot wouldn't get. So we'd be far better off later when we finished this interesting job.

This led to my assignment as one of the test pilots on the XP2H-1, which (there's a picture of it, right there) was the largest airplane ever built in the United States at that time. It was the first four-engine airplane, land-based or sea-based, that was ever built in the United States.

Q: Tell me what all those letters stand for.

Adm. T.: X for experimental, P for patrol, 2 is the second aircraft, the second model that Hall Aluminum, H, had built. And this was the first one without any modifications. It would have been - if it had been P5H-2, it would be a slight modification of the P2H. Hall Aluminum Aircraft built it, and one of the reasons we would ask the silly question of a new airplane, if you push the throttle forward and pull the stick back, does its nose come up? Mr. Hall - we used to call him Old Man Hall because he was quite elderly even at the time, he had built one other patrol type aircraft, small twin-engined, that the Navy had bought some of and we used them in Hawaii. But he flew a crazy airplane down there that was his own private plane he'd built. He had to look at the compass through a mirror, and the stick came down from the overhead, so that if you pulled the stick back, the nose went down, if you pushed it forward, the nose went up. And so you had to fly with backwards reaction in that airplane. That wasn't one that he was submitting to the Navy for tests, but I flew with him in it, and he wouldn't let anybody else fly it because he said it's backwards and I'm the only one that can do that. So that was why we kept asking this question, if you pull the stick back, will the nose come up?

There was one aircraft in the world at that time that was a slightly heavier - weight, I guess - and that was the German DOX, also a four-engined patrol boat-type seaplane. It weighed more empty, but it wasn't any bigger. This plane (the XP2H) had two tractor-type engines, which were rather conventional, but then it had two pushers in the rear of the nacelles. It was a Curtiss Conqueror prestone-cooled engine. You know this fluid you put in your automobiles to keep it from freezing?

Q: Yes.

Adm. T.: Well, this ethylene glycol is prestone. We had a lot of water-cooled engines, but this was the coolant for these engines. We had to carry a few extra cans of it, in case we sprang a leak. But it was a very efficient airplane, because it would carry a bigger load than it weighed itself, and that was something interesting.

Q: That sounds impossible.

Adm. T.: No, it isn't. The thing weighed around 24,000 pounds empty, and when I took it off, full load, to fly nonstop from Norfolk to Panama, it weighed 52,000. We weighed it before we took off.

Q: How many in the crew?

Adm. T.: There were three pilots, two engineers, as we call them these days, a chief mechanic and a helper, and one radio man. That's the crew that I used. Had it gone into service, it probably would have had to have an additional radioman for relief, because the thing would fly almost forever. As a matter of fact, I had it in the air for more than a day. I had it in the air for 25 hours and something on the test flight, which was a fuel-consumption test. We wanted to fly from Norfolk to Panama at the most economical fuel consumption for range, not just for endurance, not just stay in the air, but for range.

So this was a test I was running to determine what was the best - if we knew the best fuel-throttle setting as the plane became lighter and lighter. You'd take off and fly at a little higher speed while heavy because it was more economical range-wise, and as you lightened the load burning up the fuel you would ease back and fly at a slower speed for maximum range. And although it took me 25 hours because I ran into some horrible head winds that weren't forecast, I still had quite a bit of gasoline left, enough to fly something like 500 more miles without fueling. And it had other very nice figures on it. It was very good on the water, taxiing. You could rev those liquid-cooled engines down to such a slow speed and still have them tick over that in a slight breeze you could sail backwards and tack into crowded quarters in a harbor. One thing that was bad about it that finally stopped it was that it had a - it was so light construction, it had a sort of egg-shell hull bottom that wouldn't stand too much rough water carrying a heavy load.

Now, at that time, there was sort of a controversy in the Navy about whether or not we would build an extra extension to the breakwater at Coco Solo, Canal Zone, on the Atlantic side. I was a lieutenant junior grade at the time, but I was put in charge of this test and I was eventually supposed to bring it on around to the West Coast. I was pulled out of VP squadron 9 to do this job, on temporary duty . . .

Q: Why did they select you?

Adm. T.: Because I was in a patrol squadron, the airplane was coming to be based under the patrol wing, and I was the only one available, who had been a test pilot on it. So they picked me. There was some question about whether the patrol wing in the Pacific wanted to accept this thing on a sort of a one-airplane experimental basis. They sent a message to

OpNav saying we would like to know more about this airplane before the decision is made. And the Navy Department probably said, "Well, there's a pilot there in one of your squadrons who knows all about it, why don't you ask him, and furthermore, we're going to have him come back and do it." So, away I went.

There was a controversy about this breakwater at Coco Solo. It was mainly between the submarine - we had a submarine base there - and the aeronautics department. The sea swells would come in the opening and leave a very restricted area for take-offs, especially with a heavy load, from the naval operating base at Coco Solo, where there were three patrol squadrons based. The submariners said, oh, no, they didn't think we ought to build it because maybe sometime they would need this extra exit. They had several places to get out to sea, but they wanted, I guess, as many as they could get. Because they didn't need this breakwater, so they were against it, and they wanted to keep another opening there. So, maybe there were good arguments on both sides.

Anyway, Ernie King was one who could really put the heat on people to get the most out of 'em, but he said, "Well, what I want you to do is go on down to Coco Solo while running this fuel test, and anytime that you feel that this plane is in any trouble or you don't want to go on, just go in and land anywhere and let us know. Don't feel that there's any pressure on you." Well, this was old so-called SOB Ernie King, he was supposed to be a tough son of a gun, but he was treating me as if he was my father.

Q: Did he speak to you personally?

Adm. T.: Oh, absolutely. He put his arm around me and told me this.

Q: Where was this and how did it happen?

Adm. T.: At Norfolk, Virginia. He came down there.

Q: For the purpose of this test?

Adm. T.: Yes, for the purpose of talking to me about the test, and he came back later and watched the take-off.

Q: What was his job then?

Adm. T.: He was Chief of the Bureau of Aeronautics - a rear admiral.

Q: I think that's an interesting incident and comment on his personality.

Adm. T.: It is, yes. He realized that it was an experiment, that we were pioneering in this field and there was a lot of stuff in the newspapers about it, and what kind of record I was supposed to try to break. I wasn't trying to break any records. I wanted to get the test done, as the Navy Department did. And I didn't want to try to get there too fast. I wanted to find out what were the best throttle settings or power settings for the maximum range. You could tell that by going to Coco Solo and then see how much gas you've got left.

He said, "Now, when you get there, I want you to load this plane in an overload condition," (which was in the book, just how much you put in) "absolute overload condition, and see how difficult it is, or whether or not you can get off - whether you can take off in those ground swells down there. We may need a new breakwater there, but let's find out." Well, of course, I might have been being used to demonstrate that it couldn't be done, because it couldn't. We didn't get off. In fact, I had a Dutchman, a young JG, as a co-pilot; he was a pretty stubborn young man, and he was brought to the project from a squadron in Panama, so he was quite familiar with the area. So he said, "Are you going to let me try this full-load take off?" I said, "Sure, you go ahead and take it, you are familiar with the take off area and you know when to expect the ground swells. He got going - it took her a long time to get up to speed because she was so heavy - and he hit a couple of these things and they threw him sideways and he was headed into the breakwater, so we chopped all four throttles and we shook our heads and said, "That didn't work very well," so we taxied all the way back and tried it again. The same thing happened. By that time we had to go back and put some more fuel in because we wanted a take-off with the heaviest load. So he said, "I think we can do it this time. We'll head a little more to the left." Well, he headed a little more to the left, and he hit one big one that threw him in the air, and ker-plonk, he hit the next one and he wasn't cutting the throttles, so I reached out and cut them because I knew we'd had a pretty bad thump. Then about that time we hit the next one and it was real bad, and lost one of the wing tip floats. So we quickly put a man out on the other wing, so that this wing wouldn't go down, and taxied back in. We had sprung the hull a little bit. A lot of so-called experts looked over it. The assembly and repair officer came out rubbing his hands with glee, because he wanted to get a big job. He made an estimate and said the keel was broken, and this was gone, and this, and this - made it look horrible - and then said it would take him about eight or ten weeks to fix it, and it would be so much money.

Well, my chief and I didn't agree with this at all, but the dispatch went out that way because he was the technical expert. Then the Navy Department came back and asked some questions, maybe that we'd better scrap it, and then he came in with another dispatch and said he thought they could do it in five weeks and it would only cost this much. But, by that time, they decided, well, if we're going to have it done, we'd better do it at the overhaul and repair shop in San Diego. So instead of flying to San Diego, we hoist this thing aboard the USS <u>Wright</u> and bring it to San Diego. I would much rather have gotten it fixed down there and have it flown, but I was overruled.

Q: Was it the ground swells that prevented your taking off?

Adm. T.: Oh, yes. They were bad.

Q: Did it stop the controversy about the breakwater?

Adm. T.: Yes. The breakwater was built.

Q: Was the plane itself structurally sound?

Adm. T.: Pretty delicate, on the whole. It wouldn't take too much of a pounding, but I think it might have done the same thing to any other plane that size and that heavy, but I think that it should have had a little stronger skin and weighed a little more, then without the ability to carry quite so much fuel and not go quite as far. It really went farther than we needed to go - in range. But you can never really say that because you want something that is going to be a predecessor of long-range patrol bombers. But I think the real reason - when they got it to San Diego and they looked it over, they agreed it wouldn't take too much to fix it, but by that time another design had come along that was called a monoplane - see, that's a biplane. This was right in the middle of the transition period from biplane to monoplane, and the monoplane was obviously better, so they decided, we won't continue with this project, we've learned an awful lot from it, we'll just scrap it and go to monoplanes, which they did, and the PBY was the final successor to it.

Q: On the trip down there, were there any incidents that you want to relate?

Adm. T.: There were several.

We discovered that an aircraft crew shouldn't try to stay awake for 25 hours, especially after working day and night to get the airplane ready to go, and being under considerable tension due to the project itself. It was something new and different. So we weren't in the best of shape, as far as sleep is concerned, when we took off. I tried to last as long as I could before taking a nap. Finally after we'd past Cuba and gotten out headed on down over the Gulf, I decided, well, I'd better take a nap, I want to be fresh near the end, in case we don't hit the marks we are shooting for. So I started to take a nap, and about that time I just dozed off, two of the engines quit. We had eight tanks and four engines. You could run any engine off of any tank, and there was a battery of valves and one of the tanks supplying two engines ran dry and this was all right, if you expected it. But, here, I was asleep and those two engines quit and it just brought me up real sharp, and I cut my head on the overhead I came up so fast. So I decided I wouldn't try to take any more naps.

But the radioman wouldn't go to sleep and I tried to get him to, and the last four hours of the flight he went to sleep involuntarily and we couldn't wake him up, no matter if you'd shake him, he was just completely exhausted and he couldn't send anything on the radio. But we got there all right, and it was a very valuable experience for everyone.

Q: And you did receive a "well done" from CNO?

Adm. T.: Oh, yes. It was a successful flight down there. We learned what we intended to, we didn't get lost, and we didn't get into any trouble, and everything went fine. Two days for one flight.

Q: I think we ought to put in the date on the tape, Admiral.

Adm. T.: Yes. This nonstop flight from Norfolk to Panama was January 15 and 16, 1935.

The USS Wright was the tender and flagship for the wing commander, patrol wings, Pacific, and Patrol Squadron 9 was attached to the Wright for administrative purposes and also on advance base exercises the squadron would be tended by the Wright. At other times certain bird-class tenders would go to the location where we wanted to have a base, wherever it was, and tend the patrol air-craft which were kept anchored out.

Q: And you were with Patrol Squadron 9 for two years?

Adm. T.: That's right.

Q: July 1934 to June 1936.

Adm. T.: Yes. We were scheduled in 1934 - no, I guess it was 1935, to fly up to the Aleutian Islands, and we had PM-1 open-cockpit, twin-engine biplane type flying boat aircraft. When I heard that we were going to make this advance base cruise, I decided finally I'd better have my appendix out before we went, so I did, and it was all right, chronic.

This was a fascinating flight we made up there with two squadrons of aircraft - patrol planes - which, in those days, amounted to twelve airplanes. We had, at that time, very few navigational aids along the coastline of Alaska and the Aleutians. In fact, we didn't know where the coastline was, and our charts would have a dotted line, which, according to the cartographer, meant the coastline, we think, is about here but we're not sure. Furthermore, there were certain small peak-like islands sticking up that were not on the chart. When one of these suddenly loomed up ahead in a fog, it became a very interesting sort of thing.

Q: I like the use of the word "interesting"!

Adm. T.: Well, we found that the best thing to do when we

ran into a fog, which we did often, was to fly right down a few feet over the beach. You can see white water when you can't see anything else. We had to make short flights.

For instance, we flew from here to San Francisco, and from San Francisco to Bremerton, Washington, Seattle, and, incidentally, anchored in Lake Washington right by the Naval Air Station there. And then on to - various short hops until we finally got out to the vicinity of Dutch Harbor. We had very few navigational aids and not very good weather forecasting. We had a little bird-class tender, the USS Sandpiper. There was another one, the USS Gannet, and we called them the Sandpaper and the Garnet. They were very small. Little things almost like ocean tugs, but they could carry food and gasoline. You could hoist one of these PM-1s aboard the stern of one of these little things, but they were still very small. The airplane stuck out all over both sides of the little ship.

Q: What time of year was this?

Adm. T.: This was in July, I believe, when we were up there. Latter part of June and July, 1935. We kept hearing from the local people up there, the cannery people - there were a lot of salmon canneries. Some places we'd go there'd be nothing but a salmon cannery or nothing. They would say, "Well, if you don't get out of here by such-and-such a date, you might as well wait 'til next year." That's the way they felt about it, and they were natives. This disturbed us somewhat. But one of the things was the very high tide. We went into Kodiak, for example, one of our first stops in the Aleutian Island chain, and the tender had planted these buoys with a 500-pound anchor on each, so we just landed and had a line of buoys, one for each airplane to moor. Then we went aboard the tender, and the next morning we came out and looked, and all the airplanes were high and dry up on the rocks. The tide there is anywhere from 20, or it could be 30, feet. So the position they laid the buoys, at low tide just wasn't in the water at all. But it didn't seem to damage the planes much because it was inside a protected harbor and the wind wasn't blowing. So, as the tide came up, they just moved the buoys into deeper water. Then with the next low tide, the aircraft didn't end up on the rocks.

It was much colder than I thought it would be. Ice all over the place and on the ground. Our next stop was at a little anchorage in the Shumagin Islands - I believe that's the name of them. There wasn't any settlement there. But that was the last take-off place before we were going to get to Dutch Harbor. We took off and it was a nice sunshiny day and started flying along, and we passed by an island that was near the tip end of Unimak Island - and went on a few minutes more, and all of a sudden we were in the worst looking blizzard I've ever seen. You could just dimly make out the plane you were following, the plane ahead of you in this formation of six aircraft. We held our same course for about an hour hoping to run out of this thing and then the skipper decided we'd better turn 'round and go back. I remember the last place we had seen was a kind of clay-looking cliff, anyway it was a different color than the rest of the rocks that we'd left about an hour before that. We turned around and in about seven minutes there we were right back again. You see, the wind had come up to about 60 or 70 knots and our cruising speed was 80, so we had just been almost standing still in that blizzard. When we came back we weren't sure it was the right place but we were in a few minutes where we'd just left an hour before.

Q: Were you aware of that?

Adm. T.: Well, we saw the point . . .

Q: I mean at the time.

Adm. T.: I wasn't. I didn't realize how strong the wind was blowing until we took only seven minutes to return to a spot we had left 60 minutes before. You couldn't see anything but snow. It was a sort of a bitter cold thing, but we had these bearskin flying suits, very heavy, and they kept you pretty warm, with gloves, but your face got cold in an open cockpit.

We finally wound up finding a landing place in Morzori Bay. It may be called Cold Bay now - you can see that on a map. It's near where we went through False Pass also near Unimak, on the northern side of the Aleutians.

The wind was blowing hard and, of course, the tender was nowhere near us, because they didn't expect that we were going to land there, but we had to. We were showing about 50 knots on the air speed meter, just sitting on the water, and we were sheltered from the wind behind the land. The wind was coming over, although we were sort of in the lee of this land, we were still getting 50 knots on the air speed meter, and each one of the planes was dragging its anchor. We had these light-weight anchors in the plane itself, that would hold in a light breeze in good mud, but with these rocks that we were anchored over and the wind so high, we'd pull the anchor up when we found ourselves drifting and the flukes would be bent back. We decided, this is no good, because you had to crank and crank the engines to start 'em up before you drifted clear across the bay onto the rocks on the other side. Somewhere, we couldn't even see. The skipper was Henry T. Stanley, skipper of VP-9 at the time, and he decided that we'd better get the hell out of there, and looking at the chart, it looked like we would maybe find, hopefully, some kind of a sandy beach if we followed the coastline. Well, I had an engine I couldn't get started. I could start only one. So everybody went off and left me. I knew where they were going. He sent a message saying what he planned to do. I gave up trying to start that engine. We were all exhausted from cranking the flywheel starter up to speed and we were soaking wet. When those bearskin coats get wet, they're not only heavy but they don't smell very good.

They get a stinky thing about them and it might even make you sick at the stomach.

So, we got this one engine going and decided, well, we'll drag a bucket in the water on that side off the wing tip and that will keep us from must going 'round in circles. If you have just one engine going, you give it throttle to make some progress, and when you start to turn too much off the desired course, slack off on the throttle. The bucket drogue drags in the water and straightens you back out again. So you go kind of like this -- a zig zag. That's a lot slower than being able to get up on the step and zoom along taxiing on the water. But I finally saw the other planes just about dusk, and they all had their noses up on what looked like a beach, with not very big rocks. There isn't any sand in that vicinity. There are just jagged rocks or round rocks. Well, they'd found some round rocks, anywhere from the size of a football to the size of a baseball or a golf ball, and they had left one small opening for me. It was a very short little beach. There was just nothing else but cliffs. So I was supposed to get into that little opening, or else spend the night going round and round. I decided I could make it, and approached parallel to the beach with it on the dead engine side, going close along the tails of the other planes. When I got to my slot, I gave it full gun and it just swung me right around into there, and then they all grabbed the plane to hold it and we took the anchor out and took it over a little hill and buried it and put logs on top of it. We found some logs from an old pier.

Then, that night, all of the planes, one after another dragged and pulled that anchor right out of the ground over the hill, after it had been buried, and each of us had to crank up again several times.

Q: Were you still in this bad storm?

Adm. T.: Yes. We couldn't take off. There was nowhere we could go. You know, we didn't do much instrument flying in those days. We didn't have the instruments to do very well with instrument flying, certainly not precise enough to avoid mountain peaks and jagged islands and so forth. Of course, there were no landing approach aids whatsoever. So it was the better part of valor to stay put until the storm blew over. And after all that, we thought, well, boy, half of us are going to be sick with pneumonia and everything else. Not a single person even caught a bad cold. The tender finally arrived in there, we got some hot food and the weather cleared up. We moored to the buoys laid by the tender and went aboard the ship to get some much needed rest.

Anyone up there can tell you what the weather is going to be in the Aleutian Island chain - it is going to be unpredictable.

We had a rude introduction to how suddenly the weather can change from nice to violent. It was about midnight and I was in the after bunk room of the tender Sandpiper when the word was passed, "Flight crews man your planes -- a williwaw is building up."

I had never seen a williwaw but thought it couldn't be very bad because I had been out on deck 15 minutes earlier -- there was no wind, the bay was like a millpond and all the stars were out.

But what a change in 15 minutes! Now there was a strong wind, the water was being whipped into a frenzy of white caps. We hurried into the motor whaleboat. My plane was shackled to the fifth buoy in line and by the time we got to the fourth the wind had increased much more and the planes were dancing around almost flying like kites tied to the buoys. My plane appeared to have broken loose from the buoy and was drifting rapidly down wind. We chased it and scrambled aboard over the nose.

I wondered how many minutes we would have before being blown onto the rocks on the opposite side of the bay. We would have to get those engines started and soon! Fortunately, each one caught on the first try and we started to taxi back up wind. We were out of sight of the ship's lights but soon saw them again and the searchlight being used to illuminate the line of seaplanes moored to the buoys. My plane was the only one that had broken away. I taxied toward the gap in the line of planes where my assigned buoy was supposed to be. We couldn't see it. I reduced the throttler to let the plane drift back for another approach in case we had already passed it.

All of a sudden the buoy appeared right alongside the nose

I yelled at the man in the nose, "Grab it, grab it!" He put a boat hook through the ring on the buoy and pulled it up close. I said, "now pass a line through the ring two or three times so we won't break loose again." With a puzzled look on his face he turned to me and said, "We don't have to, we are already shackled to the buoy with our own wire cable from the keel."

What had happened was the 500 pound anchor had been dragged out of the shallow water into water deeper than the length of cable from anchor to buoy - so the buoy went under like a cork on a fishing line with a lead sinker that is too heavy. The buoy re-appeared when I taxied back and dragged the anchor into shallow water again.

Soon the wind died down to a flat calm and the stars came out again. It was difficult to realize that this williwaw took only about an hour from beginning to end and yet at its peak gusts to 75 knots were registered on the ship's anemometer. I do not need to see another williwaw.

Q: What was the purpose of the trip?

Adm. T.: It was to exercise and test the squadron in deployment to various out-of-the-way places for advance base exercises, in case we had to operate there, to go and scout out some enemy submarine or ship or whatever, and be in a forward base. It was an advance base in the wilderness, as far as I was concerned.

But I talked to a doctor about why we didn't get sick

because we were so exhausted from all this 24-hour business, and he said, "Well, whatever germs you had brought up here you were used to them and there just don't seem to be any up here, so you were built up with a certain immunity to the ones you had, you didn't get any new ones, so that's it." And that may have been the reason.

Q: Good as any!

Adm. T.: Yes. The fact is we didn't get sick. No one got a single little thing wrong with them.

Q: It sure is hard to believe.

Adm. T.: From VP-9 I received orders to Scouting Squadron 6B based aboard the light cruiser division ships, and my ship was the USS Cincinnati, and this was my first command of an aviation unit when there weren't any other aviators senior to me aboard the ship and I reported directly to the gunnery officer and the captain of the ship.

Q: How many were in your squadron?

Adm. T.: Oh, well, the squadron was - let's see, there were eight, two based oneach of four cruisers, and mine was the Cincinnati. The Squadron Insignia was appropriately a little seahorse. The Omaha was the flagship. We often operated together at sea. There were only two planes based aboard each cruiser, and I had three pilots - myself, Ensign Eastwald, and a very wonderful enlisted pilot, an AP named Sorensen. I had the good fortune - yes, good fortune. The reason I hesistated about whether it's good fortune or not is because I relieved a man by the name of Sid Harvey. He was then a Lieutenant Harvey, and later when I reported to a fighter squadron, he became the second commanding officer of that squadron while I was there and I was the third. But that's another story that will come later. Well, Sid Harvey always did an outstanding job and anyone who followed him really was . . .

Q: He was a hard act to follow!

Adm. T.: He was a hard one to follow, because you couldn't top him. He had E's with hash marks on all his planes and everything he did was an outstanding performance. Everybody realized what a fine officer he was. Just the best in every way. So, in order to live up to what he had done, we had to work very hard, which I guess in the final analysis was good. But you couldn't do much improvement, although we did a little improvement because of a slight accident. The skipper of the ship was Captain C.C. Baughman, and he was a real, tough seaman. He scared everybody to death. I remember one time we were towing a sleeve for the smaller guns - 50 caliber machine guns that we had in the foretop as well as other guns aboard the ship, and we were running a certain practice, or training for it, in accordance with the OGE. The captain had seen the E's on the planes and noted that not only Sid Harvey but I and my other pilots had fired E scores in this airplane too, so we put another hash mark under the E. He called me up one time and he said, "Now, you're apparently a good gunner. I want you to, during this exercise, I want you to train these machine gunners in the foretop to hit that sleeve and then maybe that will help 'em, help the ship for regular practice." I said, "Aye, aye, Sir," so everytime we practiced this exercise, I would climb up in the foretop and try to train these gunners to hit a sleeve. Most of the time I had to stop them from shooting too soon. They always wanted to shoot too soon, and sometimes by the time the . .

Q: Yes, and get the plane!

Adm. T.: Well, not necessarily get the plane, but shoot before the thing was even in range. It would come across at an angle. And if they started shooting too soon, not only they wouldn't hit, but usually the gun would jam before - by the time they had a good shot, so they couldn't hit. I had to hold them back.

Anyway, we had these sleeves - sleeve and towline were flaked down in a certain form of a bent figure eight, and then the sleeve folded in such a manner that it would hold the towline underneath it on these tow boards that were attached to the bomb racks on the wing, and then bungee cord was brought across the sleeve that was all folded up, so you could fly with it and then, by pulling a little toggle from the cockpit, you could release - trip the bungee cord and the sleeve and towline would all fall away and you could tow. Then, there was another one that you could release and drop the whole thing.

Well, the practice was to fly, after the firing training, fly by the ship and drop the sleeve in the water, and they'd send a boat out to pick it up and haul it in. It took time and this Captain Baughman was very impatient and he said, "There ought to be a better way to do that. It wastes too much time.

Interview #2 with Vice Admiral John S. Thach, U.S. Navy
(Retired)

Place: His home in Coronado, California

Date: 8 August 1970

Subject: Biography

By: Etta-Belle Kitchen

Adm. T.: If we could fly real close to the ship and release the sleeve so it would land aboard, that would save a lot of time. I had been thinking about this previously but I didn't dare suggest it to Captain Baughman because I thought he would jump down my throat and say, "you're going to tear all the antennas off my ship." But there was a heavy guy wire running from the foretop down to the bow of this class cruiser, and I thought that we could fly alongside the port side and then make a right turn ahead of the ship, this would bring the sleeve tow line in contact with this guy wire and it would slide along, then, if we could drop the sleeve precisely at the moment that the sleeve appeared over the ship, or just slightly ahead of that, the sleeve itself wouldn't drop in the water. If the sleeve ever got in the water, it would act as a drogue or a sea anchor, and you couldn't pull it out with the ship mooring. So he said, "all right, let's try it." He said, "We'll try it the next time we tow a sleeve." I said, "Well, I'd like to be on the bridge and give a signal for the officer of the deck to blow the whistle and the pilot in the airplane will see the steam pop out from the whistle and that way there'd be instantaneous recognition that that's the time to drop." So, we tried this. I waited until the sleeve was coming up very close and then gave the signal. The pilot saw the steam puff from the whistle, and the very first time the sleeve dropped right into the hands of the commanding officer and he could count the holes that the gunners had put in it. This was even better than I had hoped for. Once or twice the signal was given too soon and the sleeve did get in the water and we had a hard time keeping the sailors aboard from trying to grab the line because we knew that it would rip the skin off their fingers.

But then the captain got so interested in this he wanted to give the signal himself, which he did, and he got very good at it.

It was about this time that I became qualified to stand officer of the deck watch underway, and I remember the first time I had the bridge all to myself, we were on our way to San Francisco, and the requirement was to be at San Francisco at a certain time in order to hit the right tides in the bay to go alongside. I had the mid watch, and about twelve o'clock the captain came up on the bridge and said, "We haven't had a star sight and it's been overcast now for more than twenty-four hours, so it's very important that we pick up the navigation light off the entrance to San Francisco." I think it was the Farallon Islands light. "And I expect that about 2:30 a.m. you'll see it, and when you see it, why call me and call the navigator." So I said, "Aye, aye, Sir," and I put a sailor in the foretop because with a higher height of eye he should be able to see it sooner. This was a young man by the name of Rogers, I talked to him personally to tell him how important it was, and that the currents along the coast were very tricky and if we drifted in too close to the beach we might run on the rocks. He seemed to be impressed. Well, we were all looking very hard for this light and 2:30 came along and no report from the lookouts, and I couldn't see any light, and I told them it was supposed to be about one point on the starboard bow, but to look in other places ahead because any light that he saw I wanted to know about it and if we picked this light up and it was on the port bow we were running into danger. So, I called him again and said, "Do you see that light yet?" He said, "No, Sir, I don't see it." Five more minutes went by and I called him, and I said, "Rogers, don't you see that light yet?" And he said, "No, Sir, but I can almost see it." I didn't worry about him anymore because I knew that he wanted to see that light. He wanted to see it so bad he could almost see it but he wouldn't say he saw it. He may have been beginning to get a little inkling of the loom of the light over the horizon and that was the reason he said, "I can almost see it." Then, about two minutes later, he did report it and a little later we could see it. I've thought often that if everybody wanted to do a job as much as that young man, we wouldn't have too much trouble.

"Baughman's Bellow"

One time when we were required to tow a sleeve for small-arms firing from the ship, Swede Eastwald, who was the other commissioned pilot aboard the Cincinnati, was flying and when he was catapulted both the sleeves fell off on the deck and the lines started running out from the towboards under each wing of the plane, but he kept - of course, he had to keep going, he was catapulted - and the lines broke at the sleeve because they caught on the rail, but here he was flying along with these long bow lines scraping in the water and he had on full power but it just gradually pulled him down the more line went in the water, it wouldn't break, and he didn't realize for the moment what the trouble was, but he knew he was going down so he just landed with full power on, landed on the ocean. I was up in the foretop ready to supervise the machinegunners up there the captain had asked me to train, and I heard the captain let out a bellow and I came, half falling, down the mast to get to the bridge. By the time I got there, he said, "Look. Look what's happened," and I said, "I saw it, Captain." He said, "Well, the plane's going to sink," and I said, "I don't think so." He said, "Well, it's damaged." I said, "How do you know it's damaged?" He said, "The navigator told me it was going to sink and he's an old aviator." I said, "He's a lighter-than-air aviator. He can hardly be considered an expert witness in heavier-than-air." "I saw the landing and I think the airplane is perfectly all right. We'll have to go over there and pick it up and get those lines loose." We went over. We had to stop the ship and the plane slowly taxied alongside under the crane. Fortunately, it wasn't very rough weather - rough water.

Q: It had floats?

Adm. T.: Yes. It was an SOC-1 aircraft, a single center float, and little pontoons under each wing.

What had happened was that the bungee cord that held the sleeves on the tow board had gotten weak and gave way due to the force of the catapult shot. The captain was very unhappy about that. Of course, we all were. He said, "It seems to me that you aviators would be smarter than to build a thing like that. You ought to do a better job, somehow. We can't put up with failures like that." So I said, "The first thing we're going to do, of course, is to put new bungee on there and I think it'll hold next time, but I agree that this is a sort of a poor rig and we should be able to do better." I also remarked that I thought it ought to be more streamlined because with those tow boards, a big square wooden board hooked onto the bomb rack, it created a lot of drag on the airplane and you couldn't fly as well. I went back and talked to my ordnanceman and told him to think about it. So the next day he came to see me and said, "I think I've got an idea." I said, "All right, let's go see it." Well, he had taken one of the water-fillable practice bombs - it is filled with water to make it heavy, and it was just made out of light metal. We used to call them tin bombs. And he'd cut it, cut the rear half off, and showed me how he could capsize the front flexible metal ring of the sleeve into a figure 8 - fold it over and it would just fit into this bomb, and that we could use the same fittings on the bomb that we used to attach a practice bomb, attach it to the bomb racks, and rig up a release mechanism so that you could release not only the sleeve but, if necessary, the whole bomb with a tow line wound in it. I told him, "You ought to build a hinged door and then we'll put the line in, stuff the sleeve in last, and make it so it would spring out against the door when the door was opened." Well, we all worked on that, with an idea from one person and another, we got what we called an Ollie bomb, because the ordnanceman's nickname was Ollie. And it worked. So the captain was very enthused about this and he said, "Now, whenever you invent anything, you want to write it up and tell the Navy Department all about it." So we wrote the letter and forwarded it through him, he put a nice endorsement on it, and it went back to the Bureau of Aeronautics and they accepted it and made it a standard piece of equipment for carrying a sleeve on, not only that type of aircraft, but the other types as well.

Q: That was a real advance for gunnery practicing!

Adm. T.: Oh, yes. It was sure better than that old way.

For many reasons it is highly desirable to bring the aircraft back aboard the cruiser without stopping the ship. An ingenius way of doing this was developed called the "Cast Recovery Method."

When the ship is ready to recover her aircraft she comes to a course which will leave the wind broad on the starboard bow. Then a turn $90°$ to the right will swing the bow of the ship through the wind until it is blowing from broad on the port bow. This turn knocks down and smooths out the waves creating a slick area where the little seaplanes can land more safely and taxi up to the starboard side of the ship where a sled is being towed from a boom which sticks straight out from the side. The sled is about 4 by 5 feet and covered with wire rope netting.

The pilot must taxi the plane so that the nose of the center float rides up on top of the sled. He then reduces power to let the plane drift back so that a hook on the keel of the float will catch on the sled.

From that position the engine can be turned off and the plane hoisted aboard by the ship's crane.

The slick made by the ship's turn is not large and it doesn't last very long so the pilot must have a delicate sense of timing as to the precise moment when he should be in position to settle on to the slick. His landing must be just inside the edge of the slick to avoid the rough water and still not overrun and slide into a collision with the ship. He must land directly into the wind. Therefore his approach will be a glide path heading toward the side of the ship. There are no brakes on a seaplane.

With sufficient practice a pilot can land so close to the ship that he could swing right just at the end of his landing runout, be on a course parallel to the ship and up on the towed sled in less than sixty seconds from touch down time.

One of the difficulties is the fact that the pilot must taxi crosswind approaching the sled and then wants to weathercock into the wind which if permitted would back the eggshell-like float into the side of the ship. Because the pilot has a big air-cooled radial engine in front of him, his vision from the cockpit over the nose is somewhat obscured. It is difficult to see just where the sled is - so he sticks his head way out to the left and incidently gets a continuous bath of heavy salt water spray picked up by the propeller.

These float planes looked like top-heavy bugs sitting on the water and in fact they were top heavy and could easily stub the toe and capsize if the waves were at all high and the plane was not handled skillfully.

I noticed that every time we recovered aircraft by the

"Cast" method there were numerous spectators all over the top-side of the Cincinnati. If there was going to be a mishap they wanted to be there to see it and explain to their friends just how and why it happened. It was difficult enough but looked even more so. I think it is a sad thing that this interesting sporting event is no longer conducted.

Another exciting event, at least for the pilot of the plane, was the catapult shot from the light cruiser. I have been shot off of ships by gun powder catapults, hydraulic catapults and compressed air driven catapults. By far the most sudden kick in the pants is provided by the air catapults of the Cincinnati. In spite of the number of times I was launched in this manner I never got used to it. Everyone blacked out during the launch. The big question in my mind was always "Will I regain consciousness in time to keep the plane flying straight and level in order to gain an adequate margin of speed above stalling?" I always came to wondering who was flying the airplane!

One time I had a novel experience in addition to becoming unconscious at the end of the catapult. I almost flew into the water after a catapult shot and I was not unconscious at the time. We had a navigation board made from a flexible plastic sheet. It fitted into a metal framework that would slide in and out from under the instrument panel when needed. This nav board fitted loosely and I had to tie it to the framework with string to keep it from getting loose and being blown around in the cockpit on take off. The gunnery officer borrowed it to use as an "is was" or circular slide rule to help solve some of his gunnery ballistic problems. When he returned it, instead of giving it to me personally he just placed it in the sliding framework without tying it down. On the next cat shot after I regained consciousness I couldn't see. There was some thing wrapped around my face! I took a quick slap at it but failed to dislodge the thing. The wind was holding it close until I took my hand off the throttle and pulled the nav board down into the cockpit just in time to pull up the nose and avoid flying into the water. I learned later what happened on the bridge during this incident.

The catapult is trained to point as far forward as possible to take advantage of the relative wind created by the ship's speed. Consequently the aircraft flies close to ship's bridge after leaving the end of the catapult. The captain, the navigator and the O.O.D. as usual were out on the wing of the bridge during this launch. The O.O.D told me later that Captain Baughman said, "What is Thach doing with that thing covering his face? How can he see where he is going?" Mr. Fisher, the navigator who couldn't stand to have anyone think he didn't know exactly what was going on said, "Why captain, he doesn't want to see anything. He is practicing blind flying."

Q: And after a year in the Cincinnati you went to Coco Solo in the Panama Canal Zone?

Adm. T.: Yes. When I got my orders to Coco Solo from the Cincinnati I thought, "Oh, boy, they're sending me to Siberia. Maybe I talk too much." I wasn't very happy with those orders. I didn't want to go for two reasons. I didn't particularly want to go to Panama, and I was hoping to get back into fighter-type aircraft. But the policy in those days was a good one. It was to give officers well-rounded experience when young so that, later, if they were promoted enough to get a large command with various types of aircraft and ships, they'd know something about them, having been there themselves. This was a good policy, but I did object to it at the time. I didn't make any official objection. I just griped to some of my friends, and they said, "You'd better just go and keep quiet," which I did, and this turned out to be one of the most interesting and valuable tours of duty I had at that point in my career, both professionally and otherwise.

Q: That would have been in 1937 when you were with Patrol Squadron 5F.

Adm. T.: Yes. The commanding officer of that squadron was Warren Berner, and we had some interesting experimental work

Thach #2 - 110

to do in that squadron. We were given the job of developing night illumination with series of flare droppings and to figure out the tactics and the best way to illuminate a ship or a group of ships so that they could be bombed at night.

Q: It didn't have anything to do with carrier landings or that type of thing?

Adm. T.: No, these were boat type seaplanes, patrol aircraft. We called them "big boats."

Q: I mean the illumination was just . . .

Adm. T.: It had nothing to do with landing. It was to illuminate an enemy, illuminate a target whether it's an enemy ship or a target on land, so that a bombing group - we had to work out the coordination between a bombing group and the illumination group, (the flare group) and work out the tactics which became pretty complex when you have a wind blowing and the flares, of course, hang on little parachutes when you drop them, and you have to drop enough of them and just at the right place at the right time, so that when the bombers arrive at the dropping point, they have the maximum illumination of the target. This took a lot of trial and error and experimentation. Most interesting, the squadron devoted itself to actually working at night instead of in the daytime. We just worked all night, so we didn't fly very much in the daytime for the first six months that I was in the squadron. And there were some aviation cadets who reported to the squadron. At that time, unlike later, the Aviation Cadet students who finished the course of flight training at Pensacola weren't commissioned, they were still aviation cadets when they reported to the Fleet, the Fleet squadron, and then, if they were successful - I think about a year later - they were promoted to ensigns from aviation cadets. This was one of the first groups of aviation cadets we had in the Navy and they were really top-notch people. They were good pilots and they were very fine young men in all respects. I remember one of them was Bill Von Brach, another was Park Sager. Some of them have now been selected to Flag rank. Park Sager is now a rear admiral. The interesting thing about their particular experience in the squadron was the fact that they had never seen these particular airplanes before, yet they had to qualify to fly them as copilots, so we had to do it at night. And so, here, these young men were having to check out in a new airplane, learning how to fly them at night instead of in the daytime. They were flying and making landings in these airplanes, became qualified to take off and land in the harbor there at night, and they had never flown in the daytime but they had months of experience at night.

I never will forget the horror stories that they all came in and told when they had to make a day landing. They said they didn't realize they were coming so close to this obstruction or that obstruction to get into this little bay right in Coco Solo.

Q: Scared them to death when they could see what the danger was!

Adm. T.: They said we can see too much. At night they were coming in mostly on instruments, especially as far as altitude was concerned, making the approach . . .

Q: Was the harbor well lighted at night?

Adm. T.: Not too well. It had obstruction lights, you know. At night you don't see things as well. You know you're going to miss the obstruction lights, but they didn't realize how close they were coming to these things. We had to come right over France Field where there were some buildings. France Field, an Army Air Corps base, was right next to Coco Solo. Anyway, I thought it was interesting that they were so shook up when they had to make a landing in the daytime.

Q: What was your particular job?

Adm. T.: My job was communications officer. We went through the usual gunnery qualification, gunnery competition program and we were not doing very much antisubmarine warfare exercises, most of our training was scouting, search, and then bombing, horizontal bombing. A number of us qualified for E scores in bombing and in training our crews in free gunnery, flexible guns.

Q: You were always good in gunnery!

Adm. T.: Well, yes, I seem to have a knack for it. I could picture what the problem was and I learned early that success in gunnery depends an awful lot on very smooth flying. In other words, if you fly your plane perfectly, you have a better chance, whether you're bombing or whether one of your machinegunners is shooting at a sleeve, or whatever. Then those who qualified for an E score were given an opportunity to attempt to qualify as Master Bombers, and this was a title that - there were only a very few people in the whole Navy who ever qualified as a Master Bomber. I think you could count them on one hand, as I remember. I wanted to become a Master Bomber, if possible.

Q: Tell me what was involved.

Adm. T.: To get an E score, you had to drop four bombs

separately, with separate runs, inside of a ten mil circle.

Q: From how high up?

Adm. T.: A mil is one in one thousand. If you're a thousand feet up, a mil is one foot. If you're ten thousand feet up, you have a ten-foot radius that you can play with. But to qualify as a Master Bomber, you had to get within six mils, and you had to have four different practices on different days, so that the weather conditions would be sure to be different. You have to contend with different kinds of weather conditions, and if you failed on any one of those four qualification efforts to get the bombs inside of six mils, you were finished. And this is the reason that it was extremely difficult to do it.

Q: Translate that six mil into a distance I would understand.

Adm. T.: So, to make a long, painful story short, on two qualification attempts I was successful, but the third one I failed to get all the bombs close enough. And I said "painful" because I think I still have corns on my knees from leaning over a Norden bomb sight - this was the horizontal bomb sight. It's a very interesting gyro stabilized mechanism, and later was procured by the Army Air Corps for their big bombers, but Mr. Norden wouldn't sell them directly to anyone but the Navy because he was afraid nobody else would take care of them. They required expert maintenance. So, in order for the Army Air Corps to get any, the Navy had to buy them from Norden and then turn them over to the Army Air Corps.

Q: Isn't that interesting?

Adm. T.: It's the fact.

Q: I can understand why there were so few Master Bombers when you describe the difficulty.

Adm. T.: Oh, yes. I think the only ones that existed were at Dahlgren, the ordnance proving grounds, and they were in the process - they were testing equipment, and they would drop hundreds of bombs every day. They did nothing else, and they got really good, of course. I was disappointed, though, because I thought I could do it. But my skipper, he wasn't so disappointed that I didn't do it because, he said, "You know what would happen to you if you got to be a Master Bomber? You'd get detached and be sent to Dahlgren and spend the rest of your life dropping bombs and testing bomb sights!" So there was a silver lining in this failure.

Q: But you've been so excellent in all phases of gunnery that I'm sure it was a personal disappointment.

Adm. T.: Well, it's one of those things that when you had a particular day when the wind was blowing in a different direction at altitude than it was half-way down, and it was almost impossible.

Q: In the long scheme of things, I'm sure it was relatively unimportant.

Adm. T.: Oh, yes, it was probably a good thing. Being based at the Fleet Air Base, Coco Solo, periodically we would go up to Guantanamo, Cuba. This was one of the places we went for what was called advanced base exercises, and other times we'd go to some small protected harbor, or water, between two islands and simply live off of the seaplane tender. This kept us mobile and ready to move, and able to move, with all of our equipment and all of the things we needed to maintain the aircraft, to keep them in shape. Guantanamo was, of course, not quite as austere as far as a truly advanced base was concerned because we had some buildings we could live in and we didn't need a tender there, so we didn't take a tender. There was a long flat building we used as a BOQ, a kind of a barracks. We had a difficult time sleeping at night because of "gig 'ems." Gig 'ems are little sort of gnats that can fly right through a small screen, although when there was a screen it kept out the mosquitoes. There were plenty of mosquitoes, but the gig 'ems went right through. This could have been the same sort of a little bug that they call a sand fly, and it has a heck of a bite. It just stings like the very devil when it bites you, and you can barely see it if you look closely. Some people were very allergic to this and I've seen people who've been bitten on the legs and their legs just swell up, the whole leg, and get infected and they have an awful time with it, but I wasn't - they didn't bother me too much except while they were biting me. That was a great irritant.

I remember we didn't have very modern facilities. We had an outdoor "Chick Sales" place, and this was really a masterpiece. It was one, I think, unique because it was constructed hanging over a cliff about 500 feet above the Atlantic Ocean, and the way they did this, they took some old ship anchor chains, huge chains, and anchored them in the ground and used them as a kind of a suspension bridge construction to support this thing that was simply sitting out beyond the cliff. If anybody ever fell through there they would go right into the Atlantic Ocean. This was quite sanitary, but it was a strange one. I remember one night we heard a great commotion outside BOQ on the pathway to this place. Several of us ran out. We had a Chinese cook and he was running up this path with his pants still down. You've heard stories that a man can't run with his pants down. Well, it was disproven. This fellow was really running and he was terribly excited and frightened. Lieutenant Cam Briggs was the first one that got to him and said,

"What's the matter?" And he said he was sitting out there reading a funny paper and he thought there was a bug on his ear and he slapped at it and he slapped a great big snake in the face - the snake was looking over his shoulder. So Cam said, "Well, now, pull up your pants and tell us about it." So he described this snake and I went and got a 9 iron - I had my golf clubs up there. There was one overhead bulb in this place so we got some more searchlights and we went out there and, sure enough, here was this big snake still reading the funny papers.

Q: It hadn't bitten him, fortunately?

Adm. T.: No, it hadn't, but he said that he slapped at what he thought was a bug and this snake was tickling his ear, and he said he looked around and the snake just stuck his tongue out at him and he said, "That's when I left."

Q: I can't imagine anything more horrible.

Adm. T.: I killed him with a 9 iron. The snake, not the Chinese cook. He was over 6 feet long. (The snake).

Q: What kind of a snake was it?

Adm. T.: It was a mahout, which is a water snake, a type of

moccasin. They're not found in very many places, but it was native to Cuba. The same type of snake crawled in an airplane that we were flying up to Pensacola, Florida, and the crew didn't know the snake was in there until the radioman was sitting at his station, near the stub wing, inside of the airplane, and this snake stuck his head out of the wing. He'd been in the wing while they were flying along between Guantanamo and Pensacola. The radioman picked up the intercom and reported to the pilot, "There's a snake peeking out of the wing at me." The two pilots looked at each other and said, "Where was he last night?" They didn't believe it. And he said, "Really, there's a snake back here." So one of them got out of the seat and went back and looked, and, sure enough, there was one of these mahouts in the wing. There's an opening in the side of the hull, you know, where you look into the wing for inspection, and that's where this snake was. And here they were in the air and they didn't know what to do about it, so they didn't do anything. They just waited till they got to Pensacola and they got him out after they got there.

Q: I assume they're poisonous?

Adm. T.: I don't know how poisonous they are. They have a head that is triangular shaped. It looks like a poisonous snake, and it is a moccasin.

Q: A moccasin's very poisonous, isn't it?

Adm. T.: Some of them are. Cottonmouths. I grew up with cottonmouth water moccasins. I know the cottonmouth water moccasins are poisonous because I've had quite a bit of experience with them in my youth, when my father and I used to go camping. My whole family would go camping and in order to get enough food, we'd fish, catch a couple of fish, and then we would have - often be able to get frog legs which is, of course, a delicacy. We would go out at night to get these frogs and on this river if the current swept you down and you bumped into an overhanging weeping willow - many weeping willows were along the edge growing from the shore onto the river - and if you bumped one of those, usually a water moccasin would fall out, sometimes in the boat, and whenever one of these moccasins fell in the boat, we left the boat because we'd heard that a moccasin can't strike at you when he's in the water, but if he's in a boat, of course, he can. I don't know whether that's true or not, but we didn't want to prove it one way or another, so we left the boat and then the boat would usually drift on down and come up against a bank somewhere and we would be out on the land and if the snake was still there we'd have to get him out with a paddle or kill him. We had this experience frequently, having a snake drop in the boat at night. You have this light and you have to hold it on the frog that's on the bank, big bull frog. You can see these frogs for 150 feet or more. You can see them from 50 yards because their two eyes reflect in the strong light - spotlight - they just look like two fiery rubies looking at you. But if you keep the light on the frog it won't jump.

Q: It hypnotizes him?

Adm. T.: Well, it just can't see you coming. But if you take the light off, then his eyes adjust quickly and he sees the boat sliding up and before you throw the gig at him he's gone. There's nothing better than frog legs for breakfast that have been caught the night before.

We were flying P2Y3 aircraft. They were built by Consolidated, now part of General Dynamics in San Diego. But it came time that we should get new airplanes and the PBY had been developed, so the squadron was ordered to turn their old aircraft in at Norfolk, then go to San Diego and pick up new PBYs, which we did, and after installing the bomb sights and the new equipment connected with bombing so that the bomber could fly the aircraft through an automatic pilot arrangement - this was a complicated thing in those days, it's not so much now - and this took quite a few weeks to get all this new equipment in and get ready to fly back to our home base at Panama. One day we finally took off with fourteen aircraft and headed for Panama. One day we finally took off with fourteen aircraft and headed for Panama from San Diego on a nonstop flight. The C.O., Warren Berner, had asked me to work out a procedure for foul weather deployment in case we ran into bad weather while we were in formation. So, I did. I worked out a system so that the leader (the skipper) could hold his course and altitude and the other aircraft, starting with the ones that were fartherest out in the formation, would turn out, fly for a certain specified time, then climb up a certain assigned number of feet above his former position. Each aircraft would do this, and I figured it out so that we could spread the formation very quickly this was in case we were all suddenly in the soup. Then, everybody was supposed to go back to their original course and hold their altitude, because no one would ever see anyone else and there'd be a cloud full of 14 airplanes. But we would have lateral as well as altitude separation.

Well, we took off and near the Gulf of Tehuantepic, about midnight, we ran into a pretty husky front, and the captain ordered the foul weather spread, we called it, and everybody started going to his newly assigned position, but this weather got real bad. The captain then called me and said, "Maybe we can get over the top of this thing. You climb up as high as you can and see whether we can get over the top of it or not." I didn't like this very much because I knew there were other planes wandering around up there and I didn't know whether they were still on their track or not, or whether they were over where I'd butt into them as I was going up, but of course I had to do it. So I went on up . . .

Q: What position were you in the formation?

Adm. T.: I was the second section leader of three planes. We had 14 airplanes in three-plane sections (except for the last two) the sections were flying a V of Vs sort of thing. I climbed and climbed and climbed and finally got up to around 22,000 feet and couldn't get over it and I was beginning to climb more slowly because it seemed we were getting close to the aircraft's ceiling, and I looked out and saw the instrument lights reflected on a big strut that looked like it was coming right down into the side of this seaplane hull and we didn't have any strut that was anywhere near there. I thought, well, I wonder if something has gotten loose from the aeroplane and was swirling around and stuck in the side. I just couldn't understand, so I asked the copilot to get a light and shine on it and look at it up and down. It was about as big as your arm, it looked like. He did, and he said, "It's ice. It's the antenna all iced up!" I looked at my altimeter and we were beginning to lose altitude, so I called my skipper and I couldn't get him, but we went on down a little and the ice fell off. Then I could get him and I told him my experience, that I'd iced up and we couldn't get over it. By this time, we were getting very turbulent air and lightning started striking. Lightning struck my aircraft and burned my radioman's fingers, a big heavy spark, and his fingers were all blackened and little black spots on his hand. And the strange thing, which often happens, I understand, blue balls were drifting around in the cockpit. Kind of roaming around. Like a St. Elmo's fire thing. It's a phenomenon that occurs sometimes when lightning strikes something.

Q: How big were the blue balls?

Adm. T.: They seemed about as big as a baseball. I slapped at one of them and it just stood still and looked at me. So I decided that I might be beginning to lose my mind and I'd better pay attention to my instruments because we didn't want to turn upside down as well as being struck by lightning. It turned out that 13 out of the 14 aircraft were struck by lightning, some of them a little worse than others, but most of them, because the aircraft parts are bonded one to the other - by bonded I mean there was a little pigtail wire that makes an electrical contact between the ailerons and the wing of the aircraft and between the tail and the fuselage, any movable part. So electricity can surge through the airplane without jumping in a big spark and doing too much damage.

Q: But those balls of blue fire must have been a frightening experience!

Adm. T.: It was frightening. Also sort of eerie.

Q: You'd think you'd gone to another world.

Adm. T.: Yes. I thought we were. I thought we were going to another world, anyway!

Q: How do you react in that circumstance?

Adm. T.: You can't believe it, at first. You don't know what it is, but you've got a job to do. Fortunately, you don't just have to sit there a long time and let those things roam around. Finally, they went away.

Q: You say you have your job to do and you just go ahead and do it and hope for the best, is that . . .

Adm. T.: I realized what it was, finally, because the radio-man came up from wrapping his hand that was mesermized and I said we must have been struck by lightning. A little bit later, when we were still on instruments and I was back down supposedly in my position, a light, as I thought, in the rear of the aircraft, back in the hull somewhere, was bothering me because it was reflecting on the glass in the

the cockpit and it irritated me a little bit, and I called the crew on the intercom and I said, "Put that light out back there. It bothers me." There was no answer for a while, and I called specifically to the radioman. He said, "Captain, I don't see any light back here. I'll check with the other people." So, there wasn't any light back there. I looked back and I noticed it was outside the aircraft, not in it, and it was so close it was reflected and bothered me. It turned out it was one of my wing men, and he could see my lights. I called him and told him to go away, get back on his station, and he said, "Well, I can see you all right. I've been with you all the time." He didn't deploy.

Q: He'd gone up with you as well as down?

Adm. T.: Yes. Apparently he did. He doesn't know whether he did or not and neither do I.

Q: How long did the whole episode last?

Adm. T.: It was several hours. It actually lasted until about daybreak. We began to come out in this clearer weather just before dawn, which I don't know what time it occurred - maybe it was 5:00 a.m.. I know we went into the thing at midnight.

Thach #2 - 127

Q: Had you not had weather predictions which would have told you the severity of the weather?

Adm. T.: You can't get good weather predictions even today in the Gulf of Tehuantepic.

Q: It was a particular geographical area.

Adm. T.: Well, you can't even get them at sea down there. In fact, sometimes they fool everybody on the West Coast of the United States, especially down to the south. You still don't have good weather reporting.

Q: A civilian doesn't realize that. You hear the weather reports and you take them for gospel without realizing that maybe they're not reliable at all.

Adm. T.: Well, you see, when you get down off the coast of Central America and Mexico, then out at sea, where the weather comes from, there are very few ships, very few fishing vessels and they may not report. You're out of any traffic lanes of large ships that have a good aerological unit aboard and make good reports from which predictions could be made. You could run into the same thing today down there, and not know that it was coming. Also, little fronts build up and huge thunderstorms. All they could predict in that case would be "thunderstorms in the area:

the weather is conducive to thunderstorms." But where?

Q: Or how severe they're going to be.

Adm. T.: How severe, nobody knows. And they don't know today. So, we finally came out of it and I saw two aircraft ahead of me which looked like about where the skipper was supposed to be and I joined up on them and my wing man came on. Then we couldn't find anybody else, couldn't see anybody else. Finally we were in communication with everyone, and Ruff Johnson had hit severe turbulence and was struck by lightning, and he decided he wanted to go down so he went down low on the water. That delayed him a little bit, but he knew approximately his position, and so the captain said we'd rendezvous over the coastline nearest San Salvador, the country of El Salvador, which we did, and then we headed on down over Nicaragua. I've forgotten what time it was. It may have been late morning, this huge black cloud that stretched almost half of the horizon over Nicaragua, so the captain said, "Now, let's have this foul weather spread and do it right this time." In we went. This wasn't as severe as the Tehuantepic storm, but it was heavy rain, zero-zero visibility at 8,000 feet or whatever it was, and we came out of that storm and everybody was exactly in the right position. You could see everybody just as soon as we came out. So we learned a lesson. We finally landed at Coco Solo after about twenty-four hours' flying.

Q: It had been nonstop, however?

Adm. T.: Yes, it was nonstop.

Q: Your nerves and physical condition must have been just at the breaking point after an experience like that!

Adm. T.: Let's say it was somewhat hairy, but after an aviator has had enough experience, those things - oh, of course, he's tired - but he doesn't feel it too much as far as feeling near a nervous breakdown because he's been conditioned to it. By that time we had flown many twelve-hour patrols, six hours out in the ocean and six hours back, for example, to an unlighted coast down in Central America during fleet problems, and flying in Alaska. There are some flights, such as that one, you're glad they're over and you hope you never run into a thing like that again, but since you handled it once, why can't you handle it again - and that's the way you feel. It's the same thing when you've had a forced landing. I had a forced landing in a PM-1 when I was with VP-9. It was near El Salvador, too. We were flying round-the-clock search patrols because there was a big fleet problem in the Pacific and we were searching out from the

The Thach Weave

This defense maneuver helped our carrier fighters to down 14.3 Zeros for every single loss in spite of the fact that the Zeros had all three fighting advantages—speed, climb, maneuverability. Admiral McCain wrote that the "genius (of the Thach Weave) broke and defeated the air forces of Japan."

Some of the many variations and the exact technique of the Thach Weave are still confidential. However the basic maneuver is well known because it was not only adopted and used by the U. S. Navy but by the U. S. Air Force, the R.A.F. and the Russians. It is a defensive maneuver and counter attack but the same principle is used in escort and attack on bombers to deliver that 1-2 knockout punch. The higher the speed the more useful it will be.

Let Capt. J. S. Thach tell you about it. He talks with his hands.

"The Fighter Combat Team is four planes. They fly in pairs (two-plane sections). the wingman follows his section leader closely . . . . . .

section leaders fly far enough apart so that, if an enemy approaches the tail of one of them, they can make a . .

quick turn like this. The quick turn toward each other does two things to the enemy pilot. It throws his aim off and . . . .

because he usually tries to follow his target, it leads him around into a position to be shot by the other part of our team . . . .

suppose an enemy had attacked the left hand plane which has now turned away. The preoccupied enemy is suddenly confronted by . . .

another plane (right hand), at which he cannot point his plane. But the right hand is in position to make a kill. After you have . . . .

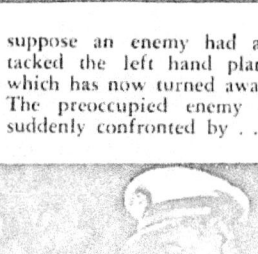

thrown a few red arrows into him you had better start to turn back and repeat the weave. There may be others coming at you . . . . . .

if they attack in quick succession you can continue to weave, shoot and then return to that all important initial position. Fight as a team and you'll live longer."

coast. There's a gulf there, the Gulf of Fonseca, where the USS Wright was anchored tending us, and we would either take off at midnight and come back at noon, which I felt better about. Or else you'd take off at noon and come back to that black coast with mountains behind the bay. If you didn't hit the bay just right and kept looking for it, you might run into the mountains.

One time I was out on one of those things. I had taken off at midnight and I'd gotten back about 15 or 20 miles from the coast when one engine let go and the propeller just stopped, frozen. In the PM-1 we couldn't fly on one engine, so I landed on the ocean, and I radioed the Wright that I was down and I added that I wished they'd hurry up and come and get me because it was kind of rough out there and we were all going to get seasick or we thought we were. Then I told them that I'd put a bucket over the wing tip on the side of the good engine and I was taxiing in toward the coast making about eight knots, I thought, in a zigzag fashion. I knew which direction to head in. They radioed back and said, "Keep on coming. We're not going to get the Wright underway." So I taxied right on into the harbor. Finally, after hours and hours, I got in there late in the afternoon. I was sort of upset that they didn't come out to try to get me. Suppose we had sprung a leak and sunk?

Q: Yes. It occurs to me that that was the first thing

that they were there for!

Adm. T.: They sent out another airplane to look at me every now and then.

Q: To be sure you were still floating!

Adm. T.: Yes, to be sure I was still taxiing and making headway for the harbor.

Q: Again, that must have been a miserable experience. I'm sure, of course, it was.

Adm. T.: Well, it was. All of us felt we were going to get seasick but nobody did.

Q: I've often thought when one was so scared you don't get seasick.

Adm. T.: Yes, I think so. You worry. You have a problem on your hands.

Q: So, after two years, you got ordered back to the place you wanted to go originally, which was a fighter squadron. Is that correct?

Thach #2 - 132

Adm. T.: That's right. VF Squadron 3, which was the Felix Cat Squadron. It had a little Felix Cat as an insignia. I was given the job of gunnery officer, which was very much to my liking.

Q: Where were you?

Adm. T.: VF-3 was a Saratoga-based squadron and our shore station was North Island, Naval Air Station, San Diego. One of the first things that happened to me in VF-3 was that I got a letter of admonition. The way this occurred was the fact that I had the fleet air officer-of-the-day duty, and our station was an office in the administration building quite a distance from West Beach, where the aircraft were. The policy then was to have an assistant in the control tower who handled the course changes that indicated which direction to land. Now it would be called the choice of designated runway use. And if a certain number of black shapes, or black balls, as we called them, were hoisted, it would indicate that you landed to the north or the west, et cetera. On this particular morning, I checked the weather report and it looked a little too bad to hoist the course signals and put the field into commission. But also, it was each squadron commander's decision - he made out the schedule, and it was his decision about when and if they would fly. The regulations were a little bit loose, or, rather, not too specific, concerning whether aircraft could take off when the black shapes were not hoisted. On this particular day Bombing Squadron 2 under the command of Lieutenant Commander Don Felt had a scheduled exercise which involved them going over into the desert, so the aircraft took off. In my office I didn't even hear them, I didn't know anyone had taken off. They tried to get through the pass to go over the desert and apparently the weather closed in on them. There was a low overcast all over the coast and it extended up into the mountains, and three of them crashed into the mountains. Well, this was a bad thing, so an investigation started. I was not called as a witness in the investigation. The investigating officer made the statement that the regulations needed to be brought more in line with reality, and he suggested that I make a statement to that effect and criticize the regulations, saying that they weren't adequate. I saw no point in doing that, since he said he was going to do it anyway. So, the next thing I knew I was called into the office of the chief of staff of Commander, Aircraft, Battle Force, who was Captain John Hoover - we called him Genial John Hoover, and this "genial" part was probably the most sarcastic of titles, I guess, that anyone ever had because he was a martinet and a cold, mean man. He questioned me about what I had done that morning and why I hadn't stopped the airplanes from taking off, why I had permitted them to take off.

And I said I didn't permit them to take off, I didn't know they had taken off. I did not have the field open. He told me that I should have stopped them and he handed me a letter that he had had already written out, a letter of admonition.

Q: Did he suggest how you could have stopped them?

Adm. T.: No. He didn't know how, either, I'm sure. Anyway, I felt that was pretty unjust, but the letter went on down officially through to my commanding officer and I was pretty unhappy about that. I had the privilege of writing a letter of rebuttal which was sent to Washington along with the admonition. Genial John also had a program on, or a campaign, for security which is a very good thing if it is done right. He worked on it and changed things around. He put on more sentries and so forth. Then he made the statement one time that now the place was finally secure. Well, one of the duties of the fleet air officer of the day was to go round and check the sentries to see if they were on the job and he had challenged any of us, "you can't get in there without being recognized. You can't get into West Beach or any of the other hangars, but I want you to try." I had developed a huge dislike for "Genial" John and wanted to prove him wrong. So, I put some black on my face and put on a pair of coveralls and crawled across the field and watched the sentry moving back and forth. Timing it just right, I got into three hangars and put sabotage tags on the airplanes, then made out my report. He called me in and raised cain with me because he said that maybe the officer of the day could do that, but that nobody else could. And I said, "Well, I was somebody else because no sentry ever saw me. I was not challenged. Anybody can do this. I don't see how you can put enough sentries on to stop somebody from getting in sometime. In the first place, they're out in the open and maybe they could have caught me had they been inside the hangar. Once I was inside the hangar I was free. All I had to do was get out without being caught." I used to do this frequently, but one time I did get caught. The sentry was smart. He apparently saw me crawling into the hangar and I didn't know, and without my hearing a thing, all of a sudden I turned around and there was a great big .45 pointing right in my face. I said, "Okay, I'm the OD. You can put that thing down." And he said, "I don't know whether you are or not." I thought he was going to shoot me right there.

Q: He was doing his job right, anyway.

Adm. T.: He was. He sure was. To get back into more important things, we had this wonderful document I think I mentioned before, the orders for gunnery exercises, abbreviated OGE, which designated the gunnery practices that were to be performed and just how they were supposed to be done in order to make them not only standard but realistic, so that no unrealistic type of procedure that wouldn't occur in wartime would creep in and permit pilots to get a good score when they wouldn't have done it in actual combat. This was not a static thing. Every year a committee was designated to update this document and there were, as always, a number of what we called sea lawyers who would figure out a way to slip through the loop-holes and the description of how to perform the approaches to the target. This was especially so in our fixed gunnery practices. But I think that this book and the way it was handled, the way the exercises had to be conducted so that there was always an umpire there watching, and the umpire was from some competing squadron so he wasn't going to let anyone get away with a thing, increased our actual readiness more than anything else. It forced us to learn how to shoot the way you had to shoot at a bird when he's flying across, and to take the proper lead, instead of simply riding up on the tail of an airplane and shooting it. The reason one should not do this (unless, of course, it's a fighter with no rear guns) is that there is no point in giving the opposing gunners an opportunity to hit.

There grew up an idea in the squadrons of large aircraft, both of the Army Air Corps and of the Navy - the Navy patrol planes - that our free gun manned by gunners in turrets or swivel mounts could defend a large aircraft in the air. The Flying Fortress, the B-17, was designed with this in mind, and they expected to go without any fighter escort. But we had learned a long time ago - and I had this further demonstrated when I was in VP aircraft, that any fighter pilot who did the right thing would have an extremely small chance of being hit by guns installed in a bomber type aircraft. If he were stupid or over-eager and permitted the large aircraft to turn its tail toward him, so that they had a no-deflection shot on the fighter as well as the fighter having a no-deflection shot on them, then all you're doing is trading shots and this is not at all necessary since the fighter aircraft can always out-maneuver the bomber aircraft.

Another wonderful thing we had that was unique in the Navy - no other aircraft squadrons that I know of had it - was a camera gun. The camera gun was a camera, bore-sighted parallel to the guns, bore-sighted forward, and it had a little clock and each frame of the film would take a picture of this clock as well as what would be seen through the gun sight each time it was rolled. Each time the trigger was pressed, why, the camera would operate. By synchronizing these clocks on the ground just before flight to conduct camera-gun exercises, both fighter against fighter and fighter against large aircraft with flexible guns, it was easy to tell by looking at the film and the little clock who got the first hits and when. This kept down a lot of arguments that might not have been settled otherwise.

The scoring of camera-gun exercises was most interesting. The umpire would go into a projection room with the representatives of each opposing squadron, or each opposing aircraft if it were within the squadron in a camera-gun exercise, and run this film just frame by frame, and call out whether or not it was a hit. An experienced officer could do this. However, either opposing pilot could hold the film and argue each hit, if they felt that the umpire had made an error, and often this would be the case and then they would get out measuring sticks and measure the line the aircraft were flying and the target aircraft and calculate the angle and so forth, and finally settle it. These things could be settled amazingly well, to the satisfaction of everyone.

Q: It was a marvelous training tool, wasn't it?

Adm. T.: Oh, it was fantastic, and I was surprised that no foreign aircraft - the British didn't have it, the U.S. Army Air Corps didn't have it. We were the only ones that had it. It really surprised me when I discovered this.

I progressed from gunnery officer to operations officer, and when the then-commanding officer, Cooper, was detached and Lieutenant Commander Sid Harvey took command of the squadron, I was made executive officer, No. 2 in command.

Q: He was the man whom you'd relieved on the Cincinnati?

Adm. T.: This was the same Sid Harvey I'd relieved in the *Cincinnati*. About that time the war was on in Europe and a letter came directing that he be detached to go over to England as an observer in the Battle of Britain, and I was given command of the squadron. The orders further said that when his tour was finished over there, then he would come back and relieve me and I would go over. Unfortunately, when he stopped in Washington to get a final briefing before going over, he was playing handball and when he finished the game he went in and took a shower and fell over under the shower with a heart attack and died as a young lieutenant commander. He was one of the finest naval officers I had ever known. He had a way of leadership that was just like a magnet. He would be out in the hangars some place, either during working hours or afterwards, when some of the men were going on liberty and he would start talking to one of them just about something in general, about how jobs ought to be done and why, and, first thing you know, he'd have a crowd of people standing around listening to him and hanging on his words. And they didn't have to be there. They could have gone on ashore. I noticed him doing this many times. He was a most likable person and one utterly dedicated to his job and to the mission of the U.S. Navy. So it was a very sad thing to have him fall over so young. Because of this I didn't go to England. I retained command of the squadron, although I was only a lieutenant at the time. This explains

Thach #2 - 140

why I was given command of a squadron ahead of my contemporaries.

Q: You retained command of that then completely through the first six months of the war, didn't you?

Adm. T.: I made lieutenant commander in January 1942.

Q: But you were commanding officer of the squadron through the first six months?

Adm. T.: Yes. Up through June of 1942. There were a number of things that we proved time and time again. One of these was the fact that two aircraft of the same type and equal in performance with each power plant performing properly, if one of them had altitude advantage over the other he could generally get on the other's tail and ride him right on down to the ground or anywhere the fellow proposed to go. In other words, the fighter with initial altitude advantage couldn't be shaken off, and should win the dog fight, assuming that he made no mistakes. Of course, mistakes are easy to make under those circumstances, but with the group that we had when I was commanding officer, it was very evident that the experienced ones could do this every time. With one experienced pilot against another, if the one above made no mistakes, which he usually didn't, the one below could not get out from under and get the advantage again. In other words, he couldn't bring his guns to bear because the one with the initial advantage would always be riding in a good tail position and never could anyone turn the tables on him. On the other hand, in the case of new or inexperienced pilots who'd just come from the training command or maybe from some other type of squadron, the experienced ones could give away altitude advantage and still turn the tables on them and lick 'em every time.

So, I established what we called a "humiliation team." It was composed of myself, my executive officer, Don Lovelace, Noel Gayler and my gunnery officer whose name was Rollo Lemon. We would take these newcomers to the squadron, take them up and give them all the altitude advantage they wanted. Then we'd fly towards each other and see if they could come down and get on our tails and stay there long enough to shoot. A pilot who has just achieved the wonderful accomplishment of getting his wings is usually rather full of himself and sometimes a little cocky. So this was a good thing to let them know that they didn't know everything right off the bat and show them that they had a lot of work to do. We could even eat an apple and lick these kids, or read a newspaper. I used to take an apple up and eat it just to . . .

Q: Show them!

Adm. T.: Well, anyway, this was true with one exception. One person who came to my squadron fresh out of the training command was a young man by the name of Butch O'Hare, and the first time I took him up and gave him altitude advantage, he didn't make any mistakes and I did everything I could to fool him and shake him, and he came right in on me and stuck there and he could have shot me right out of the air. So I came down and I got hold of Rollo Lemon and I said, "Well, I've had one of these new youngsters up but I want each member of the Humiliation Team to go up with him and give him a chance. He's pretty good, and I'll just wager a little bit, that he'll get on your tail the first time and stay there." "Oh," he said, "they never do." I said, "I know that." "Well," he said, "where is he?" Up they went and, sure enough, Butch did it again. It wasn't long after that before we made him a member of the Humiliation Team, because he had passed the graduation test so quickly.

Q: How did he gain that skill? Were you able to evaluate that?

Adm. T.: I think Butch O'Hare, when he learned how to fly an airplane, he learned how to fly it real well. He was a good athlete. He had a sense of timing and relative motion that he may have been born with, but also he had that competitive spirit. When he got into any kind of a fight like this, he didn't want to lose. He wanted to win. He really had a dedication to winning, and he probably had worked a lot of this out in his own mind, then read as much as he could, and when he first got to the squadron he studied all the documents that we had on aerial combat and he just picked it up much faster than anyone else I've ever seen. He got the most out of his airplane. He didn't try to horse it around. He learned a thing that a lot of youngsters don't learn that when you're in a dog fight with somebody, it isn't how hard you pull back on the stick to make a tight turn to get inside of him, it's how smoothly you fly the plane and whether you pull back with just enough of turn on your aircraft so that it remains efficient and isn't squashing all through the air causing more drag, which defeats the purpose of what you're after, to get around in the shortest time, that is the tightest turn consistent with not losing ground due to rough handling of the aircraft or working the controls in such a way that they cause a drag on the forward motion of the aircraft.

Q: Do you think the best aviators have almost a sixth sense of how to do this?

Adm. T.: I think that, in the first place, they have to have a competitive spirit. A good fighter pilot has got to have a competitive spirit. He's got to want to go up there and do this thing. He's got to want to do it more than anything else in the world.

Q: That's innate!

Adm. T.: Yes, that's the spirit of competition, I guess, that's built up somewhere, or he was born with it - one or the other. But he must have more than that. He's got to have a feel to develop it by trial and error of how to fly his airplane so he's getting the most out of it. That's the trick. That's the difference between . . . When two airplanes are right like this and they both try to turn toward each other, what happens? They do like this. They get into a scissors. Whichever one can then turn the tightest and finally get on the other's tail, he's flying his airplane more efficiently than his opponent.

Q: I wish the picture of you describing that could go on the tape!

Adm. T.: Every aviator, especially a fighter pilot, has to talk with his hands whether he talks any other way or not.

This desire to excel has a significant bearing on how people do later in combat, I think. I'm sure that I could, after a little while flying with a pilot, flying against him in a fighter, I felt that I could tell whether he would be good, mediocre, or average, or superb, also whether he would lose his head, was he calm and cool and would he remember to do the right thing, would he have the capability to do it, physically, but not do it because he suddenly gets a mental block due to over-excitement, or fear or something. In the early part of the war I kept a little black book - I never showed it to anybody - and I listed those people in my squadron whom I thought might probably - we might lose first. That's the way it turned out, and so I threw the book away.

I forgot to mention that in the case of the three aircraft taking off and crashing, Don Felt's squadron, Genial John also gave Don Felt a letter of admonition, and years and years later he told me one time, "Remember that letter of admonition we got?" And I said, "Yes, I remember. I'll never forget it." He said, "Well, that wasn't a very good start to get four stars, was it?"

Q: Didn't you have a chance to answer that?

Adm. T.: Yes. I answered it, and I thought maybe they might retract it, but they never did. Sid Harvey was very upset about this. He said, "Genial John thought he had to punish someone, make somebody else the goat, so he wouldn't receive any criticism himself." Don Felt said, "The fact of what anybody did on the field had nothing to do with the crashing.

If they went up to the mountain pass and it was closed and they couldn't get through, they should have turned round and come back. That was the reason they crashed. They tried to get through and the weather was too bad and they didn't have enough altitude." It was as simple as that, and it still happens to aircraft. They try to go through a mountain pass with not enough altitude. It has nothing to do with the condition of the field or whether they take off or whether they - or when they take off or why they take off or who permitted them to take off.

Q: Fortunately, it didn't interfere with your career.

Adm. T.: Apparently not.

Q: Maybe that was like the Humiliation Team?

Adm. T.: No, but it told me that I didn't know everything - about the character of some people in positions of authority.

It was in the spring of 1941 when we received an intelligence report of great significance. This report had come out of China when the Japanese and Chinese were having aerial combat in connection with the war there. It described a new Japanese aircraft, a fighter, that had performance that was far superior to anything we had. It said it had more than 5,000 feet per minute climb, it had very high speed,

and it could turn inside of any other aircraft. Well, those
are the three advantages that a fighter pilot would like to
have, or rather, that he needs if he's going to be successful
in combat. He'd like to have at least two out of the three:
one is high rate of climb, one is a tight turn, and the other
is speed. Now, you can turn altitude into speed just by
putting your nose down, but you can't change the rate of
climb or how tight an airplane will turn. That's built
into it. So, when I realized that this airplane, if this
intelligence report were correct, had us beat in all three
categories, it was pretty discouraging. Some of the pilots
just didn't believe it. They said, "Why, it couldn't be.
This is a gross exaggeration." We discussed it in our
squadron in every way, and I remember noting the language
in which this was written, whether it had been interpreted
or not, I don't know, but it was fighter pilots' language.
I felt we should give it some credence because whoever wrote
it talked like a fighter pilot, like he knew what he was
talking about. I told my squadron, "All right, let's assume
that it is exaggerated. Let's say it's only half as good
as this report says it is, and let's put down those figures.
Say it only has 2,500 feet per minute of climb. We have
1,100. Suppose it doesn't turn quite as - do the things
that the writer of this report describes as to rate of turn,
cut that in half and it still looks like it can turn inside
of us. And the speed, the same thing. If you take off half

his speed, he'd be about the same as we were." As it turned out, he did have about 3,000 feet per minute climb, he could turn inside of anything, and he had a lot more speed than we did, even carrying more gasoline. This was the Zero, and I decided, well, we'd better do something about this and remembering my days on the football field and basketball court, if you have somebody who's faster than you are, you have to trap him somehow so that he can't use his superiority, whatever it is. You've got to bait him or do something. I believed we had one advantage, if we could ever get into a position to use it. We had good guns and could shoot and hit even if we had only a fleeting second or two to take aim. Therefore, we must do something to entice the opponent into giving us that one all important opportunity - it was the only chance we had. So every night when I came home - I lived in a little rented house in Coronado, California, where we are now - I used to work on this problem. I used a box of kitchen matches and put them on the dining room table and let each one of them represent an airplane. In this manner I could get as many airplanes in the air as I wanted in various formations and try to decide what they ought to do. Usually, I would work on this every night until about midnight. My wife, Madalyn, was worried for fear I was not getting enough sleep. So about 11:55 p.m. she would come to the table and say, "Jimmy, you know you are going to fly tomorrow. Don't you think it's time you got some sleep?"

She was right. She knew I lost track of time when fiddling with those matches. So I would put them away until the next night.

For years when I was flying in a fighter squadron, one thing that sort of irked me, made me a little unhappy, was the kind of formation we flew, with three-plane sections, a leader and two wing men. If you're going to fight and do radical turns, this was an unwieldy formation, because if the leader made a tight turn, say, to the left, if it was as quick and tight as he might want to turn, then he would cause the inside man to slide over and probably right into the other wing man, especially if the inside man was trying to get his sights on something at the same time the leader was. So, in order to fight in a three-plane section staying in that formation, I decided that we had to have three eyes - three eyeballs, one to look at the leader, one to sight through the gun sights to hit anything, and the third eye to keep an eye on that other wing-man so you didn't run into him. Starting with that premise, it was obvious that if we were going to be able to do something sudden to fool an enemy, we ought to throw away one of those planes and just have a two-plane section, which is what I did. At that time, everybody was flying around in three-plane sections, both in our country and Europe.

Q: Japan, too? Or do you know?

Adm. T.: Yes, I think so, at that time. Finally I decided what would happen if, say, we just had two-plane sections, and we had a four-plane division, or combat unit, and when you're in the air and you see an enemy aircraft and you know either you want to get him or you want to avoid getting shot down yourself, you don't run away from him unless you're sure you've got a headstart, assuming that he has a greater speed, so you have to turn toward him. If you're afraid of him you turn toward him and hope that he won't get a good shot and that you will. So, assuming that you've got enemy aircraft out here and they're going to come in to attack you, say, they're off to the side, you turn toward them. Well, they've got to pick out some target, so they pick out one of the airplanes and, in that case, if we split a little wider apart, into a sort of a wide formation, he'll have to take on one section or the other, and if he goes after the one on the right, the one on the left, presumably, might have a chance to shoot him in a cross fire. So, I thought, let's try that. We tried it, but it became apparent - I'd work on these things every night, then the next morning we'd try them in the air- it became apparent that there wasn't any use in flying these four planes very close together, you might as well start them out split. That way you could separate them far enough so that if an enemy came after either one, either from ahead or astern, or above, you might be able to confuse him by doing something that he didn't expect.

Then I decided that we would have a standard distance equal to the tactical diameter of the aircraft. The tactical diameter of anything, ship turn or aircraft, is the diameter of the tightest circle it can make, or half-circle. Being in that position, if an enemy plane or planes came in from ahead, why, the one they were coming after could have a head-on shot at them, and this one could also have a shot at them, the one that they weren't attacking. Now, if they come in from astern, we had a lookout doctrine that the two planes on the right looked out, watched over the tails of the two planes on the left and vice versa. If you were on the right side, you never needed to look to the right, you always kept an eye open over to the left. So that somebody would know if another plane was coming up on its tail. Often I talk to myself while working on a problem - it seems to help. I said, "Well, if we're going to really fool him, we won't use any signals, we'll have to wait until he's almost within lethal firing range and then the one who's watching him - (the other won't be able to see him because he can't see straight astern)- he makes a sharp turn toward the one being attacked, and that's the signal that somebody is right within firing range on his tail. So if he is the one on the left, he turns also. He turns right. What does this do? The attacking aircraft has to take a lead, if he's diving in on you, he has to take a lead. If he takes a lead, an extension of your flight line as he sees it, and you suddenly turn after he's committed himself, it throws his lead off. He's not going to hit. And if he tries to follow on around, to get back his aim he's got to do at least two maneuvers, he's got to put his wing down and then pull his nose back up again. That takes time. It brings him right in the sights of the right-hand section of aircraft which should have a good shot at him either head-on, if he continues to follow his target, or a good side approach, if he pulls out." We, then, although he has superior performance, we then have a shot at him but he hasn't shot at us - not accurately. So, this looked like it was, maybe, the only thing to do. I was very excited about this discovery with matches on the table. I went into the bedroom. I thought maybe my wife was asleep - she wasn't - just waiting to tell me when it was midnight. I said, "Madalyn, I've got it! I've got it! I know you can get enough sleep for a change." I wrote this all up and then I presented it to the squadron and we discussed it and I said, "Well, we've got to practice this, but who's going to be the Zeros and who's - how are we going to find the airplanes? We don't have airplanes that are that fast and that high performance. So, I'll tell you what we'll do." I told Butch O'Hare to take four aircraft and use full power, and I would take four and never advance the throttle - we put a little mark on the throttle quadrant - never advance it more than half way. That gave him at least a superior performance. Maybe double, maybe not, but somewhat.

Q: But by not exceeding a certain rate . . .

Adm. T.: Power setting.

Q: Because he's going at full throttle it gives him a relative superiority.

Adm. T.: Relative performance given to his four aircraft.

Q: To represent the superior Japanese characteristics?

Adm. T.: Correct. We went up and I had told Butch, "You attack from any direction you want to and keep a good eye out and see what it looks like. Does it look like it's any good? Is it giving you any trouble?" So, he made all sorts of attacks, quite a few of them from overhead and coming down, this way and that, and I figured it looked like a pretty good thing to me. I noticed every time that - (you can tell when an airplane is in position to shoot) - he came in to shoot, we just kept weaving back and forth all the time these streams of aircraft were attacking. After we landed he came over to me and he said, "Skipper, it really worked. It really works. I couldn't make any attack without seeing the nose of one of your half-throttle airplanes pointed at me. So at least you are getting a shot, even though I might also have got a shot, at least it isn't one-sided. Most of the time that sudden turn, although I knew what you were going to do, you can't tell exactly <u>when</u> and I didn't want to anticipate it, but it always caught me a little bit by surprise because it seemed to be timed just right. When I was committed and about to squeeze the trigger, here he went and turned and I didn't think he saw me." Of course, he didn't. That's the beauty of this also, you needed no communication. You were flying along watching the other two and they suddenly made a turn, you knew there was somebody on your tail and you had to really turn in a hurry, and that's all there was to it. Didn't need any radio. Radio could be out.

So we felt a little better about the situation. We had been proving, you might say all of our fighter lives, that an airplane with superior performance could knock you out of the air and that's it. No question about it. If you met him, he was going to get you, assuming he wasn't a stupid pilot, and you can't assume the enemy is not going to be experienced and able to shoot. But now we had something to work on, to keep us from being demoralized.

Q: Actually, I would think if you knew you were going against a superior-performing aircraft, I wouldn't know how you could get anyone in the air against him.

Adm. T.: Well . . .

Q: Naturally, you go because you're ordered to, but without some kind of . . .

Adm. T.: You go for the same reason that everybody goes. You're dedicated to it. But it gave us something to work on, and it gave us a little sort of plan and I've always felt that in athletics, football or basketball or any competitive sport, and the same applies to combat, that you've got to have a plan. If you don't have a plan - and I told my people this often, have some kind of a plan, even if it's a lousy plan and you're working your plan, at least, it's better than having none. The enemy isn't working his, - because if you start working yours, his may not fit in with it and you can keep him off balance. (I keep wanting to talk about what happened in the war, but I will stay away from that for a while).

Q: What you're describing, of course, is what's known as "Thach Weave," but I hadn't realized that you had developed it this early in your career.

Adm. T.: That's right. I developed it before the war, in

the summer of 1941 - summer and fall - on my kitchen table in Coronado. A lot of people don't realize this. I've read in various places that I studied the combat reports of the Coral Sea Battle and then figured it out just before the Battle of Midway. This is not true at all. We'd been practicing this for a long time. Jimmy Flatley gave it the name Thach Weave. I didn't. I'll tell you about that a little later.

Q: Also, if you had not gotten the intelligence report, you might not have had to go to these measures.

Adm. T.: Oh, I'm sure. I think we would have gone right along, fat, dumb, and happy, and run into this thing and not had nearly the success that we had. We'd have been much worse off. In fact, we would have been in far worse shape in the early battles in the war.

Q: We'd have lost a lot of planes before realizing what we were fighting.

Adm. T.: Yes, that would have occurred.

Q: Do you know where that intelligence report came from?

Adm. T.: All I ever knew is that it - they said it came out

of China and that apparently a Chinese pilot who spoke English and was a fighter pilot had witnessed or himself tangled with these airplanes and was amazed and wrote up a report and our intelligence people got hold of it. In those days, and, of course, during the war, the intelligence people never did, and they should not have, told us the source of intelligence. So that's the reason we didn't know. All we knew is it came out of China.

Q: One could say thank God it did!

Adm. T.: Yes. Later in the summer of 1941, my squadron was aboard the Saratoga and then we went out to Pearl Harbor and were based there for a while. We'd had some difficulty with our engines. We'd had an oil-seal leak and it leaked on the windshield. Apparently someone was trying to save money and bought some much cheaper oil seals than the original ones (the old ones couldn't have cost more than a few pennies apiece) for the Pratt and Whitney engines we had in our aircraft, they leaked, and the propeller would pick it up and throw it all over the windshield. When you're coming in for a carrier landing at night with a little rain, the one thing you don't want is oil on your windshield. And this worried me because we had some new people who were learning pretty well, but some of them were a little marginal about getting aboard, especially at night. A night landing aboard a carrier is a sort of a scarey thing anyway. I wrote a real critical letter on this subject and said I didn't think that a Fleet squadron should be utilized as a laboratory for trying out new and cheaper oil seals or anything else like that. So they took action fast. We got the old good oil seals back again, but it took us some time to take each engine down and get them in and so forth, along with a few other difficulties, so we missed out on a lot of time that we should have been firing at a sleeve and getting real good and getting everybody qualified to be able to shoot from the hip, so to speak, if necessary, snap shots or any other kind, and hit. We couldn't get our airplanes in the air enough. Finally we got a new engine, whole new engine, and we had to put that in each aircraft. Well, that took more time. In the meantime we were getting a turnover of personnel and I had a number of people who were not qualified in various things that we had to do.

I remember that the squadron was ordered to get aboard the Enterprise - by this time the Saratoga was in for a short overhaul - because there was going to be a big Fleet problem and we got the operations order for it and everything. All of a sudden, out we went. I was getting more and more uneasy, so I wrote a letter saying that our readiness was not up to where it should be at all, we were unready, we were not ready to fight, period. I showed it to my good friend Everett Burroughs, who was a lieutenant commander on Admiral Halsey's staff - his flagship was the <u>Enterprise</u>, we got aboard the <u>Enterprise</u> - and he said, "Look, don't just mail that letter in. It looks too routine. Why don't you go to the chief of staff and tell him you want to see the admiral and hand it to him?" So, I did. I fought my way up and got to see Admiral Halsey, and I said, "We're way behind and I have a feeling we may have to be in a war pretty soon. After all, the Japanese have told us to keep out of the Western Pacific, and things look like to me they're building up. We've got a war going on in Europe, and I just don't think that this squadron ought to be in this condition. We've had all kinds of things, including inspections and this, that, and the other, we have to get ready for, and it just seems like they keep us off balance all the time, and I've got to have a 30-day period at least where I would like to fly day and night, including weekends. I hope that you can give me permission and arrange for me to do that." He looked at it and asked me a number of questions about how many people and so forth, and I said, "I'm not sure I could even hit anything. I'm pretty experienced. I know my kids can't. They haven't had an opportunity to fire a gun." He said, "When do you want to do this?" I said, as soon as possible. He said, "How about this afternoon?" And I said, "Wonderful, but we're going into this Fleet problem." So he said, "I'll just let you out of the Fleet problem. Do you want to fly ashore this afternoon and do it?" And I said, "Yes, Sir, and would you just please do one more thing? Send a message and tell the commander in there at Ford Island to have his supply department with somebody on duty to handle gasoline and supplies, day and night, for this squadron." He said, "Sure. Go ahead."

I flew in that afternoon. We missed the Fleet problem. Started my day and night 30-day business. But then we ran into another problem and that was a shortage of ammunition, shortage of .50-caliber ammunition. I knew it had been getting kind of bad but I couldn't get any. It had all been used up and no new shipments were coming, and here I was, out of ammunition and had permission to fly the pants off these people all day. I didn't anticipate this. I thought surely somewhere I could get some ammunition. So my chief gunner and I used to sit out in the gunnery shack watching them prepare those guns to fire a record practice, and it was really an interesting thing. He had some good assistant ordnancemen and they took those machineguns apart, every little piece, and felt them carefully and any burrs on the moving parts hone them with an Arkansas stone until they just moved beautifully like a perfect piece of machinery that hardly makes any noise, it's so smooth, except a little clicking.

Another thing that he had the idea of doing, but he said he'd need some help - this was earlier. I just want to tell about this so that I can give you an idea what kind of wonderful gentleman this chief was. He said, "If you want to be sure that you don't have a jam on a record practice" - you know it's a horrible thing to happen to a young pilot, he gets up there firing record practice and he fires a burst of twelve, he's sure he got some hits and he starts in to fire some more - he's going to fire six bursts of twelve rounds each - and his gun jams, the one gun he's using. You only use one gun on practice. So he said we should fit every round of ammunition that we were going to use in a record practice - the day before, we should fit it in the chamber, take it out again and put it in the belt. So I said, great idea, because we were always getting slight aberrations on one round a little outsize, not manufactured to fine tolerances, and it would stick and you couldn't eject it, and that's the end of that record practice. You don't have another chance. So I got hold of all the pilots and I and everybody else, as skipper of this squadron, would go out there in this gunnery shack and fit each round into the gun that we were going to use, the round that was going to go into that gun, and then belt it and you'd be ready for record practice. And we didn't have any jams -

Q: How tedious that was!

Adm. T.: Tedious, but worth it.

He came to me and he said, "Captain (I was a lieutenant, but he said, captain - captain of the squadron), I heard about where some ammunition is - some .50 caliber ammunition." And I said, "Where is it?" And he said, "Well," he wasn't sure whether he ought to tell me or not, he thought he could get it, and I said, "Maybe I can help. We need it in a hurry." He said, "You know this squadron that's based next door to us and we use the same ammunition locker, VF-2, Lieutenant Paul Ramsey's squadron (Paul Ramsey's a classmate of mine, always been a very good friend, ever since we were midshipmen together),"he has a lot of ammunition and his squadron has completed their gunnery training phase and they're doing something else now. Maybe we could take some of that." I said, "Chief, are you suggesting that we steal that ammunition from my good friend Paul Ramsey?" And he said, "Well, I'm suggesting that I go take it, just borrow it, maybe." I said, "I will have none of that. If anybody's going to steal anything I'm going to steal it myself. You go get the keys from this other chief for his side of the ammunition locker and tell him you want to borrow some Verey's pistol rounds, that we've run out, and we'll pay him back next week. Get those keys and we'll go in there and steal that stuff tonight." So, we did. We went in there and we stole about half of his ammunition. We didn't want to steal all of it because we didn't think that was fair, and also he might notice that it was gone. So we took it, but it still wasn't too much. They never knew anything about it and, to this day, I haven't told Paul Ramsey that I stole his ammunition.

Q: If they didn't notice, it wasn't much of a loss!

Adm. T.: And I play golf with him every week, and one of these days I'm going to tell him.

Well, what we had to do because it was so little, instead of firing twelve rounds in practice at a sleeve - a twelve-round burst - I decided we'd better just fire one round, like a single-shot rifle, one round out of one gun on one pass at the target, one approach. This is what we did. It seemed pretty puny, and if you didn't hit with that round you came back with a clean sleeve, no holes in it, but, amazingly, the youngsters got so that they could put that one round in there, and in a way this may have been a blessing in disguise because it taught them to conserve ammunition. When you get in a big dog fight, milling around, it taught them not to open up too soon. The common error of every gunner, and this is true right now in Vietnam, is to waste ammunition. They see a target and long before they're in range they just start spewing out ammunition. This is no good in aerial combat where you only carry a certain amount and you don't know how many airplanes you're going to have to confront. So, I preached conservation of ammunition and don't open fire until you know you're within range. This firing with one round helped to really get them in the habit of doing that, and I think it saved us an awful lot in the Battle of Midway later, because we all came back with some ammunition, and this was amazing with the number of targets we had. So we managed to do pretty well in spite of this loss of ammunition.

About the time we finished this 30-day period uninterrupted, and got most of the people qualified in what they had to do, we got a message which said, "Transfer all of your guns to this Marine squadron (I've forgotten the designation of it, but it will come out later), all of your .50-caliber guns to them, and you will get new guns later." Well, this just really hit me, with what my ordnancemen had been doing with these guns, making them so perfect, and here, I thought I was now in pretty good shape and I'm going to lose all my guns. I couldn't understand why the Marines couldn't get their own damned guns, and I was really upset about it, so I again went down to see Everett Burroughs, who was the gunnery officer on Admiral Halsey's staff and said, "Look," I started crying all over his desk and I said, "I don't understand. This is ridiculous. This must be a mistake. I can't give up my guns. Let me tell you . . . ." and I told him about what good shape they were in and how many hours of work these ordnancemen had put on their guns to be sure that they didn't have any burrs or malfunction in them. And Ev Burroughs said, "Yes, we heard about that. That's the reason you're going to have to give these Marines your guns." I said, "Why? Why don't they have guns?" And he said, "Well, they haven't gotten any. They were getting new planes and no guns. I'm going to have to tell you something that I wasn't supposed to, but this Marine squadron is going to Wake Island and they're going to be way out on a limb and they've got to have the best guns and the best of everything, so we're giving them the best that we can find anywhere, and your guns are part of it." So, I couldn't argue any more. We waited and finally got some more guns and went through the same process again.

Q: Do you remember the date when this happened, Admiral?

Adm. T.: This would have had to be about September or October 1941.

Q: Getting very close to the crucial period!

Adm. T.: Yes.

Q: You were telling me about some of the personalities that you had served with, and let's take a time right now to tell a couple of those anecdotes.

Adm. T.: One of them was a great guy. I think I mentioned that he rowed on the Olympic champion crew, the Naval Academy crew that won the Olympics in 1921. The reason they called him "Country" Moore was because he looked like a big overgrown country boy and there were some things he wasn't too familiar with, such as the kind of perfume that women wear, and he had a girl friend and he wanted to get her something. The Saratoga was in Panama at the time on a cruise and "Cat" Brown and Jack Tate told him about a very good buy on perfume that sort he liked, he could get it very cheaply, so they told him the name of it and told him where to go in Panama and he went and bought six bottles and sent it to his girl friend. He didn't hear from her for a long time, until we got back to Norfolk, Virginia, and he called her up and said, "Did you get the six bottles I sent you?" And she said, "Yes, but I didn't know that I needed it. I don't know why you should send me six bottles of O-do-Ro-No."

Q: Maybe, for the record, we ought to say O-do-Ro-No is a deodorant.

Adm. T.: Maybe so, because I don't know that they sell it any more.

Q: I haven't seen it for a long time.

Adm. T.: Anyway, O-do-Ro-No was probably one of the few and

maybe the first deodorant that was on the market. Jack Tate was a great storyteller and he apparently had had some amazing experiences and he loved to get in a room with a number of people and start telling about some of them - things that had happened to him. Most of us refused to believe these stories because they sounded so fantastic, and we were determined to catch him in one and prove that these weren't his experiences, they were just a figment of his imagination. So, one time in Norfolk, Virginia, when I was in the experimental division, Country Moore and Freddy Wegeforth, Jimmy Dyer and I were all there at this party, and Jack Tate started telling about an amazing thing that had happened to him when he was flying in an airplane and it had crashed in the water in the Panama Canal. He was in the plane with one other person, and he managed to get out of the airplane after it sank and the other pilot didn't come up, and he dove back down and found him with his foot caught, and he said that he remembered that there might be a bubble of air in the wing, so he took a little pencil that he had and poked a hole in the bottom of the wing and slit it and stuck this fellow's head up through the fabric in the wing so he could breathe and Jack would come up and get enough air to go down several times and finally free his foot, and thereby saved his life.

Well, we thought this was one of the usual stories and we figured that it didn't happen, and again we were determined to catch him. He had mentioned this other pilot's name, and, lo and behold, a little while later somebody said that this fellow was in town, that they'd seen him that afternoon, so we got on the phone and invited him over. We told him it was important that he come over right away, which he did. As soon as he walked in, we asked him if he had ever crashed in the Panama Canal and he said, yes, as a matter of fact, I did and Jack Tate saved my life, and he told us how he did it, exactly the same story. So, we stopped trying to catch Jack Tate in these fantastic stories because apparently most of them were true, but unbelievable. That's the end of insert.

Q: I think it's interesting to tell about these various people as an indication of the type of man who was your compatriot at that time, and I'm sure they probably have fantastic tales to tell about you that maybe you're not putting on the record.

Adm. T.: Maybe. I'll tell you another one about Country Moore. One time- again Cat Brown was in one this one - they arranged for an officer to come in and pick a fight with Country, needle him until he lost his temper or something, and make himself thoroughly obnoxious, to get Country Moore to swing on him. This fellow was a good boxer and he figured he could duck any blow that Country threw and it wouldn't hurt him. The whole scheme worked out. They got the fellow in and, sure enough, he was terribly obnoxious and finally Country half swung and half pushed him and he fell over near the bunk and then very cleverly dropped down and hit his fist against the side of the bunk. It sounded like he hit his head. Country was so mad he walked out of the room after doing this. He was sort of irritated with himself for doing it, and he left. Then they got to work real fast. They got some flour and whitened up his face, took his clothes off and put him in the bunk and covered him up with a sheet, and then went and got Country Moore and said, "Country, something terrible's happened and we don't know what to do about it. You killed this fellow, and he's in there dead. Country said, "Oh, it couldn't be. I guess he did hit his head a little bit, but . . ." They said, "No. We've been trying to get the doctor but we haven't yet. You'd better come round and take a look at him because he's dead." So they brought Country around there, pulled the sheet back and there was this white face, and Country just wasn't going to look at it and fled.

Q: That was a terrible thing to do!

Adm. T.: Horrible, but later he discovered what it was . . .

Q: How long did it take him to find out?

Adm. T.: Oh, about two or three more hours. He went and got the doctor and the doctor came up and wiped the flour off the fellow's face.

Q: At least, he had the proper reaction.

Adm. T.: Yes, he did. I'd like to go back now to catch up with the sequence of events in VF-3. Later, in October or November, we came back to the West Coast and on December the 7th 1941 we were based at North Island on West Beach and we were in Coronado. The Saratoga was tied up at the pier at the Air Station and we were scheduled to get underway on, I believe it was Monday, the 8th of December, to deploy out to Pearl Harbor.

My wife and I were driving along in a little Ford automobile, going down Orange Avenue in Coronado. We were going to have lunch with my executive officer and some other squadron people, and we'd gone to get some beer, and we heard that the Japanese had attacked Pearl Harbor. It was very apparent that it had happened. My first reaction was, they can't get away with that. Our carriers will intercept them and I wish I were out there because I think they've made a bad mistake and they won't get away. But, of course, I didn't realize how well they had done it, how successful, although in my air group and in other squadrons, oh, from the time of VF-1, way back in 1931 - 1930 and 1931 - we'd been having exercises in the Pacific and sometimes they involved attack on targets in and around Pearl Harbor, the island of Oahu, and whenever we did this we always came in unopposed. We knew that it could be done and we knew how to do it because we'd done it time and time again. At that time, the U.S. Army had the responsibility of defending any target on the Hawaiian islands against air attack. This has never been brought out very clearly in all the hue and cry about the Navy getting caught unprepared. It's true that if we had known we would not have had so many ships in Pearl Harbor, but at that time the Army Air Corps had a policy of never flying over water. I don't know how they expected to intercept an incoming air raid if they were going to wait until after he got over the target, but that wasn't my problem, and they didn't even wear life jackets, Mae Wests or anything like that. They didn't have them in their inventory, because they didn't want to fly over water, and at one time there was a rule that no Army Air Corps plane would go more than 15 miles from the shore line. This was all right with us because we felt that we had the responsibility on the ocean, but I think that a better arrangement should have been made for naval fighters to have some definite role in the defense of an island, or at least some arrangement where airplanes could get out far enough to intercept, especially since we had radar. But - that's the way it was.

Q: How did you hear about Pearl Harbor?

Adm. T.: Heard it over the radio.

Q: Car radio?

Adm. T.: Yes. Then we - I just turned the car right around and went charging out to the Air Station, and soon everybody in the squadron was out there, and we got word that the Saratoga would have to change their loading. We weren't going out on a peacetime mission any more and since ours was supposed to be an 18-plane squadron - we had 12 airplanes in commission and we were going to take those. The reason we didn't have any more is that there was a man by the name of Josephson who was a labor union leader of a union that worked for Allis Chalmers and he called a strike. Allis Chalmers produced the little electrical device that was needed in the electrically controlled variable pitch propeller that was on our aircraft. He was later convicted for some subversive activity as a Communist and spent a few years in jail.

Q: Because of that, or among other things?

Adm. T.: Not necessarily that incident, but his actions in connection with the Communist Party in the United States.

He called this strike at a very difficult time for us. I think he knew what it would do to us. In order to get airplanes out of the factory, we had to put a propeller on them, fly them out to San Diego, and take the propeller off and ship it back, put it on another airplane and fly it out. This was in December 1941 - November and December - and we were going through this process - this is the reason we were short of airplanes, and had to go to war with not a full complement. There were four in major overhaul at North Island and we managed to get two of those out that were almost finished because we looked at them and decided that our mechanics could do the finishing of them on the hangar deck on the way out. All this was done and the decisions made on this - on December the 8th, on Monday morning, and the Saratoga had to delay getting away while we pulled these airplanes half-finished out of overhaul and got other equipment loaded aboard the Saratoga. And so the Saratoga finally got underway in the late afternoon of the 8th instead of early in the morning of the 8th of December. We made a high-speed run out to Pearl Harbor. I guess it took us about four and a half or five days, anyway. We got there and the battleship Arizona was still on fire, smoking, and we pulled into the pier and the people who came aboard had a certain look in their faces that really rather surprised me. Every one of them looked like they were frightened. They'd been through a pretty harrowing experience and were pretty well shaken. We didn't really feel this way at all. Of course, we weren't there and we were just mad because we wanted to get out and catch those people that did that to Pearl Harbor.

They did make a very professional attack. They hit the airfields right early before aircraft in any significant numbers were able to get off the ground. As I remember, there were only a handful in one field up north of Wheeler that got off the ground to do any defending or attempt to, and one of them had a very harrowing story. He confirmed that a Zero could turn inside of anything we had. He said he had pulled up and was on this fellow's tail and was just about ready to shoot him and the Zero just flipped right over his back and was on his tail and shot him down.

A number of people came aboard, of course. I didn't know exactly what the plans for the Saratoga were. They weren't telling anyone at that time. But I noticed one thing, that whereas before I d had a little difficulty in getting certain supplies that I wanted, such as a carburetor or something, because they had a policy of - well, let's put it this way, it wasn't a policy, it was a misinterpretation of the supply department rules - they said when you get down to three carburetors, for example, on the shelf, then more should be ordered, but it was interpreted that when the supply department storeroom got down to three carburetors, that's as low as they can go. So, if they have three carburetors on the shelf and I need a carburetor, I can't have it, because there are only three there. I don't know what they're going to do with those three, except they misinterpreted the order. Anyway, these same people that I'd been having problems with concerning supplies came aboard and said, "What do you want?" And I said, "Well, I'd like to have three spare engines"(and I named off a whole list of things), and they said, "When do you want them?" I said, "This afternoon." And they said, "They'll be here." I said, "What about the paper work?" and they said, "Forget it." Shows how people suddenly change their attitudes. Some of the people felt that they owned this material and that they were doing us a favor to give it to us. An unfortunate attitude that wasn't true in all cases, but my favorite target used to be the supply department. But it was much better than I realized it was, at the time, and it so proved later.

We got underway, I think the next day. Admiral Aubrey W. Fitch came aboard. The Saratoga was his flagship of the Carrier Division and we headed West. When we got to sea, they told us we were going out to support Wake Island. They'd had some information that Wake might soon be under attack. So, we got out near Wake Island and I learned that the Lexington was somewhere behind us, in that part of the ocean, anyway, and the day before we were to arrive in position to - we also got information that the Japanese were attacking Wake Island and that they had some transports and apparently they intended to make a landing and take the island. Of course, our job was to knock them out and prevent this. The day before we got within striking distance of Wake, a message came that said, "it was impossible to relieve or support Wake Island, return to Pearl Harbor." This was a very great surprise to all of us, and I was on the bridge when the message came in and, having known Admiral Fitch when he was a young captain and we used to call him the "gray-haired ensign" because he could stay up later than anybody else and still look good the next day. I went to him and I said, "Admiral Fitch, there must be some mistake. This message couldn't be true. I would like to strongly recommend that you do what a British naval officer did many, many years ago. Look at this message with your blind eye, and let's get going after these invaders of Wake." He looked very sad and he said, "I'd like to look at it with my blind eye, because I don't like it any better than you do, but it could be that they have more information than we have, either in Washington or Pearl Harbor, and they have a reason to pull us back." Well, as it turned out, I think this message did come from Washington. It may or may not have been relayed by the command in Pearl Harbor . . .

Q: Admiral Pyne?

Adm. T.: I guess it was. Nimitz hadn't arrived then. Anyway, this disappointed us terribly and, as it turned out, we could have polished off that one little carrier they had and we could have knocked off all the transports and saved Wake Island for a while, anyway. As it was, Wake Island finally fell, but held out for a long time.

Q: And all those guns that you'd sent out there . . .

Adm. T.: And all of my good guns went to the Japanese or were buried in the sand at Wake. We got back to Pearl Harbor, then the Saratoga was sent on what was called an offensive patrol round Oahu. I wondered why that word "offensive" was used because it was very offensive to us to be tied there, but I know that wasn't the meaning of the phrase! I think somebody just coined that phrase. It certainly didn't describe the kind of operation, but apparently they wanted to keep the Saratoga out of the harbor for fear of another attack, so they just put her out there patrolling. We would run searches, hoping to pick up something as it came in, but they also got a message that we were short of oil. I think a tanker had been torpedoed by a Japanese submarine somewhere in the Pacific and didn't get to Pearl Harbor, or they were playing it very defensively, I thought at the time, and I thought it later. I might as well say now that most of the actions where we lost were due to overcautiousness and just being on the defense, instead of having a plan to go out and attack something and catch them by surprise, and this was an example of it. So the Saratoga was patrolling around, and, one time, late in the afternoon just before dinner, I was sitting out on the gun turret and the dentist walked out, looked down at the water, and said, "We're not going very fast, are we?" and I said, "We're making six knots." I had already asked about it because we were awful slow. And he said, "Gee, if there was a Japanese submarine anywhere in this part of the ocean, it would seem like to me it could catch us easily." I said that's what I think, too. "I don't know why we're going so slow. It would take a long time to launch an airplane if you had to get up speed to do it." That night, at dinner, I was sitting in the wardroom eating, when it sounded like the bottom of the ship blew out, a whole big explosion, all the dishes went up in the air, and I remember seeing my executive officer, who was sitting right by me, reach up in the air and catch a roll that was coming down. I don't remember hearing "general quarters" sounds, any gong or anything. Everybody went to general quarters immediately. It was a huge, loud, ear-splitting explosion. We got to the ready room and word came from damage control that we'd been hit by a very large torpedo, obviously from a submarine. It had knocked out two boilers.

Well, the Saratoga cranked on 27 knots and moved out with that big hole in the side. Instead of 33 we were down to 27, which speaks pretty well for the watertight integrity of the ship. We had a hole big enough to drive two trucks through, side by side, and knock out two boilers - flood two boilers - and still move at 27 knots.

Q: Did you ever find out why they were going at such slow speed?

Adm. T.: Yes. The captain had been ordered to conserve fuel. That's the way to do it.

Q: How about conserve ships?

Adm. T.: Well, that's a risk you take when you conserve fuel, but if you don't have enough fuel, where do you put the compromise? I think we should have come into the harbor until we were able to have enough fuel to steam at a proper speed, and have out submarine search patrols. But, as it turned out, the submarine wasn't our greatest threat. Japanese carriers were our greatest threat in the Pacific. So my squadron was put ashore. Oh, I forgot. We got up into the ready room and the ship was beginning to heel over a few degrees, and we would watch some water somebody had spilled on the deck, and we'd see the water roll this way and run back that way, and I said, "Well, if we're going to be hit again - I was waiting for the next one because I thought if a submarine had hit us once, there may be more than one submarine and we'd catch another one - let's everybody get in his flight gear and maybe we can fly off even if the ship does sink, we can get off." I turned to my exec and looked in his hand and he still had his roll, this piece of bread in his hand. I said, "Don, I see you're prepared in case you get hungry. You've still got the roll in your hand." And he didn't realize he had it, so he put it away like it was hot! This is what happens to people, you do things you don't realize. Anyway, we did fly off and the ship came back into Pearl Harbor, amid all kinds of alarms concerning submarines at the entrance, and there were a bunch of depth charges dropped in places where there was suspicion. Maybe there were some submarines there but they didn't hit the Saratoga because she came really boiling in there, having had good air cover. We were put ashore at Kaneohe, the Naval Air Station at Kaneohe. That was before it became a Marine Air Station. And we continued to train there, and then we were ordered to fly out on board the Lexington. This was about early February, I guess, or late January, 1942, and we headed for the South Pacific. The Lexington got underway without taking on very many provisions. It was apparently planned that we would meet a provision ship at sea. Maybe the Lexington didn't come in, we just flew out. Anyway, the Lexington went to sea with about two weeks' provisions and we stayed 60 days, eight weeks with no additional food. I remember because the average loss of weight among the people on the ship was 12 pounds. We got down to two meals a day, and we ran out of everything except spinach and canned beans. We ran out of pepper and salt, a lot of staples that we really should have had. I remember we would have canned spinach for breakfast, and beans and canned spinach for a mid-afternoon meal, and that was it, and we were flying combat air patrols all the time. It was getting hotter and hotter, we were near the equator.

Q: You needed salt, didn't you, from that standpoint?

Adm. T.: I think they were either short of salt or didn't have any. I don't remember. But I know they ran out of pepper and most of the staple things that you usually have with food. Ran out of all kinds of seasoning, and those pale, tan-colored beans were the most tasteless things I ever ate. They weren't good pork and beans, they were the worst brand of beans I ever saw. I had a dream one night, and I dreamed that I had caught some enemy spies down in the store rooms opening cans of beans and skinning each bean and stuffing some clay in them and putting them back together again and putting them back in the can and sealing up the can, and that's why they tasted so bad.

We had a plan to attack Rabaul on the northern tip of New Britain Island in the Solomon Islands group. We had, I remember, little charts of the area and the location of Rabaul, and the plan was that the Lexington, with its few cruisers and destroyers, would steam in close enough for us to launch from the north, fly over New Ireland, and go in and attack Rabaul. It was expected that there would be a number of heavy ships in the harbor and an unknown number of aircraft on the field. We realized that among them would be the famous Zero fighter, and we hoped to catch these airplanes on the field right at the crack of dawn, and hoping that they wouldn't have too many in the air. I was to lead the group - the attack group - and go in with the fighters and strafe the field and keep enemy fighters from taking off, while the dive bombers and torpedo planes were doing their job of bombing and sinking any ships in the harbor.

The afternoon before the day - either the afternoon before we planned the attack or the previous day - I think we were probably about 400 miles from Rabaul, and I was on combat air patrol with Butch O'Hare leading another two-plane section, and Bert Stanely leading a third one, so we had six planes on combat air patrol. We'd been keeping radio silence. In fact, I hadn't even heard any conversation in the Navy between aircraft or aircraft and ship from the day the war started. This was real honest to goodness, no-fooling radio silence. No one dared open up, because we figured if we did they might get a bearing on us, either a submarine or something. So I was almost jumped out of my seat when this loud voice of the Lexington fighter director came in giving me a vector to course 240, and said there's apparently a snooper about 35 miles away. I started out after him and Butch O'Hare started to follow me, and I turned around and looked at him and motioned him back. He didn't want to go back, but, inasmuch as I knew there couldn't be fighters in the area and it could only be large aircraft, I figured that my wing man and I could take care of that, anything like that. So I made him go back, and he went back like a good boy, back over the ship. I also calculated that if there's one snooper since they obviously sent out searches on various sectors, there'd be one on one side and there'd be probably another one, so it was better to have the other four planes back there ready to be vectored out in case we found three. And of course it was important to get these planes and knock them out before they could report the location of the Lexington and the Lexington task group.

Well, I went on this heading, getting a few little changes of course from time to time, and I noticed he was heading me right into a big thunderstorm. So I called back to the fighter director and said, "You're heading me right into a heavy thunderstorm," and the answer was, "Well, that's where he is." So I went right into the soup with my wing man tucked close under my right wing tip - Doc Selstrom. Once we were in the soup, of course, we couldn't see very much. Sometimes in a thunderstorm especially, there'll be a slight rift so there will be an opening and you can see a few feet - and we came into a kind of a rift, an opening in the cloud just for a second and right below me was this great huge Japanese insignia. I could only see a part of the wing and the rest of it was stretched out the other way. I saw two engines on one wing and then just as quickly we were in the soup again, and here he was right below me.

Q: How many feet?

Adm. T.: Like about 20 or 30 feet.

Q: Oh, that's close!

Adm. T.: Yes. About that time the fighter director called and said, "We have a merged plot." I called back and said, "We sure do. If it had been any more merged, we would have crashed into him. I just sighted him. It's a large patrol plane."

Q: Couldn't that plane hear you?

Adm. T.: I don't know, but we'd already been talking. If he knew and was listening on high frequency, but until I got the first vector there wasn't anything on that frequency.

There was radio silence. Anyway, I decided that maybe he didn't see me. I could see the guns sticking out, a part of the wing, the right side of the fuselage and guns sticking out. So, I held my course, pulled up a little bit because I didn't want to collide with him, and my wing man was flying stepped down a little lower than I, and we came out into the open and no airplane. Nothing. I thought, well, he must have seen me and he knows I'm after him and he's turned and gone down. And just about that time, the fighter director called and said, "He's off the screen. I don't have him any more." Then I thought, well, he must have gone down. So I circled round under the rain and I saw him - just a vague outline and he was at about the extent of the visibility, and I didn't want to go for him then because I figured we'd be playing cat and mouse in this storm and that wouldn't do any good. So I quickly ducked back in and made a turn or two. He seemed to be on a steady course and I thought he hadn't seen me, the second time, anyway. And I thought this isn't a very big thunderstorm. I mean it doesn't stretch for miles, and he'll come out of it pretty soon, then I'll catch him out in the clear. And that's just exactly what happened. When I came out again I saw him heading south, right out in the sunshine. So I climbed up to get a little altitude and we went after him and, since we had only two planes, I drew up on the right hand side and told Doc

Selstrom to bracket him. He didn't understand me for some reason, and I said, "Get on the other side." If the enemy plane turned away from me to bring his tail cannon to bear on me for a no deflection shot, why it would give Doc a good chance for a high side approach. But he didn't turn. He held a very steady platform, which is really the only thing he can do, because he can't thwart a couple of fighters from getting in good runs, and if he turns tight he makes the problem for his free gunners much worse. So he was trained, as we were, in big planes to hold a perfectly steady platform and give his gunners every chance possible, hoping that they'll damage the fighter and knock him off. It took Doc so long to get over there, I decided I'd better start my attack. So I made a high side approach and I'll never forget thinking, "with all of this training I've had over all these years, I'd better do it right this time." I even looked at my ball leveller while I was in the approach to be sure that I wasn't slipping or skidding, everything right, nice and easy, and took just what I figured was the proper lead on him, and waited until I got close enough, coming in from the side, and opened up with all six of those guns. I hadn't fired six guns at once before. It was really a good blast of tracers. I took a good lead on him and on the engines on the right wing. Bullets would carry into the cockpit, through the engines or round the engines into the cockpit, and pulled out, looked back, and nothing happened. No smoke, nothing! I thought, have I got blank ammunition? By that time, Doc was just about in position to make a run and just as he was turning in, I had recovered and was going to come in for another run when the whole wing just jumped with flame, all along - jumped sideways - the whole length of the wing, all four engines. This was an Emily. We'd never seen one. We had no intelligence that they had that kind of an airplane, but I knew it was huge, and also I could tell it had cannon in it, because when the cannon was shooting it would make smoke rings and you could see the tracers coming at you from the cannon, where you couldn't see the tracers from the smaller caliber, unless you looked back. After they went past you it looked like rain - red raid. So that's the way we knew he had a 20-mm. in the tail and one in the top turret in the back, side guns and - a lot of guns. I really felt sorry for him because here he was doing his job, and obviously had gotten off a message on the location of the Lexington task group, and I hadn't hit him soon enough because I couldn't find him in the soup. But we didn't have to make any more attacks, just watched him. He started burning and there were about six huge long bombs and they dropped in the water. A few minutes later his nose went down and in he went with a splash. Made a big cloud of smoke and they could see it all the way to the Lexington, and I told them that I had splashed this big airplane and I wanted a vector back, so they gave me one. On the way back I heard them take another section and send it out to the northwest, and this was Stanley and his section. They didn't pick Butch O'Hare. So they went out and they found another Emily, large patrol plane. They went in on it on an overhead approach. They had plenty of altitude so they could turn over and going in the opposite direction turn over on their backs, run it down and get a perfect shot at it, and with a couple of attacks like that - it didn't burn, it was a little closer to the Lexington and they could see it too. It just splashed.

Well, those were the only snoopers, so by that time my patrol was up and we were relieved by another combat air patrol in my squadron and I landed aboard. Butch O'Hare was fit to be tied. Here, he tried to go out with me and I sent him back, and they didn't pick him to go out after the second snooper.

Q: He did have a combat spirit, didn't he?

Adm. T.: Yes, he did. He wanted to get in quick. This was the first airplane - enemy airplane - any of us had seen.

Q: You speak of being sorry and you said sorry because you

hadn't gotten him before he got the message off. Did you feel sorry in any other respect? You said you felt sorry for him, and you did mean him personally?

Adm. T.: Oh, yes. I felt sorry for the crew of the aircraft because I'm sure that at least some of them, maybe all of them, had convinced themselves that they could defend with all those guns against a fighter type aircraft. After all, how else could they feel? It was the same feeling that I found in VP-5, when I was in Panama and we were doing gunnery training, and the same sort of propaganda that our big bombers were putting out to bolster their feeling of being able to survive against attack by fighters, and I'm sure a lot of them believed it. I never believed it. I knew otherwise, and that's the way it's always seemed to turn out when you have a fighter pilot who is at all well trained. He doesn't have to be the best fighter pilot in the world if he does the right thing and he's had some training and knows how to shoot and hit, he won't get hit by these guns and he will hit them. He's throwing four to six guns straight at them right on the line of his flight and he has a much easier gunnery problem, his sighting problem is far easier than the gun that swivels controlled by a man.

I might, at this point, explain why this is true. The problem that a - I'll call him a free gunner, that's what we always called them, either a turret or a gun in a swivel - the problem he has when the opposing fighter gets within range, that fighter is doing some things that are not stable. He's turning, for one thing. He turns in and then reverses his turn to make the final shooting approach. His speed in increasing, if he's making a high-side approach or overhead. His rate of turn is changing. His rate of change in speed is changing. So everything is changing. In order to hit, you've got to lead the target the right amount, depending on all of those things. You may have the right lead at one second, but by the time the bullet gets there, it's different. Even with the most sophisticated computer to control guns like that, the best computer we have today, would have to be based on tracking the target (the fighter) for a certain period of time, and what that fighter is doing, his speed, his course and everything, and his rate of turn just goes into the computer, and then aims the gun properly for what the computer had in it during those few seconds that it tracked before firing. By the time it fires the data in the computer is bound to be erroneous, with all this change in angles, turns, rate of turn, and change in speed and rate of speed, if you don't want to get hit you hope that the computer or the enemy gunner is perfect, because he'll surely miss you. You hope he's perfect, because if he makes some bad mistake in the "right" direction he might hit you. So that's the problem that they have.

I talked during the latter part of the war with a number of mathematicians and scientists trying to help figure out some way that they could - where a free gunner should aim to get the best chance of hitting. I never got hit attacking a bomber and no other good fighter pilot ever did. Some fighter pilots have been shot down attacking a bomber, but they either weren't good enough in the first place, in fact, I would say that they were rank amateurs, or they got excited, were overanxious to get there, and let themselves get pulled back in a tail chase so that the gunners that could bear on them had an equal chance to hit. And, later that day, one of my new pilots was shot down by a Japanese bomber. I saw it happen. He made a bad mistake. He was charging in from dead astern and the 20 milimeter cannon in the tail of this "Betty" bomber hit him right on the nose.

Q: We haven't specified the date. Is this February 20th?

Adm. T.: This was February 20th 1942. We landed aboard, had lunch. Of course, everybody wanted to know what it was like - what happened when we made the attacks, what kind of attacks, were they the same way we did against the sleeve, and we all said, yes, the same thing you've been doing all the time, so don't worry about it, just go do what you know how to do. That afternoon, I was in the ready room and Noel Gayler had a section - no, Don Lovelace, my executive officer, had a section on combat air patrol, and Noel Gayler was on standby. I was in the ready room, in the after part of it, poring over these little charts we had and also the intelligence manual that didn't have an Emily in it, I didn't know what to call the thing, and the flight order sounded, "Fighter pilots, man your planes," so I knew we had something coming and I figured it must be an attack because - or else another snooper. Lovelace's outfit was ready to go - no, Gayler was on deck, Lovelace was in the air, but it was near the end of his patrol so he was low on gas, so they manned their planes and started warming up. By that time, they had vectored Don Lovelace out, just about the time Gayler got in the air, so they had 12 planes to go to work on these people if Gayler could get up there in time. It wasn't long before we could see from the flight deck, in the distance, some smoke and airplanes falling. I'd manned my plane and so had my wing man, but he was back in the pack somewhere, and they were trying to straighten the deck out so we could launch mine too. We didn't know how many attacks were coming.

After Gayler had gotten off, they turned and apparently weren't going to launch me. Then I sat in the airplane watching and I could see these bombers in close formation headed for us. The enemy was at about 8,000 feet. Later

I learned that Noel Gayler had called down, having gotten up there, telling our own antiaircraft fire to please shorten their fuses down to 8,000 feet, because that was the altitude of the enemy bombers, and he was being bothered by the bursts of our antiaircraft fire above them where he wanted to maneuver to make attacks. Then, we didn't have influence fuses. We had time-set fuses, so many seconds. A fuse set is working all the time when they feed in the information from the AA fire control director that sets the fuses. But all the bursts were above the enemy and among our fighters. This was the situation the first part of the war. We did half of our fighting in the middle of our own AA fire, and the other half in the middle of the enemy's, so we didn't think much of AA fire at that time, and it wasn't very good. It got a lot better later. Then suddenly the Lexington turned into the wind and decided to launch me. I don't know whether they launched - I think they got off me and Butch O'Hare and his wing man and my wing man, but that's about all, because the bomber formation was getting pretty close and the skipper wanted to be able to maneuver.

I started climbing up in the direction that they were going so that if I ever did get to the altitude maybe I could get some of them, all the time looking back, watching these airplanes falling out of the air. It was a fantastic sight. Sometimes there were three and four falling at once just coming down with dark red flame and brown smoke coming out . . .

Q: How far away from you?

Adm. T.: Well, they were getting close to the dropping point, nearly over the ship, and I was climbing out in the direction that they were going, hoping I could get up there and get some of them, if there were any left, because it didn't look like there were going to be many. But there were a few, and some of them dropped their bombs. I forget exactly how many. Out of the nine of them, I think, maybe three or four got to the dropping point, and by that time I was almost at altitude. We didn't have a very high rate of climb, only 1,100 feet a minute when we were fully loaded with our 1,800 rounds of ammunition and full of gas. But I managed to get up there and was able to start working on them after I saw three of them still in some kind of a formation and then they split and they were starting to run away individually. I made an attack on one of them from the low side because I didn't have enough altitude, and this one burst into flames, started down, and I saw this other one. About that time I saw one of my planes coming in dead astern, boiling and a flash right on his windshield where, apparently, a cannon had hit him and he just went into a spin right on in. That was the one that I mentioned earlier. He made a bad mistake by coming in on the tail of a bomber that has a cannon in it. So I was pretty mad at this character who had shot down one of my pilots and I wasn't going to let him get home free. So I decided I was going to get up ahead of him and really get in close. I managed to get up a little bit above his level and I looked all around before starting the approach and I was amazed that, to my way of thinking, I was definitely out of his range but he was shooting all kinds of stuff at me. You couldn't see it looking right at it, you had to look behind to see it. I went in and put what I thought was a real good burst into his wing root and fuselage and nothing happened, so I got out and made another run, pulled out and looked at him again, and, just all of a sudden, he disintegrated, just blew up. With the delayed action, I decided then that if you put holes in his engine, his oil tank - oil seemed to burn better than gasoline, and I think I know why. Because oil in the engine is very hot and under pressure, so when you puncture the engine or any oil lines, this extremely hot oil comes out in a spray, so it's very flammable.

Well, I chased another one and I chased him too far, obviously. I didn't realize how far from the ship I was getting, but I didn't have my wing man with me and I couldn't see him. We were a little disorganized because we never had had a chance to join up after taking off, and it wasn't really necessary because against bombers you didn't have to defend yourself with maneuvers. So it was all right to go just hell bent for election and the airplane that can get there the first gets there. Then I heard over the radio - I got the impression there was another wave coming in and as it turned out, this is what happened. I started back to the ship, and Butch O'Hare hadn't gotten up in time to do any chasing after the first wave, the second wave came in later, another nine-plane group of Bettys. We didn't know they were Bettys at that time. We didn't know what they were because they were entirely different from anything we'd had in our intelligence manuals.

Butch was vectored out after these people and intercepted when they were about six minutes away. He went out with his wing man and, as we had a practice of doing, charge all your guns and fire a short burst to be sure that you've got 'em charged and your gun switches are all on. His wing man did this and nothing happened. He apparently had a short or some open circuit. He couldn't get any gun to fire. Butch realized this and waved him back over the ship, but he didn't want to go. Butch shook his fist at him and tried to get him to go back, but he came on with Butch and maneuvered around to try to draw some attention to himself while Butch went in and made the attacks. Butch made one side approach after another recovering on the opposite side from first one side and then the other, and he lined up these - you see, they stayed in a rigid formation. This was the best thing for them to do. First they've got to have a bomb pattern if they want to hit the ship. So if they have a whole proper formation for the right bomb pattern. Furthermore, it gives all their guns from each airplane a chance to shoot to defend themselves. So he got in and lined them up, up the echelon, and apparently he knocked down two of them in one pass, and he'd go over to the other side and work on that line back and forth, and inside of six minutes, he had six of them down. He was given credit for only five, at first. They thought antiaircraft had shot down one but after that one of them came down and made an approach like he was going to crash into the <u>Lexington</u>. Well, we got photographs of that airplane and one engine had completely fallen out of the wing. Butch had shot that engine out. Apparently the fire had gone out but that plane was on its way down. Antiaircraft did shoot at it and maybe they did polish it off, but I'm sure that plane never would have gotten home and I'd give Butch credit for shooting down six. He certainly shot it out of the formation. So, the net result was that I got back and one of them had its nose down and going to beat the devil, and that's pretty good speed. We had a little speed advantage over it provided we started at the same level but a long time to catch it, and that's the one that got away. Out of the 20 aircraft we met that day, nineteen were shot down. This was using offensive tactics. It is better if you've got more than one airplane working on them - Butch didn't have this advantage except that his wing man was up there fooling around, trying to make them think he had guns - coming in from each side then pulling out. I asked each one of the pilots to make a little sketch of any part of the airplane that they were sure of its shape. If they had noticed the tail more than anything else, just exactly what shape was that tail, and how was it with relation to the end of the fuselage? Or what did the wing tips look like? What did the cockpit, the nose, and everything? And it's interesting that one thing impressed them about it, that they were certain of and knew that it looked like that, they could make a little sketch of it. One fellow could only sketch the top of the cockpit, but it had a funny kind of a curve in it, from the front of the cockpit on back, then it kind of melted into the fuselage, and it wasn't humped up in back - he knew this. He didn't know anything else about the airplane. He couldn't have drawn it, he said, but he drew that.

I got an over-all impression. It looked like a moose to me. It had the nose of a moose. The after part of the fuselage, the whole fuselage looked like a big cigar, and the after end of it was - looked like one end of a cigar, a kind of a patched cigar, but still a kind of a shape of a cigar, the after part of the fuselage. The wings were tapered, and I had a very good idea of the tail. So I drew what I knew, and everybody else drew. We then laid these down and made a composite. We took what people were absolutely sure of, and put that on it, and it came out a perfect sketch of a Betty that we learned about much later. Well, somebody up the line looked in the intelligence book and decided it must be some old Kawanishi type. It didn't look anything like this and that's the way the report went in. I don't remember who made the Betty but it was Type 19 or something. Anyway, they got a picture out of the book, and I had a devil of a time convincing them that this wasn't that airplane. It was an airplane we'd never seen a picture of or anything else, and it was a pretty good airplane. It had speed and it had guns and it was manned by a very experienced crew that wasn't going to quit. They just kept boring right on in, no matter how many dropped out, the rest of them would just keep coming. Captain Frederick Sherman, of course, watched them and he was zigzagging around dodging bombs. Herbert S. Duckworth, who had been in VF-1 when I came to it earlier in my career – he was the air officer of the Lexington and a very good friend – the Captain was worried about Lovelace because his flight was very low on gas, he'd been on patrol for a long time, and he was just due to come back when the first wave showed up and they vectored him out. So he was really hurting for gasoline, and Duckworth told the skipper, "Don't worry, we'll get them aboard." And so every time the Captain would come through a course that was into the wind he'd take aboard one or two, in a turn! They were good pilots. They'd landed aboard many times and he knew they could do it. After the few bombs that were dropped had missed, the skipper, who had been busy watching the bombers and maneuvering his ship, turned around and said, "We'd better get those planes aboard," and Duckworth said, "Captain, they're already aboard."

Q: That must have been one of those things that you just can't take your eyes off, horrified fascination.

Adm. T.: That's right. I never saw so many airplanes in the sky falling at once and never hope to again. I hope I won't.

Q: Were these planes based at Rabaul?

Adm. T.: Yes, and as it turned out later they had a lot of Zeros there. So the decision then was made that, since they knew we were there and would obviously be waiting for us with everything they had, Zeros in the air and everything, that with just the one carrier we'd better not go into Rabaul. And there was another reason. The ships had got underway and gone, so the only remaining reason to have gone to Rabaul would be to tangle with Zero fighters, and that would be a little stupid, so we didn't go. Instead, we went on down into the Coral Sea. And planned an attack on a different place. Information came that there was an invasion of New Guinea at Salamaua and Lae. There was a harbor full of ships unloading, unopposed landing, and there were a lot of cruisers, destroyers, et cetera. They didn't know about any airplanes, whether there were any airplanes there or not, but it was an amphibious landing, unopposed, and they were there with a lot of cargo and transports. By this time we were into the Coral Sea and it was decided that the best way we could attack Salamaua and Lae - Salamaua and Lae are two little names on the harbor that's shaped kind of like a horseshoe, Salamaua at the southern end of the horseshoe, Lae at the northern - they were unloading at Lae and Salamaua, both, not too far apart, when you're in there you could be between them and see each place. So the Yorktown joined the Lexington. The Lexington had been alone with its task group of cruisers and destroyers. And we planned to execute an attack, getting as close as possible to the south shore line of New Guinea in the Coral Sea, just south of Salamaua and Lae, into the Gulf of Papua, with the Owen Stanley mountain range between us, and fly up over the mountain range, then come down and hit 'em.

Since there were ships in the harbor and the best way to sink a ship is to put a hole in the bottom of it, at least below the waterline, it was planned to carry torpedoes on the torpedo planes. Lieutenant Commander Jimmy Brett was commanding officer of the VT-2 based in the Lexington and he was to lead the torpedo group, he being the most experienced of the two torpedo skippers. He took VT-2 and VT-5. They launched him last because he was flying these TBD-1 Devastaters and that was the poorest, oldest airplane we had at that time. I don't know how many years old it was, but they'd been around for a long, long time, and they were absolute fire traps, and they were underpowered and carrying a huge torpedo and all the gasoline, they could just barely get off the deck if they started from right at the stern and the ship making 25 or 30 knots, they could just barely stagger into the air. I was to go along and protect the torpedo planes and stick with them all the way, because we didn't know what we were going to run into. The Owen Stanley mountain range is - I can't tell you the exact altitude of the lowest part of that jagged ridge, but it must be somewhere in the neighborhood of 10,000 feet more or less - anyway we couldn't go around because it would be too long, couldn't go all the way down around Port Moresby and up the other side of New Guinea, we had to take the straightest short cut right across the Owen Stanley mountain range. Well, it was planned that - there was a lot of calculation done about whether or not the torpedo planes could get over that ridge carrying a torpedo, carrying a few bombs I'm sure they could, but it was a question still in everybody's minds, including the pilots' of the torpedo planes. So, they started out and climbed and climbed and climbed, and got to the mountain range. They were still below, looking up at the ridge, and I was sitting right on top of them, and it looked like they weren't going to make it. They went right at the ridge and then had to turn away. They milled around and tried to get more altitude, couldn't seem to do it. In fact, it looked like to me they were losing altitude, and I didn't know what to do. Jimmy Brett called me and he said, "You'd better go ahead. I don't think we're going to make it. You go ahead." And I said, "No, I'll wait here a little bit. I've got enough gas. I can wait a little bit." There was a signal that everybody would recognize. When Jimmy Brett got his torpedo planes over that ridge, he would sing out "Halfway house." Every naval aviator that went through Pensacola knows what halfway house means. It's a little place you get a good cold glass of milk and a sandwich and a soda pop, half way between downtown Pensacola and the Air Station at Pensacola, and everybody stopped there. Just a little roadside sandwich and cold drink place, and every now and then on a Saturday night they would have a combo and have a dance out there. So everybody knew what halfway house was, they didn't have to be clued. Well, he didn't say "Halfway house," but when I said I'd wait a little bit, he said, "All right, hold it. I've got an idea." I said, "I'll stick with you," and he started to go parallel to this ridge. He'd seen a sunny spot over some lush fields. Now, this young man had been trained as a glider pilot. He was one of the few that went through Pensacola when they had to take glider training before they got into powered flight training, and he loved gliding. He knew the glider pilot's business, and he'd gotten real good at it. He saw this sunshine shining on the fields and he remembered that this is where you get a thermal updraft of air, and that's how gliders stay in the air so long. So he headed for this thing and, sure enough, he started to rise, and just circled round there, rising, and finally got enough he just washed himself right over the ridge and yelled "Halfway house." By that time, he'd used up quite a bit of gas, but he was over, and the glider pilot experience was what did it. That's how the torpedo planes got to Salamaua and Lae.

Q: How many torpedo planes were there?

Adm. T.: I think about a dozen in each squadron. No, I think there'd be fourteen.

Thach #2 - 205

Q: And he led them all in this pattern?

Adm. T.: Yes, and they all got over in formation. Just scraping the top of the ridge. So, away we went, and it was planned that . . .

Q: What time of day was it by the time he finally made it over?

Adm. T.: It was midmorning, breakfast time to the average person. We always took off pretty close to daylight. So I figure it was about 8:30 or 9:00 a.m. when he got over. So, we went on into Salamaua and Lae and, sure enough, there were the cruisers. We saw them getting underway, pulling up the anchor chains and there were a lot of transport. So he went in with his torpedo planes for the conventional anvil attack, and I took my fighters in. I had Noel Gayler and Butch O'Hare. I left Butch upstairs. He didn't like that, either. But we didn't know whether we were going to run into some Zeros and we wanted to go down and strafe just ahead of the torpedo planes, to give them some chance. Butch didn't say anything, but I think he was expecting that, maybe, I knew there was some action he was going to get. And, anyway, if I was going to leave anybody up there, I wanted to leave Butch up there. I figured that no matter how many planes there were coming in, he could give them a busy time before they got down to us.

We went in and did some strafing. The torpedo attack was beautifully executed. You could see the streaks of torpedoes going right to the side of these cruisers and nothing happened. I saw one or two torpedoes go right on underneath and come out the other side and go over and bury themselves in the bank on the shore. Some obviously hit the cruisers and didn't explode. So we had bad fuses and very erratic depth control, and I didn't see any torpedo explosions, and what a heart-breaking thing after all of that effort and all of that training, and the use of this wonderful experience Jimmy Brett had to get over there, and then to drop these torpedoes and they're practically all duds. So, about this time, there was a little float plane that came along and was milling around shooting a small-caliber gun at the - at one of the - torpedo planes. I saw it and I looked up and Noel Gayler was coming down to strafe. He was strafing the cruisers, and he just turned out a little bit, gave a squirt at this airplane, blew it up, and turned right back and went on the same run to strafe the cruiser. So he was the only one that shot down an airplane that day. It was the only airplane anybody saw. Poor little float plane got mixed up with Noel Gayler, which was a bad mistake. The dive bombers got some hits on ships but I didn't see any roll over and sink although some were on fire.

We got back, and there was, of course, a serious investigation concerning the readiness of our torpedoes. This stemmed from the same sort of thing that we've been going through in the Pentagon in recent years. For example, Mr. McNamara and his figures boys claimed that we didn't need to practice with live ammunition. We didn't need to shoot a live rocket or drop a live torpedo, that you could make dummy runs and why waste the ammunition. Save money that way. Look at all the money you'd save if you never shot a rocket - air-to-air or air-to-ground rocket - or a torpedo. And that was his theory, and it's the same theory that caused - same sort of theory, that you couldn't drop an expensive torpedo, a live ammunition torpedo. They dropped them in practice and then recovered them, but they didn't have a warhead in them, so we didn't know whether the fuse was really any good or not.

Q: I knew about the submarines' torpedoes, but I had not heard before of the torpedoes from the planes being ineffective.

Adm. T.: All of our torpedoes were that way. I don't know how often this country has to learn that lesson, but of course new people like McNamara come in who are so "intellectual" that they won't listen to anyone with experience and they say experience doesn't mean anything. You just give me the facts that I direct you to provide and I'll do the figuring and make the decisions. And this is the sort of thing that it leads to. I don't know how many times we have to learn it before we do the right thing. And right now, today, pilots who are supposed to be able to fire air-to-air missiles, or air-to-ground missiles, are very fortunate if they ever get to fire one missile in training, and it's due to this McNamara-type policy.

Q: This action on February 20th, however, you got your first Navy Cross and for the period of - actually for the first six months of the war you received your Distinguished Service Medal.

Adm. T.: That's right. The Distinguished Service Medal at that time was the highest medal the Navy could give. It was higher than the Navy Cross, took precedence over it. Later, the Navy Cross was put at the top and took precedence over all other Navy medals.

Q: The Distinguished Service Medal did take care of - did cover - the entire six months, whereas the Navy Cross was . . .

Adm. T.: Primarily for developing the tactics that Jimmy

Flatley named the Thach Weave.

Q: And then you received a letter of commendation from Admiral Nimitz.

Adm. T.: That was for the Salamaua and Lae action, the strafing of the cruisers and shooting up a few gun crews.

Q: The date for the New Guinea . . .

Adm. T.: The Salamaua and Lae attack was March the 5th, 1942. The Lexington finally came back to Pearl Harbor and we flew ashore to continue training, and then I got word that Admiral Aubrey W. Fitch was going to take out the Lexington as his flagship and go to the South Pacific again. Inasmuch as we had been shifted from the Saratoga, which was back by this time in a shipyard in the United States getting repaired, to the Lexington, I thought, of course, that we would go back aboard the Lexington. But Admiral Fitch asked for me to come and see him, which I did, and he said, "I'm going to sea again, but we've decided that you'd better stay here at Pearl Harbor because there's a big training job to be done. We're getting more airplanes and more pilots coming out and there are not very many people who have had any combat experience, and you're going to have to stay back here and teach them how to fight."

Well, that really hurt me. I begged him to take me with him. I said, "I don't think you ought to go to sea without me, without my squadron." He said, "Oh, I'm going to take your squadron. I'm going to take all your pilots and give them to Paul Ramsey." And I thought, oh, for heaven's sakes, he's found out about my stealing Paul Ramsey's ammunition! But that wasn't the case. The point was that VF-2, Paul Ramsey's squadron was the Lexington squadron, and he had a rest when we went down there and he should come back aboard, and I was still basically a Saratoga squadron. Also he said, "Your squadron is finally going to be increased to 27 aircraft, but I'm taking all your pilots and giving them to Paul Ramsey and that will build up his squadron. Then you'll get some more people, some more pilots, and 27 airplanes."

Well, the pilots didn't arrive right away, but the airplanes did. So, there I was at Kaneohe with 27 airplanes and I was the only pilot, and I didn't have any officers, so I called the Chief Petty Officers together and I said, "Well, starting today - pointing to the gunnery chief - you're the gunnery officer and you'll do all the things that the gunnery officer is supposed to do. And to the line chief, I said, you're the operations officer, and to the old head chief, I said, you're my executive officer. He had a big grin on his face. He shook his head and said, "I've never been executive officer of anything." And I said, "But you can do it. Don't worry," and then I got the storekeeper and said he was the supply officer of the squadron, and so on. Then, the line chief spoke up and he said, "Well, as operations officer I'm not going to have very much to do because if we only have one pilot we sure can't fly much," and I said, "I'm going to fly every one of those airplanes, one after the other, because I've got to get them in the air to check them out, to be sure that there's not anything seriously wrong with them. I would like to be able to also check the guns." I looked at the new chief who was the gunnery officer and he was shaking his head. But, it worked. I flew every one of the airplanes and I did a lot of flying in the next few days, checked them out and wrote the discrepancies on whatever I found and they got to work and fixed them.

About this time, we did get a few pilots. Some of them had had some experience. I remember a young chief who was a pilot by the name of Sam Cheek, a very fine young man. He came to me, and one or two others who had been in squadrons before and had been on shore duty or something. Then I began to get a stream of young fellows right out of training, out of Pensacola. About this time my executive officer - he didn't go with Paul Ramsey - was detached and he was shceduled to go back to San Diego and get a new squadron, get command of a squadron, going from exec of my squadron to command, and that squadron was going to be VF-2. He was going to relieve Paul Ramsey, eventually, but, in the meantime, the Coral Sea battle occurred and the Lexington was sunk and that squadron was pretty well broken up. And we began to hear about something big coming up and I'd better get ready. They were sending out messages for anybody who'd had fighter pilot experience, get 'em to Pearl Harbor, and report to me. So Don Lovelace, who had his orders in his hand to be commanding officer, came back on his own and said, "I know that you need fighter pilots and since my squadron is not going to be for a while, anyway, I want to do something so I'll come back and help you." I said, "Boy, I think it's wonderful that you came back when you didn't have to. You've got orders, you can be on your way back to San Diego." He said, "No, I want to do something. I'd like to come back if you'll have me," and I said, "I'd rather have you than anybody I can think of," and I sure needed him. About that time Jimmy Flatley came along and he was willing to help, too, although he wasn't attached. Don Lovelace just held his orders but he didn't get himself detached.

We started training these new people, whipping them into shape. The Army Air Corps heard about our gunnery training and they had a P-39 squadron based at Kaneohe, part of the defense of Oahu. They would go up and fly combat air patrols, and so would we along with them, and they wanted to learn about firing on a sleeve. They'd never done anything like that. They didn't have any planes that could tow sleeves. They didn't have any equipment, and I said, "How do you train for aerial combat?" "We strafe targets on the ground and we just fight without shooting," and I said, "Well, if you want to come out with us you can load up your guns and fire on our sleeve, at the same time we're shooting at it. We'll just put a few of you with each gunnery group that goes out." So they just loved that. It was great. We liked it, too, we felt so sorry for them, they didn't have any training. They didn't know anything, and no equipment, which was horrible, no cameras or anything. So we towed sleeves for them and they'd fire on them, and they got so they were making approaches the same way we were, except for the overhead approach. They said, "With this P-39 you can't make an overhead approach because it picks up speed so fast, it's so streamlined that we just couldn't do it." So Jimmy Flatley said, "How about checking me out in the P-39? I'd like to find out about them." So, they checked him out. He went out and made beautiful overhead attacks, led a P-39 group right through an overhead attack and showed them that they could do it. They were still more delighted with that, and they got so friendly with us that whenever we'd come back, we had a practice, a sort of doctrine, of when we approached the field we didn't approach it like we were landing on a field, we pretended that the short righthand corner of the runway was a carrier deck. We'd put a landing signal officer out there and we'd come round in a tight turn and pick him up, and he'd keep our hand in with field carrier landing practice. The P-39s started coming in and doing the same thing. Finally one of them got so enthusiastic about it, he wanted to check out in one of our Wildcats, which I let him do. Then he said, "I'd like to go aboard a carrier," and I said, "Well, I don't know about that, but I will get my bosses to approve it because I think it's a good thing, if you can get permission from whoever your boss is." It was the commanding general out at Wheeler Field. So I went to the Commander, Carriers, Hawaiian Islands, and said I'd like to have this fellow join my squadron the next time we went to sea as a loan from the Army Air Corps. He'd already checked out in the Wildcat and he was pretty good, made good carrier approaches. The Army pilot fought that thing right on up and, finally, he got permission to do it, but that was much later. He didn't go with us in the Battle of Midway. It took him a long time to get the Army to approve. Our people certainly okayed it, if the Army approved. He finally did go aboard after Butch O'Hare relieved me in the squadron.

Q: He became a member of the squadron?

Adm. T.: On a loan basis. I guess this was the first exchange pilot that I knew about. Whether we started it or not - somebody else may have done it at the same time, I don't know, but I think it was probably the first. Later on, and even now, you know, we have exchange pilots between the Air Force and the Navy all the time. In the Korean War we had a few Air Force officers, maybe one or two for each squadron.

We didn't realize it, but the Battle of Midway was getting closer all the time and I was working real hard, flying an awful lot, training these people, trying to teach them how to shoot and we were beginning to get a few holes in the targets. This was about the time that my wing man, who was a very fine, wonderful young, cheerful, eager fellow, little blond boy, we were at Ford Island but he had left his laundry over at Kaneohe. He wanted to get back over there and get it, and it so happened that there was one of the dive bombers going over there and he had an empty rear seat, so Doc said, "Let me ride over with you and pick up my laundry." So he got in the airplane and they took off. There was a strong wind that afternoon, and there was a crane sticking up near the end of the runway, the wind had apparently drifted them over and they flew right into that thing and burst into flames, fell on the ground. They got both people out but Doc Selstrom was very badly burned. In the hospital he was conscious for several days, knew exactly what was going on, knew he was badly burned, and probably couldn't be saved, so he died a few days later in the hospital. That was a sad blow.

Q: You spoke of him as your wing man?

Adm. T.: Yes, he was my wing man when we were down in the South Pacific in the previous engagement. He was killed before Admiral Fitch took all my pilots away from me.

Q: I was wondering because I had a different . . .

Adm. T.: Yes, we were at Ford Island then. We'd been over at Kaneohe and we were at Ford Island. We bounced back and forth quite a bit depending on what was up.

Q: But this was while you still had your squadron with you?

Adm. T.: It was just before I got the 27 airplanes. I still had my squadron with me. I think that they were just getting ready to, maybe to go aboard the Lexington to join VF-2, Paul Ramsey's squadron. I've forgotten the dates. Yes, I know that it was before this. Between the time that Admiral Fitch told me I had to give up my pilots but I was going to get 27 planes. That's right. Anyway, it was a very sad blow. He would have gone on with the rest of them.

As other pilots began to come in, of course, I was able to designate one of them my gunnery officer and another one to various jobs and the good old Chief Petty Officers went back to doing what they'd rather do in the first place.

Q: And all your officers were ensigns?

Adm. T.: No, they were various ranks. Most of them were ensigns. I had another doctrine that I established, oh, some time back, but it still held in the Battle of Midway. If there was a Lieutenant JG that was new, right out of Pensacola and an ensign that had experience in combat, I would tell the lieutenant that he was going to be a wing man and the ensign was going to be the section leader because he'd had more experience, and I asked if he had any objection to that and he said, "No, thank goodness. I'd rather follow somebody for a while . . ."

Q: A good man would take that attitude.

Adm. T.: Yes. They all did, and he said, "I hope to eventually become a section leader." I said, "Don't worry. If you live, you will: and if you're good enough maybe you'll live." Gradually we got people assigned jobs, but right up to the time we deployed we were getting a few people - not right up to the time, but within a week or two - so I had to concentrate on the newer ones, and all the new ones, although they had landed some kind of an airplane, a training plane, perhaps, aboard a carrier and become carrier qualified in some type, none of them had landed a Wildcat aboard a carrier, and this Wildcat was not an easy plane to handle. It had narrow landing gear and the right wing had a tendency to drop on landing, so you had to watch it a little carefully. Most of them, the first time they got in the plane and took it off and came back and landed, quite often the wing would go down and they would get a little nervous and let the plane ground loop. Sometimes there were some pretty wild looking ground loops. One guy ground looped right through a bunch of parked aircraft. I don't know how he ever got through, there were planes parked all over the parking area and somehow or other he ground looped close to three or four of them and ended up between them and the hangar and didn't touch a one. We gave him some kind of a medal for that, some kind of a phony medal. Anyway, some of them were a little concerned about landing aboard a carrier and this was because they hadn't had too much time in the airplane, although all of it had been good hard work in gunnery learning to shoot pretty well, and I got them together and I said, "Look, you have landed aboard a carrier, right?" and they said, "Yes, Sir." I said, "You have landed this airplane, right?" "Yes, Sir." "All right. You are hereby qualified to land this airplane aboard an aircraft carrier. All you've got to do now when you go out is you just do it and prove it. Then that'll be that. I don't want to hear any more about it." There was nothing else I could do.

Q: I bet that was good psychology!

Adm. T.: I think so.

Q: In the first place, it let them know that you had complete confidence in their ability, whether you did or not!

Adm. T.: You couldn't act any other way. So, we got the 27 airplanes and 27 pilots, and they called me up and gave me an inkling that there was something big coming up in the Central Pacific. They said it looks like the Japanese are going to try to hit us again.

Q: Who told you?

Adm. T.: It was a member of Halsey's staff, although Halsey at that time was in the hospital with skin problems.

Q: Shingles, I think.

Adm. T.: Something horrible. Yes, shingles. Herpes Zoster is the technical name for shingles. I know because my mother had it. Anyway, I knew we were going aboard and they told me what day to be ready, but they told me not to talk about anything big to anybody, just to tell them we were going aboard. We didn't know where we were going, as a matter of fact. They didn't tell me where.

Q: Did you know what ship?

Adm. T.: Oh, yes. The Yorktown. The Yorktown had been damaged several times and was in pretty cripped shape, but as we all found out since then she was rushed back from the South Pacific into the Navy yard, and those Navy yards were working around the clock at a fantastic job of patching that ship up and even gave her a nice ice cream machine that was vanished. So, although the ship wasn't as strong as it would have been had it been a complete repair - overhaul-type repair job - it was patched, a lot of good patch work. And so, one morning, about the 1st, 2nd, or 3rd of June - I forget which now - maybe about the 1st of June, we were scheduled to fly out and land aboard the Yorktown and go somewhere. I was forming up the tactical organization. I was so thankful to have Don Lovelace back as my strong right arm as executive officer, and I told him, "You can have the pick of any of these people for your wing man. You decide. You've flown with them." So, he did, he decided which one he wanted, and then I took another one by the name of Ram Dibb. He was my wing man in the Battle of Midway, a fine young man, but very young.

Q: An ensign?

Adm. T.: Yes. We had ensigns running out of our ears. We had one Lieutenant, Don Lovelace, but not very many JGs. A day or two before embarking in Yorktown about fifteen pilots from VF-42 reported to me to fill out the roster of 27 pilots.

Q: But no one who'd had any combat?

Adm. T.: They were experienced in carrier operations and some of them had been in air combat in the Coral Sea but I had no idea how well they could shoot.

Q: Frightening, isn't it?

Adm. T.: Well, other squadrons went out with little or no gunnery training especially with the Army Air Corps - for example, Tom Lanphier, who shot down Yamamoto told me if it hadn't been for a big red-headed Navy pilot that he met in the South Pacific and showed him something about tactics and let him shoot on their gunnery sleeve, that they don't know what they would have done, because, he said, at that time they just didn't know anything about aerial combat or aerial gunnery, how to do it.

Q: In a book about him called <u>Get Yamamoto</u>, he said in his inscription, "To Jimmy Thach, to whom I and all Air Force, Marine, and Navy fighter types owe more than we can convey for his intellectual and combat leadership and skill, with affectionate respect, Tom Lanphier." That's a nice tribute and obviously well deserved.

Adm. T.: It's certainly nice. Tom is a very fine gent, and I got to know him much better than I ever did just in very recent years because he was a fighter ace, so am I, and we worked together in putting on a fighter aces' rendezvous for the benefit of charity, such as the USO and Aerospace Museum, and he is a wonderful man and has done a terrific job. Anything he sets out to do, he really does it in fine fashion.

Q: Is there a camaraderie between pilots that exceeds your own service?

Adm. T.: Oh, yes. Well, I won't say "exceeds." I don't

know what you mean by "exceeds". It doesn't exceed the loyalty to your own service, but it's something that - you have more in common with another fithter pilot, whether he's U.S. Air Force, Japanese Air Force, German Air Force, or any air force, than you do with some people in your own service, because they haven't had similar experience as fighter pilots have had.

Q: And they don't know how you think.

Adm. T.: True. They can't speak our language and understand the things that we talk about any more than we could understand people at a dental convention who were talking shop.

We're getting aboard the Yorktown now. I mentioned that I'd given Don Lovelace the pick of wing men, and I'm glad I did because I would feel even worse than I do now, in view of what happened. We were bringing the 27 planes aboard. I'd already landed aboard and was in the ready room and Don Lovelace, after my division came in, brought his in. He landed and he had taxied across the barrier, the barrier had just lifted behind him, and his wing man landed too hard, bounced clear over the barrier, and landed right on top of Don Lovelace and cut his head off, and that was the end of Don Lovelace. That was a pretty bad blow at any time. It was especially a difficult thing to accept at that moment, because by this time we'd all been briefed on what was coming along, not only a sad thing to lose the life of a good friend, but to lose his ability and leadership and everything else in the air was a doubly bad blow.

Q: And to think he didn't have to be there!

Adm. T.: He didn't have to be there. Had he carried out his orders strictly according to the letter, he would not have been there. But he was a dedicated, loyal individual, and he knew that he was needed. He knew he was badly needed.

Q: I'm sure you weren't able to let yourself think about it at the time.

Adm. T.: No, but right away it was such a shock for the youngsters. I had enough people so that the flight leaders, for instance, the ones leading a combat air patrol or the section leaders going with the strike group, those people had had some experience, but maybe nobody following them, nobody else.

Q: You started to say it was such a shock to the young kids.

Adm. T.: It was. Here they were going into something that was utterly new to them and things had been moving pretty fast as far as they were concerned. I got them all in the ready room immediately and told them that they had to just wash that out of their minds, that if I could do it, they could do it, because he was one of the best friends I ever had and the loss to me was far greater than they may imagine, and I was going to forget about it right now. We have work to do, we're going to do it. We're going into a big battle, and we can't let something like this affect our performance in any way. So that's the end of that, and I don't want to hear any more talk about it. So, they took it that way.

Q: Again, that was your leadership that influenced the whole squadron.

Interview #3 with Admiral John S. Thach, U.S. Navy (Retired)

Place: His home in Coronado, California

Date: 6 November 1970

Subject: Biography

By: Etta-Belle Kitchen

Q: Admiral, I know we're approaching the Battle of Midway and because it's such an important battle and also significant in your career, would you set the stage, give me a little framework of exactly where the Yorktown was and what date we're talking about?

Adm. T.: The Yorktown was about 50 or 100 miles off Pearl Harbor when the air group, including the augmented VF-3, landed aboard. I forget whether this was 1 June or 2 June . . .

Q: It was the same date as the Yorktown had left Pearl Harbor?

Adm. T.: Yes, the Yorktown left Pearl Harbor after a hurry-up repair, a patch-up job, from her damage in the South Pacific, and we were to join the Enterprise and Hornet. Actually, they formed two task groups. Captain Buckmaster as commanding of the Yorktown and Admiral Frank Jack Fletcher and his staff aboard as Commander, Task Force 17.

Admiral Halsey was in the hospital with a very severe infection of the skin, so Admiral Spruance was sent to take his place. Admiral Spruance, TF-16, had most of Admiral Halsey's staff with him. But Admiral Fletcher was the senior officer although he had, as I remember, a more or less non-aviation staff, in other words, it was not a staff designed to operate aircraft carriers.

Q: Did you know, did your squadron, had you been briefed on the importance of this impending battle? How much did you know of what you were going into?

Adm. T.: Before I left Pearl Harbor I was given very brief indications of the fact that we expected an attack and there was obviously a big battle coming up in the middle of the Pacific. That's about all I was told before I landed aboard the Yorktown. That night, after we were all aboard and everything was buttoned up and we were headed out toward Midway, all of the squadron pilots and the air group were brought into the wardroom and Lieutenant Commander Murr Arnold, the air officer of the Yorktown, gave us a complete briefing on everything they knew about the opposing Japanese forces and their probable intentions. So we had, then, a day or so before we arrived in position and before the Japanese arrived to think about . . .

Q: There was no doubt in your mind of the vital importance of the impending action?

Adm. T.: There was no question about it because of the indications that there was a large Japanese force coming. They didn't tell us at the time that the Japanese code had been broken and they were getting most of their information that way, but very soon, of course, the Navy VPs, the patrol planes, did pick up a large force, and so that was all verified then, that they did obviously have the intention of coming in towards one of the Hawaiian islands, and the obvious objective must be Midway first. And they had more than enough to take Midway, so after doing that they probably would consider charging on down the Hawaiian island chain. Midway being, of course, about 1,000 miles from Honolulu.

After getting this briefing, it was obvious a very serious and crucial engagement was coming up and we were all mightily impressed. It meant that if we could win this one, we might be able to stop the Japanese advance. So the time that we had between getting aboard and before we finally launched our strikes, we utilized in getting all the ammunition ready, carefully checking and re-checking each airplane. I remember the night before we had been having trouble with one engine and I wanted every plane we had in commission - remember, we had lost two and instead of 27 planes we were down to 25. I went down to the hangar deck and talked to my engineering chief and he said, "I know what you came down here to see, if that Number 7's going to be ready. It's going to be ready." I said, "I don't want to push you. We're going to have a long tough number of days, and I want the maintenance people to get enough sleep." He said, "Don't worry about that. We're working in shifts and all the planes are going to be up." And I knew they would be. There wasn't any question about it. This man knew what he was doing and he had a good crew working for him.

I got word that Max Leslie and Lem Massey - Max was the commanding officer of the dive bomber squadron, he was going to lead the VB-3 and VS-5, part of VS-5. Lem Massey was commanding officer of Torpedo Squadron 3 - that we should have a conference. I agreed. I'd talked a little bit to Lem Massey before that and told him I thought that the escort should go with him instead of at high altitude with the dive bombers. He said, "I think you ought to get up with the dive bombers because that's where the Zeros are going to be. That's where they were in the Coral Sea battle." So we had our conference and we were trying to decide whether the fighter escort should go with the dive bombers or the torpedo planes, and we knew we weren't going to have enough to split them and send a few with each. I had a plan and I thought it was approved to take eight because I wanted two divisions, that was the basic tactical breakdown that we had developed, and I couldn't believe that anybody would try to break this up, because if you're going to send any number of airplanes, it's got to be divisible by four, the number that you send, otherwise you've left two planes without wing men.

Q: And it was the pattern you'd already practiced, wasn't it?

Adm. T.: Oh, yes.

Q: So you didn't want to change at this late date, I wouldn't think.

Adm. T.: No. So we planned to take eight. Max Leslie said he thought that I should go with the torpedo planes, and I said, "How about letting me decide it?" Because they were playing Alphonse and Gaston, trying to give the fighters to the other squadron, and I decided that, since in the Coral Sea battle the torpedo planes had gotten in pretty much unopposed and done the work in sinking these ships, the Japanese would be more concerned about the torpedo planes. The way to sink ships is to put a hole in the side of the ship below the waterline - that's the best way to do it. That's what a torpedo's designed for and the Japanese know this and they're going to be very concerned about any torpedo attack and they're going to try to knock it out before it gets there. So they all finally agreed that I would go with Lem Massey, VT-3.

Q: Was it up to the three of you to decide?

Adm. T.: Yes. Who would know better how to do it? It may surprise people these days but as a lieutenant I made more decisions than some very high-ranking officers have been making in the Vietnam War. I was making decisions in World War II, that McNamara made in the Vietnam War, believe me. He was telling us how many planes to send, what formation to fly and at what altitude.

Q: I understand. There was no specific doctrine established that you had to follow?

Adm. T.: Yes. A doctrine called good common sense. If you had enough, you would stack your fighters up to and including the dive bombers. You would have at least one division with the dive bombers, and probably at least one or more with the torpedo planes. The torpedo planes were the old fire traps that were so slow and awkward and no self-sealing tanks. They needed protection more than anyone else, so that governed our decision in this case. The doctrine was flexible, and, depending on what you anticipate as to where the enemy fighters might be.

Q: How fast did the torpedo plane go?

Adm. T.: Those old TBDs would go about 80 knots, with the nose down maybe 110.

Q: They carried one torpedo?

Adm. T.: One torpedo. The dive bombers were a little faster. They were the SBD, the Douglas Dauntless dive bomber. The TBDs were called Devastaters, but were more devastating to the crews in them than to the enemy, I think. It was a sad thing that we didn't have a better torpedo plane. The fighters were, of course, the Grumman Wildcats, F4F-3, and our main armament was six .50-caliber guns, fixed, firing forward from the wings. We carried 1,800 rounds of ammunition. 300 rounds per gun.

Q: And what was your speed?

Adm. T.: We could do - we'd cruise about 140 - and we could get up close to 200 in level flight. If you can have altitude and use it, then the aircraft would withstand a great deal more speed, up to terminal velocity without falling apart.

I don't know how many people slept very well the night of the 3rd of June.

Q: Can you describe your feelings?

Adm. T.: I was very concerned about whether the torpedo planes could get in or not, and I knew that if the Japanese were together in one formation and had a fighter combat air patrol of defending fighters from all the carriers, we would very likely be outnumbered. As I told you before, we were also quite concerned with the fact that the Zero fighter could outperform us in every way. We felt we had one advantage in that we thought we could shoot better and we had better guns. But if you don't get a <u>chance</u> to shoot, better guns matter little. I was thinking about all of this and also which pilots I would take with me. I picked out the ones I thought would do a good job. I didn't sleep much that night, but we were all pretty optimistic because we felt that we were going to get tactical surprise. We didn't think the Japanese knew that we were anywhere near there, and this was a great morale-builder, when you think you're going to have one of the basic principles of warfare on your side, which is surprise.

Q: Can you remember your personal emotions?

Thach #3 - 234

Adm. T.: I was pretty busy, and I don't think I could describe any particular personal emotion. Could you say what you mean by that?

Q: Were you frightened? Were you thinking of your family? Did you think you might not come back? Were you involved with personal reflections?

Adm. T.: Not at that time. I was frightened later. I'll tell you about that.

Q: Could you have taken eight planes with the bombers and eight with the torpedo planes? You had 25.

Adm. T.: That decision was not mine, and I have to agree with it, under the circumstances. I might just say right here that I was a little appalled that we were in two separate task forces and with the Yorktown the only carrier with one of the task forces.

Q: Number 17?

Adm. T.: Yes. Buckmaster, or Fletcher, I guess, made the decision that next morning before we launched that we would have only six fighters to go, and I didn't have time to work my way up to him to talk to him about it, but I did go to Murr Arnold. I said I was appalled that the Yorktown was in one task group separated from the Enterprise and the Hornet, but I wasn't too worried at the time because I thought they would stick very close together, so that it would be close enough for mutual defensive support. But the next morning, we were separated by at least 20 or 30 miles, and Captain Buckmaster, I suppose, made the decision - I never found out who made it - that I could have only six fighters to go. He wanted to keep as many as possible back to defend the Yorktown because if you send a strike against an enemy carrier force, why, usually you can expect attack on yourself as well, on your own carriers, unless you just get 'em all right away and they had no aircraft in the air with suitable weapons. Or if their search planes fail to find you.

So I had to quickly revise the formation that we were going to fly over the torpedo planes.

Q: And six isn't divisible by four!

Adm. T.: And six isn't divisible by four, so I had Ram Dibb as my wing man with Macomber as my other section leader, and his wing man was Ed Bassett. That left two, Tom Cheek and Sheedy. So I decided that we would put them just astern of the torpedo planes, more or less under my four, down at a slightly lower altitude than I would fly

1,000 or 1,500 feet above the torpedo plane formation, which would be a formation in the shape of a triangle, a sort of a V of V's, that is, that's the way they would fly up to the target until they had to split and spread out to make the torpedo attack.

Q: How far above the torpedo planes were you?

Adm. T.: About 1,000 or 1,500 feet, and down sometimes below them, and on the same level during the battle.

Q: I meant on the way out. About 1,000 feet?

Adm. T.: Yes. It varied. We had to do S turns, to slow down so we wouldn't run away from them because they were so slow, and we didn't want to be stalling along with no ability to maneuver in case something hit us before we anticipated it.

Q: When you say a V of V's, can you describe that?

Adm. T.: There would be the squadron leader, or rather flight leader, who was Lem Massey, and his two wing men, one on each side, then at about 45 degrees to his right and trailing him would be another section, and then another section, and then another division would be

Thach #3 - 237

be flying either just under him or to his left in a kind of an echelon of V's.

Q: How many torpedo planes were there?

Adm. T.: We took in 12.

Q: And six of you?

Adm. T.: Yes.

Q: And were you in a V shape as well?

Adm. T.: Oh, no. We were flying our standard combat formation that I'd developed, with a section leader and only one wing man, and there was a combat division of four planes, two two-plane sections.

Q: Who was in the lead?

Adm. T.: Naturally, I was leading . . .

Q: You were in the lead, and who was behind you?

Adm. T.: Ram Dibb was right in under my wing, and Macomber had Bassett on his wing, but he was out parallel with me, about an equal distance so that we could turn toward each other and shoot . . .

Q: How far apart were you?

Adm. T.: It changes. It depends on the speed of the airplanes, and after you do this thing for a while you just sense about how far you should be apart, depending on the speed.

Q: And then the other two were slightly lower?

Adm. T.: We tucked them down below us because they would be more vulnerable, and hoping that if any Japanese fighters might come in low over the water and pulling up underneath the torpedo planes that we might not see, Cheek and Sheedy would take care of them. Keep them busy, at least.

Q: But you were still doing the two and two?

Adm. T.: Oh, yes. I'd made that standard before the war, and an interesting thing if I may digress just a minute. I don't know whether I mentioned this or not, but I recommended, after I'd developed this weave business, that all the squadrons accept this as a standard fighting formation. I got a message back from Commander, Aircraft, Battle

Force, that since the two-plane section was such a radical change he wouldn't force all the squadrons to do it, but that I had authority to do it in my squadron. Actually, by this time the idea was catching on anyway. VF-2 was doing it also and so were some of the others. They'd thrown away the third plane and were flying two-plane sections, but they had not adopted the weaving tactics.

Q: What about the Hornet and the Enterprise? Do you know?

Adm. T.: I'm not sure whether they did because I hadn't really seen them. The Hornet was rather new in the Pacific, and I hadn't even seen them, but I tried to circulate this around, Jimmy Flatley and I had discussed it, and as I mentioned before, when I was trying to train some of these brand-new pilots and Flatley came along and helped me for a while, and we had many discussions night and day, sometimes late in the night, about what was the best thing to do. Neither one of us knew it for sure. He said, "I think the four-plane division is good, but I think we shouldn't all try the same thing. Why don't I try six planes in a formation, and you go ahead and try the four, and we'll see which one makes out the best." Later he sent two messages. He sent a personal one to me saying the four-plane division is the only thing that will work, and "I am calling it the

Thach Weave, for your information." Six planes don't work. The two extra ones get lost. And he sent another official message describing this and saying that they were convinced that it was the only way for our fighters to fight, especially against superior enemy fighters.

Now, getting back after that digression . . .

Q: I wanted to get the picture of where the torpedo planes were, where you were, and, of course, the dive bombers are way up high.

Adm. T.: Yes. This, of course, is just on the way in, before you have any contact with the enemy. You're, hopefully, ready for them and in a position where you can do something to protect the torpedo planes.

Q: What kind of a day was it?

Adm. T.: It was a beautiful day. There were little puffy clouds up around 1,000 feet to 1,500 feet that sometimes would get a little thicker and other times they'd open up and be very scattered. It was that way all the way into the enemy formation.

Q: What time did you take off?

Adm. T.: We took off later than the Enterprise and Yorktown.

Q: Do you mean Enterprise and Hornet?

Adm. T.: I mean Enterprise and Hornet. They started taking off a little after 7 a.m., and we didn't start taking off until around 8:40. By 0900 I was in the air and departed Yorktown. A strange thing happened on the way. We were flying along and, all of a sudden, ahead of us and out a little bit to the side, were two big explosions in the water that threw the water way up high. I hadn't the slightest idea what they were. There didn't seem to be anybody around, but I sort of wondered if someone hadn't inadvertently dropped a couple of bombs, and that's exactly the way it turned out. In arming the bombs - the arming device worked in a way that released the bomb as well as arming it - and a couple of the planes in Max Leslie's squadron -

Q: Did you have a last-minute briefing before you took off?

Adm. T.: Yes, although I had spent so much time trying to get my six-plane escort changed back to eight that only a few minutes remained before take-off time. I did, and I told the people that were going with me and the others who were standing by for combat air patrol, who weren't going in on the attack, were, of course listening, and I emphasized that I wanted that formation to stick together, that nobody was going to be a lone wolf, because lone wolves don't live very long under the circumstances we were going into, and they just had to stick together no matter what happened because I was convinced, and I thought they were, too, that that was the best way to survive and protect the torpedo planes. Then I reminded them of the tricks that we had heard about being played on some people. Sometimes a Japanese fighter would fly up and pose himself in a position where it looked like you could easily go out and shoot him, a little below, you know, giving you all this so-called advantage but there were his friends waiting topside to come down and pick you off if you pulled out alone. I said our primary job is to protect the torpedo planes and keep the enemy fighters engaged as much as we possibly could, all the way in and all the way out. It was a pretty serious thing because we had gotten the information now on really how big they were. Then word came for escort pilots to man their planes.

So we finally took off . . .

Q: Who gave you the information on the course to take?

Adm. T.: This comes to the ready room from the air officer of the air department and, of course, the ship's communications system gets all messages relating to the position and disposition and so forth of enemy forces, everything we know. We didn't know too much at that time, except we had received these contact reports, but as each hour and half-hour goes by they get old and the enemy obviously isn't exactly where he was when seen an hour ago. He can be more than 30 miles away in one hour.

Q: Did the commanding officer or the admiral come down to say anything to you as you got ready to leave?

Adm. T.: No. I never even saw Admiral Fletcher and I didn't talk to Captain Buckmaster because I wasn't supposed to. Information came down through the air officer to the squadrons and the group commander.

Q: Did you feel any particular emotional reaction as you took off that morning compared to other mornings?

Adm. T.: Well, of course, you might say high excitement in with, naturally, some misgiving about my inability to get eight airplanes instead of six.

Q: Did that make you mad?

Adm. T.: Yes, but I realized that it wasn't primarily the

fault of the man who made the decision, that if he's going to be out alone with only one carrier, he's got to have enough fighters to have a watch-and-watch section of a strong combat air patrol.

Q: To me, six seems such a tiny group of fighters.

Adm. T.: Well, it's also interesting that those six were the only fighters that got any combat over the Japanese fleet.

Q: Of all the three carriers?

Adm. T.: Yes. No other fighters. And VF-3 was the only fighter squadron in the Battle of Midway that had any significant aerial combat in defense of our carriers. We'll go into that a little later.

So we went in. All of us were, of course, highly excited and admittedly nervous. I think most other people did pretty much what I did - kept going over my check-off list, and as soon as we got in the air I had each section test their guns so they'd be all ready, and all the switches on and not on safety. This seemed to work all right, so in we went.

Lem Massey made a small change of course to the right. We took off on a heading of about southwest, and I wondered why he did that. I wondered if he'd gotten some more information, but about that time, looking ahead, I could see ships through the breaks in the little puffy clouds, and I figured that was it. We had just begun to approach about ten miles from the outer screen of this large force, looked like it was spread over the ocean, and several colored antiaircraft bursts burst out in our direction - one red one and another orange color - and then no more. And I wondered why they'd be shooting at us because we weren't quite in range, we weren't even nearly in range. The bursts were obviously fired from the nearest ship which was quite a distance from the main body of carriers and battleships, but we soon found out what that was. We'd been sighted from the surface screen and they were alerting the combat air patrol. A very short time after those bursts occurred, before we got anywhere near antiaircraft range, why, these Zero fighters came down on us. I tried to count them. We'd always been trained to count things at a glance, and I figured there were 20.

The first thing that happened was that Bassett's plane was burning. He pulled out, and I didn't see him any more. He was shot down right away. I didn't see the Zero that got to him, but I realized later that they were coming in in a stream on us from astern. I was surprised that they put so many Zeros on my six fighters. I had expected they would go for the torpedo planes first.

They must have known we didn't have the quick acceleration to catch them the way they were coming in at high speed in rapid succession and zipping on away.

But then I saw they had a second large group that were now streaming in right past us and into the poor torpedo planes.

Macomber's position was too close to me to permit an effective weave and I was not getting very good shots at the Zeros. I called him on the radio and said "open out more. About double your present distance and weave." No acknowledgment. His radio must have been dead. (He has since stated it was). How ironical this situation had become! I had spent almost a year of effort developing what I was convinced was the only way to survive against the Zero and now we couldn't seem to do it. I kept wondering why Macomber was so close instead of being out in a position to weave. Of course, he had never practiced the weave. He was one of the VF-42 pilots based aboard Yorktown during the Coral Sea Battle and he had tangled with some Zeros then. But like the other former VF-42 pilots, he had reported to VF-3 just before we flew out to land aboard Yorktown enroute to Midway.

I had assumed that my exec, Don Lovelace, had briefed them or required them to read the Squadron Tactical Doctrine.

I suddenly realized Don didn't have much time to brief anyone before he had his head chopped off. I had tried so hard to wipe that ghastly accident out of my mind that I forgot Don was no longer with us.

Then I remembered telling my flight during the last minute briefing to "stick together". Macomber must have thought I meant for him to fly a closed up formation. What I actually meant was I wanted no "lone wolf" tactics.

Too late to correct that misunderstanding now. I couldn't see Cheek and Sheedy so I called Ram Dibb, my wing man and said, "Pretend you are a section leader and move out far enough to weave." He said, "This is Scarlet Two, Wilco." His voice sounded like he was elated to get this "promotion" right in the middle of a battle.

Several Zeros came in on a head-on attack on the torpedo planes and burned Lem Massey's plane right away. It just exploded in flames. And, beautifully timed, another group came in on the side against the torpedo planes. In the meantime, a number of them were coming down in a string on our fighters, so we - the air was just like a beehive, and I wasn't sure at that moment that anything would work. It didn't look like my weave was working, but then it began to work. I got a good shot at two of them and burned them, and one of them had made a pass at my wing man, pulled out to the right, and then came back. We were weaving continuously, and I got a head-on shot at him, and just about the time I saw this guy coming, Ram had said, "There's a Zero on my tail." He didn't have to look back because the Zero wasn't directly astern, he was about like 45 degrees, beginning to follow him around, which gave me the head-on approach. I was really angry then. I was mad because, here, this poor little wing man who'd never been in combat before, in fact very little gunnery training, the first time aboard a carrier, and a Zero was about to chew him to pieces. I probably should have decided to duck under this Zero, but I lost my temper a little bit and I decided I'm going to keep my fire going into him and he's going to pull out, which he did, and he just missed me by a few feet and I saw flames coming out of the bottom of his airplane. This is like playing "chicken" with two automobiles on the highway headed for each other except we were both shooting as well. That was a little foolhardy, but I think because I hit him - the first reaction on being hit is to jerk back, and it pulled his stick back and his nose went up. I wanted him to pull out. I was going to force him to pull out, which is a foolish thing. I didn't try that any more. You really don't need to because if you haven't hit him by the time you get there, you can certainly afford to duck under and you'll get away.

They kept coming in and, by this time, we were over the screen, and more torpedo planes were falling, but so were some Zeros, and we thought, well, at least we're keeping a lot of them engaged. The torpedo planes had to split in order to make an effective torpedo attack. We used to call it "the Anvil Attack," I don't know where the name "anvil" came from, but they'd break up and spread out in a kind of a line on each side of the target, of the carrier. We could see the carriers. They were steaming at very high speed and launching airplanes. They looked like fighters. I couldn't tell. I just got a glimpse, and they were beginning to maneuver. The reason the torpedo planes have to split is so that they can have torpedo planes coming in against a carrier from various points around at least 180 degrees of the compass, so that if the ship turns to the right, he's left a broadside shot for several torpedoes. If he turns to the left, then the ones on the other side get the same advantage, and only one of the torpedoes then can he comb. By "combing" I mean just head right for it and barely avoid it, so it's track extended is parallel to but clear of the ships side. We thought we were doing pretty well until they split. Then, of course, they were extremely vulnerable, just all alone with no mutual protection. The Zeros were coming in on us, one after the other and sometimes simultaneously from above and to the side, we couldn't stay with the torpedo planes, except for one or two that happened to be under us.

I kept counting the number of airplanes that I knew I'd gotten in flames going down - you couldn't bother to wait for them to splash, but you could tell if they were flaming real good and you saw something besides smoke, if it was real red flames, why, you knew he'd had it. I had this little knee pad and I would mark down every time I shot one that I knew was gone. Then I realized that this was sort of foolish. Why was I marking marks on my knee pad when the knee pad wasn't coming back? I was utterly convinced then that we weren't any of us coming back because there were still so many of these Zeros and they'd already gotten one, and looking around, I couldn't see Cheek or Sheedy anymore, so there were just two others that I could see of my own. Macomber over there on my left and Ram Dibb and me. Pure logic would convince anyone that with their superior performance and the number of Zeros they were throwing into the fight we could not possibly survive. So I said, this counting is a foolish thing. It takes a second or two to look down to your knee pad and make this mark - a waste of time. I said, well, (still talking to myself) we're going to take a lot of them with us if they're going to get us all. We kept on working this weave and it seemed to work better and better. How much space of time this took, I don't know, but the reason I tell about stopping my counting is because now and ever since then I haven't the slightest idea how many Zeros I shot down. I just can't remember, and I don't suppose it makes too much difference. It only shows that I was absolutely convinced that nobody could get out of there, that we weren't coming back, and neither were any of the torpedo planes.

Then it seemed that the attacks began to slack off a little bit. Whether they were spreading out and working more on the torpedo planes that were unprotected, I don't know. The torpedo planes went on in and I saw three or four of them that got in and made an attack, and I believe that at least one torpedo hit was made. Now, all the records, and the Japanese, and Sam Morison's book, said that no torpedoes hit. I'm not sure that the people aboard a ship that is hit repeatedly about the same time by dive bombers, whether they really know whether they got hit by a torpedo or was it one of the bombs. I'm not sure they really know. I was aboard the Saratoga when she was torpedoed and the Yorktown when she was bombed and I couldn't tell the difference. I think I saw at least one hit, but it occurred either during or very shortly before the dive bombers came in. Naturally, being pretty busy, I couldn't do any more than every now and then get a glance, when I was actually looking at a Japanese fighter I would see this as well. And then I saw this glint in the sun and it just looked like a beautiful silver waterfall, these dive bombers coming down. I could see them very well, because that's the direction the Zeros were, too. They were above me but closer. They weren't anywhere near the altitude that the dive bombers were. I'd never seen such superb dive bombing. It looked to me like almost every bomb hit. Of course, there were some very near misses. There weren't any wild ones. Explosions were occurring in the carriers, and about that time the Zeros slacked off more. We stayed around. We brought out two torpedo planes, one after the other, and tried to get them out clear and then we could go back and pick up another one that we saw, stay right with him and over him, hoping that the Zeros wouldn't have him all to themselves. Of course, they may have been badly hit and some of them were in the water and we didn't see them after the torpedo attack. I know more than two attacked. We came in a little earlier than the dive bombers by a matter of just minutes, and drew most, if not all, of the enemy combat air patrol. They were ready and waiting for us as we came in as we came in a full thirty minutes after the VT-8 and VT-6 attack.

After the dive bomber attack was over, I still stayed over there, between the screen and the carriers. A single Zero appeared flying slowly below and to one side of us. I looked up toward the sun and sure enough there were his teammates poised like hawks waiting for one of us to take the bait! We didn't. I could only see three carriers. I never did see a fourth one. And one of them, probably either the Soryu or the Kaga, was burning with bright pink flames, and sometimes blue flames. I remember looking at the height of the flames from the ship and noticing that it was about the height that the ship was long - the length of the ship - just solid flame was going up, and, of course, there was a lot of smoke on top of that. So, I saw three carriers burning pretty furiously before I left there, then came back and picked up one torpedo plane and flew on back toward the Yorktown with it.

Q: How much time of flying did your fighter have? How much gasoline? How much time? How many miles or how much time could you . . . ?

Adm. T.: We had enough gasoline to get back and get aboard, the three of us.

Q: And how long had you been gone altogether?

Adm. T.: I looked at my watch, and I thought I was over the carriers between 12 and 12:30, but that may have been a little different than the local time. I think it was probably between 10 and 10:30 local time. I was over the Japanese fleet a full 20 minutes, because I had enough gas. You see, we took off later than the other people. We (the fighters) were the last ones to take off because the other types had more gas, they could fly farther than we. They had more endurance and more range. I had more speed and caught up with VT-3 in a running rendezvous.

Q: At what point did you come to realize that maybe you weren't going to be shot down after all?

Adm. T.: Just about the time the dive bombers were attacking. It may have been that the Japanese Zeros saw their carriers being clobbered and kind of lost heart. We didn't shoot them all down, I'll tell you that. But our tactics were working and they were losing more fighters than we were.

Q: But they did ease off?

Adm. T.: They did ease off. Maybe they were trying to climb up and get at the dive bombers and didn't make it, because the dive bombers were hardly disturbed before they made their attack. I think one or two of the dive bombers were attacked by Zeros after pulling out of their dive. Wade McCluskey got a little shrapnel in his shoulder. He was the leader of the Enterprise air group attack.

Q: Certainly, your decision to cover the torpedo planes was the right one.

Adm. T.: Oh, yes. These torpedo pilots were all my very close friends, Lem Massey especially, and he was lost. I felt pretty bad about this, just sort of hopeless. I felt like we hadn't done enough, that if they didn't get any hits this whole business of torpedo planes going in at all was a mistake. But, of course, you couldn't fail to send them, and in thinking about it since then I realize that this classic, coordinated attack that we practiced for many years, with the torpedo planes going in low and the dive bombers coming in high, pretty much simultaneously - that's what we tried to do, although it's usually better if the dive bombers do hit first, then the torpedo planes can get in better among the confusion of bombs bursting. So, I realized that here was sort of the reverse of the Coral Sea battle, that these people hadn't given their lives in vain, they'd done a magnificent job of attracting all the enemy combat air patrol, all the protection that the Japanese carriers had were engaged and were held down, so we did do something, and maybe far more than we thought at the time. We engaged the enemy that might have gotten into the dive bombers and prevented them from getting many hits.

Q: How did you feel? You started to say it. Were you just terribly depressed at the time, feeling it had been a wasted effort?

Adm. T.: Yes, for a while. I felt that way while it was going on. I couldn't understand why the Japanese were throwing everything at us, but apparently they saw us first, we were the only fighters they saw, they were anxious to wipe us out and that was it. They didn't see the dive bombers, and they didn't have anybody up at high altitude.

Jim Gray had the VF-6 fighter escort. He had eight, and he was at high altitude. He had an agreement with the torpedo planes that if they needed him they would call him and tell him. Well, of course, everything happened so suddenly and the torpedo planes were getting shot up so badly that he didn't hear anything from them. He may have seen VT-3 instead of VT-6, if he saw torpedo planes down there. Being at high altitude, you can't tell. If there are any fights going on below, you don't see them, with the water right under - so he saw no enemy aircraft.

Q: What ship was Gray from?

Adm. T.: From the Enterprise.

Q: So those torpedo planes never got any protection?

Adm. T.: No. VT-8 from Hornet and VT-6 from Enterprise had no fighter escort. The dive bombers from the Enterprise, led by Wade McCluskey, who took off early and didn't find

the enemy force at the place where it had been estimated
that it would be, turned and went back northwest, and he
saw a destroyer high-tailing it with - leaving - a terrific
wake and he thought that destroyer must be catching up with
the carriers, so he followed it and, pretty soon, he saw
the carriers, which made him arrive within - almost simultaneously with Max Leslie and his dive bombers. So that
was a coincidence, the arrival of those two at the same
time, but it was no coincidence that the torpedo planes
and the dive bombers from the carrier Yorktown attacked
in coordinated fashion. That is doctrine and its plan
had been practiced for many years, and it worked. It was
a beautifully classic attack, although the torpedo planes
were almost annihilated, it still went like it was supposed
to go. There was a torpedo plane that we finally joined
up with after the attack was all over and I saw that the
dive bombers had gotten out apparently free. When I
joined up with him he was about 20 feet off the water.
So I flew down alongside of him and tried to talk to him,
but his radio was out. I wanted him to get up, to get a
little altitude because I wanted to stay with him and I
wanted altitude so that I could hopefully use it to gain
a little speed if I needed to. The rear seat gunner
thought that I was pointing to another enemy Zero over
him, and he grabbed for the gun and was looking around -

Thach #3 - 258

Q: How many of yours came back?

Adm. T.: Actually, Bassett was the only one who was killed, was lost. Cheek and Sheedy were surrounded and chased by Zeros and got badly shot up but finally got back, and I'm not sure whether it was Sheedy - I think it was - who was wounded and bleeding pretty badly. His cockpit was riddled with bullets, and he came aboard the first carrier he could see, which was the Hornet. They gave him a cut and he came in and his guns went off and killed one officer and a couple of enlisted men. Later we found that his master switch, which he had turned off, was just welded across the wires by bullet holes so that you couldn't turn it off. I mean, you could turn it off, it was in the "off" position, but the circuit was complete and when he hit the arresting gear wire he jolted forward. He hit the deck pretty hard. He was not in very good physical condition, and his hand was on the stick and that's where the trigger is, and he fired a burst into the superstructure, the island. We investigated this thing thoroughly and Captain Mitscher, commanding officer of the Hornet, recommended that we have an automatic switch in the tail hook so when the tail hook was lowered it would open the circuit of the gun switch so that this couldn't happen again.

He was pretty unhappy with me when I went against that and recommended that it not be done, because we had enough trouble with keeping these things maintained properly so that they worked. This was a rate thing that happened, and the chance of it happening again was extremely remote. Suppose torpedo planes were coming in to sink a carrier, and half of our guns didn't work because of this additional switch they had which could easily get dirty because it's way back in the fuselage, it could easily get dirty and fail to make contact and then our fighters couldn't shoot down the torpedo planes and the torpedo planes sink the whole ship and a lot more people are killed, rather than just a handful. That was the reason I recommended against it. Admiral Mitscher never did agree with me. I don't know whether he did later or not, but he didn't like it.

Q: You haven't told me what it feels like to be a fighter pilot.

Adm. T.: Just to get into an airplane, even in training, into a good fighter, make a nice smooth gunnery run and fire and hit the target is a very exhilarating feeling. It's exhilirating just to be up in the air, in the first place, but when you do these other things it's sort of like participating in, maybe, a ballet that's working very well.

Q: In the midst of this carnage and horror, what went

through your mind?

Adm. T.: I finally decided that we were going to get back and I called the other people and said, "Well, they don't like it as well as they used to. Stick together and we'll get home yet." Or something like that.

Q: Did you ever wonder, what on earth am I doing up here?

Adm. T.: Yes, but strangely enough not during the battle of Midway. Oh, many times in training I wondered what I was doing where I was, for instance, at night, in the rain, and trying to land aboard a carrier. You think, I wonder if I picked the right profession." But then, after you get aboard that's all washed out and you feel happy, or if you're in a patrol plane on a long flight and you're dead tired, and you're in a storm, and everything is soaking wet, and you're beginning to have trouble with one engine, it's cutting out, and you look down and the wind is blowing a gale and there are heavy waves down there, and you think, well, I hope I don't go down there, I know I won't survive. You get used to thinking about surviving or not surviving, and it's very exhilarating when you survive.

Q: Contest with the elements or life?

Adm. T.: Yes.

Thach #3 - 261

Q: It's interesting to have you expand on your feeling. You told me a minute ago, yes I was scared and I'll tell you about it. Is this the time?

Adm. T.: Yes. This was a pretty hair-raising experience, as they call it now "pretty hairy." There were so many of them that I was afraid this Weave wasn't working, but it still, I'm convinced, was the best thing to do. And of course many other people since then have convinced me also that it was the best way to fight at that time.

Q: Did you swear, did you pray, did you have any other - ?

Adm. T.: No, you're too busy, really, to get - you're never near-paralyzed with fright because of fear of getting shot - as long as you haven't been hit, you haven't been hit. You're so busy, and also you have a respect for your opponent. That first attack they made on us and the torpedo planes was beautifully coordinated. It was something that I had to admire, and I thought so at the time. When I described it, I said, "it was beautifully executed." I had to admire these people, they were plenty good. This was their first team and they were pros. It was the team that came in and hit Pearl Harbor in the beginning. Incidentally, I never thought that the Pearl Harbor attack should have been called a "sneak attack." They were following the basic principles of warfare, and if you're going to fight somebody, take advantage of everything you've got. I was surprised that they did it, because I felt that they couldn't finally win in the long run, but when I realized how many carriers they had and how many we had in the Pacific, I began to wonder about this. They took over one-sixth of the earth's surface in six months, and they did it with their carriers, using the carriers as a spearhead, and close air support softening up the landing spot, and they were very good military planners. They're superb pilots. Japanese carrier-based pilots were really good, and they could shoot and hit. I felt, and I said so when I came back, I wished we had an airplane very much like the Zero, because we needed a better performance.

On the way back to the Yorktown - I'm sorry I keep digressing, but little things pop into my head - you were talking about were you scared or frightened. Yes, everybody's scared, but it isn't a thing that you can let prey on your mind very long because there's always something to do. You're scared but you're still carefully functioning as best you can. And you can function just as well as if you're not scared, maybe you do a little better if you're scared. I don't know. I never have figured that out. But I was scared all over again on the way back, when we were going along with this torpedo plane, and I felt my shoes were a little squashy. I reached down and I felt this slippery liquid all over my leg, and I thought it was blood. It felt like blood, but I didn't want to look at it, so I just didn't look at it for a while. I wiggled my legs and they felt all right, except I remember a little place on my shin that didn't feel too good, and I thought, I guess I bumped it getting in the airplane. Then I picked up my glove and looked at it, and it was oil. I was never so glad to see oil on my hands in my life.

Q: I'm sure of that. You were showing me a memento of this thing that they found in your gas tank. Can you tell about that?

Adm. T.: This was an incendiary bullet that my mechanic picked out of my gas tank. He saw there was a hole in the gas tank and he removed the gas tank to fix it, opened it up, and found this incendiary bullet that was half-burned.

Q: Had that burned in your tank? No.

Adm. T.: It obviously had not because the mixture was too rich. You know, your car stalls when you get too rich a mixture and the spark plugs won't ignite the gasoline in the cylinders. This is the same principle that happened in my gas tank. It was pretty near the bottom of the tank, and it was immediately smothered by gasoline and didn't do any other damage, didn't set the thing on fire, didn't explode or anything. And apparently another bullet had shot an oil line away, and when I finally landed aboard the Yorktown - we came in and gave the signal that we were low on ammunition so that they wouldn't think that we - so they'd know what our state was, we had to do this with hand signals, fly by the bridge and shake your fist at them, that meant I'm low or out of ammunition, and we had other little signals. If you're low on gas - in those days, you know, you could stick your hand out of the cockpit if you were flying slowly - and rake it along the gas tank, which meant you were low on gas. So they were holding off Leslie's dive bombers waiting for me to get back, and I remember Murr Arnold, when we were talking about how I could only take six, and he said, "And, another thing, you'd better bring them back, because I think we're in for one hell of a fight." And I thought, I'll bring them back if I can, naturally. So I got aboard, and I didn't have any oil in the engine. All the oil was gone, but the good old engine was still ticking over and I was able to get aboard.

Q: Fortunately, you didn't know that!

Adm. T.: No, I didn't know that. However, I knew I must be low on oil because both my feet were wet with it.

Q: Your instruments registered it, too, didn't they?

Adm. T.: Yes, the oil pressure had dropped to zero by the time I got aboard. I think it was reading zero pressure when I actually landed aboard. It was dropping a little all the time.

The squadron from the Hornet took off about the same time as the Enterprise attack group and searched in the direction of the estimated position and found nothing. The dive bombers, I think led by Ruff Johnson, and the fighters by Mitchell, Pat Mitchell, continued to search beyond their combat radius and, having found nothing, the dive bombers decided they were closer to Midway Island than they were to the carriers, so they'd have to either land in the water or go to Midway. So they headed for Midway. Pat Mitchell's eight fighters couldn't even make it to Midway, so finally when they ran out of gas they stuck together and landed in formation right in the ocean, all together, and got their life rafts going and were later picked up. But that's the reason that only VT-8 of the Hornet's squadrons was able to engage, and also the reason that the Hornet fighters were not present when the attack was going on. I've already explained that Jim Gray was at high altitude. You can see aerial combat going on if it's above you, but it is more difficult to see it if it's below you. And there was a lot of antiaircraft fire, of course.

Q: That's why your fighter squadron was the only one that saw aerial combat?

Adm. T.: That's true, both over the enemy force and over the American force. I'll tell you later how that came about.

After we'd landed aboard, we were getting ready to go on a combat air patrol, and having the planes re-armed, re-fueled, and checked over, and taking stock of what we'd lost and what we had left. I was in the ready room. We had a combat air patrol of eight fighters in the air under Dick Crommelin. I was in the ready room with the remainder of the fighters when suddenly they picked up on the radar about 30 miles out an attack coming in that was reported as being about 40 aircraft. Actually, I think it was 18 dive bombers supported by 6 fighters, and they came on in. The combat air patrol did a terrific job and shot down most of them, but I think I'm correct in saying that 4 got through. Some people say that 6 got through, and maybe it was 6. The way I made my count - you can hear the antiaircraft fire in the ready room, you're not supposed to be out on deck where the bullets are flying around, that's not your job, so we were in the ready room, which is at the flight deck level in the Yorktown. You hear the heavy 5-inch going off at a slower tempo than the smaller caliber, then finally the 40-mm. 20-mm., and finally the little machine guns, so it begins to be a roar and builds up to a crescendo of gunfire. When you hear the small caliber, you know that the enemy aircraft is pretty close, and I counted this sequence four times, and we felt a couple of thuds, but it seemed rather remote from the fighter pilots' ready room. So, if only four got through, they were very accurate because they got three hits on the Yorktown. One of them exploded in the - down a smoke stack, in the uptakes, and it created quite a problem because the soot being on fire was being spread around quite a bit. This stopped the ship. It blasted out all but one boiler, I think, with the blast blasting down on top of the fire, it put it out. So the ship stopped. Then, within - I'm not sure of the time, it didn't seem very long, maybe an hour, an hour and a half at the most, we heard that the engineers had run auxiliary flexible steam lines and got underway and we received word in the ready room that they thought they could make 16 knots, could we take off? And I said, yes, we can take off if you're making less than that. We could start way back at the stern. There weren't many planes left aboard. You see, Leslie, they wouldn't let him come aboard till I got aboard, but very soon after I got aboard, why, here came the attack of the dive bombers, so he didn't have time to get aboard. So he was still in the air.

We took stock of all the planes we had. When this

attack came in, they had to shut down re-fueling the airplanes and purge the lines with CO_2 gas. They were still fighting fires in some places when they got underway. There was a fire caused by one of the bombs down near the main gasoline tank in a store room, so we couldn't get more gasoline. I said, "Let's take off all the airplanes that have as much as 20 gallons of gas and any ammunition that you can get." So we did, and we got together about 6 or 8, and the ship got underway slowly and finally built up. I don't think they were at 16 knots when I took off, because I just got over the bow and dipped a little bit. Just as we were rolling down the deck, another attack came in. These were heavy torpedo planes, which, again, was a squadron of torpedo planes from the one carrier that was unfound, the fourth carrier, and they were also escorted by six or eight fighters. We didn't have too many combat air patrol in the air at this time. I think there were about four. One of them was Bill Leonard, another one was McCluskey. Ensign Tootle took off right behind me - Tootle, III. There is quite a story about that young man. But as we were rolling down the deck, the antiaircraft fire had to open up. The torpedo planes were that close. I got my wheels up - it takes about 36 hard turns with a crank - nothing automatic about it and you just have to breathe through your mouth. I was looking out to see the firing on the starboard side - got my wheels up and started over there, but Tootle, I don't think he followed me. He was a little later. I think Ram Dibb must have followed me and Milton Tootle didn't even get his wheels up. He turned toward the torpedo planes, right into our own anti-aircraft fire, shot down a Japanese torpedo plane, and a Zero promptly shot him down. He was in the air less than 60 records. This is probably the shortest combat flight on record, where a fighter shot down anything. He shot down a VT and was airborne less than 60 seconds. He said a Zero was shooting at him but he was also, like the rest of us, in the middle of our own antiaircraft fire, so who knows who brought him down, but I think the Zero probably did.

Q: Was he saved?

Adm. T.: Yes, picked out of the water. I saw a torpedo plane. They split, just like we do, so they were coming in from different points of the compass. This torpedo plane was real low on the water, I could see a bright red colored insignia shaped like feathers on his tail that no other Japanese aircraft had, and I made a good side approach on him, and got him on fire. The whole left wing was burning, and I could see the ribs showing through the flames, and that devil still stayed in the air until he got close enough and dropped his torpedo, and that one hit the

Yorktown. So, he was a dedicated Japanese torpedo plane pilot. Even though he was already shot down he went ahead and dropped his torpedo. By that time the whole airplane looked like it was on fire, the top surface of both wings was burned away, everything but the ribs. Looking at it from above - he must have had some wing surface underneath to hold him up, but he was obviously sinking all the time and he fell in the water right after he dropped his torpedo and fell in the water very close to the ship. Usually, you know, they have to pull out to avoid the ship because torpedo planes come in so low. They were very good, excellent, in their tactics, in their determination - they were just as determined as anybody else. In fact, as far as determination was concerned, you could hardly tell any difference between the Japanese carrier-based pilots and the American carrier-based pilots. Nothing would stop them if they had anything to say about it.

Q: So it was a torpedo that sank the Yorktown, rather than a dive bomber?

Adm. T.: The Yorktown had another torpedo hit, but again most of the torpedo planes were shot down before they got in, and yet they got hits. So that stopped the ship, really and we pulled out, and I had a little tangle with a Zero. Since we never did join up, we weren't even in a formation, we just turned individually off the bow of the ship into the torpedo planes, so I didn't have a wing man. In fact, I didn't see anybody else. I saw that Zero and I went at him. He apparently had been fighting with some of our combat air patrol and he was going to catch up with what he thought was left of his torpedo planes. I was hoping he wouldn't see me, but he saw me soon after I started for him, and he just pulled up very neatly and came right round over the top of my head and right on my tail. Fortunately there was a little cloud I was heading for, and I went right into the cloud, did a split S, pulled out and didn't see him any more. He almost had me. I thought I could get a shot at him before he saw me, then I decided what I would so.

Q: Were you able to get back aboard the Yorktown after she was hit?

Adm. T.: No, the Yorktown never took any more airplanes aboard.

Q: I didn't mean to interrupt. Were you through with that?

Adm. T.: No. It was a very sad thing to see the Yorktown listing more and more. I thought she was going to roll over and capsize. Apparently so did the skipper because it wasn't long before he ordered "abandon ship." We were directed to land aboard the Enterprise.

At this time, I was mad all over again. I was angry, because, here, the Enterprise and Hornet sitting about 50 miles away with combat air patrol, plenty of it, over them and too far away to help the Yorktown. There was something wrong with this, and I was unhappy about it. If we'd just had one or two more airplanes in the air to fight this attack, the Yorktown would never have been sunk. I'm sure of it.

Q: Fifty miles away wasn't very far. Why couldn't they have come to your assistance?

Adm. T.: It was too far - too late. They started over - some of them were started over but it was too late to intercept before the attack was finished. Of course, they couldn't afford to denude themselves. They didn't start anything on the dive bomber attack. They may have started some over then, but they didn't get there in time to intercept. There they were, too far away for mutual support, and yet the Japanese, on the way home, the Japanese pilots saw the Enterprise and Hornet. It wasn't that the Yorktown was being used effectively as bait to protect the Enterprise and Hornet - that wasn't intended, I'm sure, but it didn't work in any event. We just divided our forces, or, rather, they got divided. I'm sure that the people who made the decisions to have two task groups, separate, expected that they would remain close enough for mutual support, but it didn't work out that way. When Buckmaster realized that he was farther away than he wanted to be, that's when he or Admiral Fletcher cut me down to six fighters. Neither Fletcher nor Spruance were naval aviators - they had not grown up in carrier-based squadrons or had command of an aircraft carrier, where all the experience and knowledge is absorbed which would qualify one to command a carrier task force.

Q: Who made the decision that they should stay that far apart? Do you know?

Adm. T.: Rear Admiral Fletcher directed Rear Admiral Spruance, Task Force 16, to proceed toward the enemy and launch a strike saying he would follow with Task Force 17 as soon as Yorktown recovered her scouts. So Frank Jack Fletcher caused the initial separation. Did he realize he was violating one of the basic principles of warfare? That they should be in two task groups, it was obviously Admiral Nimitz. The failure to keep them together is obviously the man in charge, the Admiral and his staff. You can say Fletcher or Spruance, but, of course, Fletcher didn't have an aviation staff, and they had no real background of experience in operating carriers. Spruance had Halsey's staff, but they were ordered to proceed southwest and launch a strike. Spruance was junior to Fletcher. The Yorktown had sent out scouts and she had to land them aboard, but I know the wind was such that we could have kept them closer together and could have kept the same speed of advance if they had paid more attention to it and realized how important it was. Later, I'll point out how this can be done. It'll be much later, though, when I was operations officer of the fast carrier task force. We operated five carriers inside of a screen and kept them together, and took planes aboard, and the wind was from the wrong direction. But you can do it, if you insist on it being done, and if you look ahead a few hours, you can do it. We operated three and four separate task groups making continuous strikes yet remaining within mutual support distance.

Q: Have you ever read anything on that point?

Adm. T.: And I was very bitter about this and was for a long time. I think one of the basic principles of warfare was violated, not intentionally, I presume. Of course, I was only a lieutenant commander then, and I couldn't fuss at anybody very much, and I'd had only about fifteen years' experience in studying warfare, plus four years at the Naval Academy, where they taught us the basic principles of warfare, and they made sense. It wasn't just an edict or Bible, because the basic principles of warfare weren't invented, they were discovered. They exist as a law of nature, and the law of strategy and tactics, and people who violate any one of them are at a disadvantage, and people who exploit one of the principles, such as concentration of force, usually do better than the other fellow, if he doesn't. The element of surprise, we had and utilized. This was the main reason for our success. Otherwise, we might have had all three carriers sunk, if we hadn't had that surprise.

Q: Were you bitter at anyone in particular at the time?

Adm. T.: Well, yes, Admiral Nimitz, Rear Admiral Fletcher, Rear Admiral Spruance and Captain Buckmaster. As I said, I was a young lieutenant commander, then, and since then having grown up and gotten to be a captain with more experience in task group, task force and fleet operations and had command of two carriers, then rear admiral of a task group, and a vice admiral of a task force, and finally a four-star admiral of forces in Europe, I haven't changed my mind one damned bit.

Q: I can tell from your comments that you haven't, but I wondered if you were bitter at anybody at the time.

Thach #3 - 276

Adm. T.: Well, not anybody in particular, but a group of people, including all the people who were in charge of the thing.

Q: You didn't say, "this man should have known better," or did you pinpoint any particular person?

Adm. T.: It was too late to say anything at that point.

Q: I know it, but in your mind did you feel that there was a person who was responsible?

Adm. T.: Well, again, we went into this battle with inexperienced commanders to fight the kind of battle that we were fighting. Admiral Fletcher and Admiral Spruance, they didn't grow up in aircraft carriers, they'd never operated aircraft carriers tactically. So, maybe, they're not to blame. Maybe, it's Nimitz. Maybe it's somebody in Washington. Whoever assigned these two admirals to operate aircraft carriers when they had no experience in aircraft or aircraft carriers.

Q: But you didn't, at the time, feel a pinpointing of bitterness at any individual?

Adm. T.: No. I was frustrated, and disappointed, of course,

I've found since that no battle works out perfectly for one side.

Q: Haven't you thought it remarkably proven, however, that your training and the fact that the people in your squadron did follow the doctrine was what brought them all home, but one?

Adm. T.: There's no question about that.

Q: So, you must have had some satisfaction in that.

Adm. T.: Absolutely. And, of course, I was very proud of the fact that my squadron shot down all these airplanes. 32 enemy aircraft shot out of the air by these interior-performing Wildcats –

Q: In 20 minutes by six planes?

Adm. T.: No. This is the total including the VF-3 combat air patrol against enemy dive bombers and enemy torpedo planes and enemy fighters. There was the Japanese attack on the Yorktown and our attack on them – the total. As I told you, I don't know how many I shot down. I know that there were three little marks on my knee pad when I got back, but I know I quit marking. Also when AA fire as well as our fighters are shooting at enemy aircraft, you couldn't be sure whether the fighters or antiaircraft fire made the kill.

Q: Yourself, a possible 16?

Adm. T.: This thing I have here may not be complete because we lost Bassett and Hoffman. We lost two pilots in the final analysis, but I thought I lost more. Cheek and Sheedy came back, and Woolsey was missing, but he landed in the water.

Q: That would be two out of how many?

Adm. T.: 25. Of course, some of the Japanese pilots that we shot down may have been picked up by their destroyers and survived. I don't know. We shot down 32 for sure. At one time I thought that we probably shot down about 52, but I don't think it was that much now.

I flew over and landed on the Enterprise. Immediately, they said Admiral Spruance wants to see you on the flag bridge. I went up and he said, "Well, how do you think we're doing?" And I said, "Admiral, we're winning this battle. We've already won it, because I saw with my own eyes three big carriers burning so furiously they'll never launch another airplane. Of course, that fourth one, an unfound carrier is a dangerous thing. We certainly ought to be able to get him. I think we ought to chase 'em, because we've got the advantage now." And he said, "Well," and he kind of smiled, "you know we don't have any battleships. All we have is cruisers, and if we start chasing them, it's going to get dark pretty soon, and we suddenly catch up with 'em, they may be able to chew us up before we can get within gun range at night, and we don't have much of a nightattack capability." I said, "I think they're on the run, and I think we ought to chase them" And I left him with that thought.

Then they decided that, since the Hornet VF-8, Squadron Lieutenant Commander Mitchell, was missing, and the Enterprise had a squadron commander and most of their fighters intact, I would go over and take over the Hornet fighter squadron, take with me what I had in the Enterprise of VF-3, which I did. And then we flew combat air patrols from the Hornet which was uneventful because there weren't any more attacks, but attacks were made on enemy cruisers that had been crippled and that story has been written many times, so I won't go into it. That's all I can think of right now that might be of interest on the Battle of Midway.

Q: Can you describe returning to Pearl Harbor?

Adm. T.: That was another bitter blow, we came back in

and people were showing us all these headlines, "B-17s Win Battle of Midway," and people would say, "Where was the Navy? Didn't you all go out there? Didn't you take part in it?" This is true. This is what people were asking. They didn't know, because the Navy was very careful and deliberate about making press releases, and, of course, it was several days before we got back ashore, and there just wasn't much press concerning the Navy's participation in the Battle of Midway. But the B-17s flying from ashore could talk to newsmen, which they did, and told them what they thought they'd done. The fact that they didn't get a single hit on anything in the Battle of Midway, they may not have realized at that time. But I suspected it, because I saw all the carriers in very good shape, steaming at 30 knots in to the wind and not any smoke coming from them, not even from the smoke stacks.

Q: You told me you took off with very little, not more than 20 gallons of gas. How much did you actually have?

Adm. T.: I took off with about 30, as I remember.

Q: How long would that take you in flying time?

Adm. T.: Including a little combat, it wouldn't last more than about 20 minutes, but we got aboard the Enterprise all right.

Q: How much gas did you have left? More than a cup?

Adm. T.: I don't remember how much, but I know I was low, but having made so many landings aboard a carrier, I wasn't worried about making a bad approach and have to go round again.

Q: And after your return to Pearl Harbor from the <u>Hornet</u>, were you then detached?

Adm. T.: Not long after that I was detached. Butch O'Hare came back from the United States, having received from the President the Congressional Medal of Honor. I had recommended that when and if I were relieved, he should be the one to take the squadron because he had been promoted to lieutenant commander and he was well qualified to command the squadron.

Q: And he'd been trained well by you!

Adm. T.: He'd been trained well by a number of us, and he was plenty good to start with, far better than the average student right out of Pensacola. Anyway, it was around early July, I believe, that he relieved me and

Thach #3 - 282

I came back to the United States. When I got back to San Diego I saw Jimmy Flatley and we got together and talked over a number of things and I said, "You know, we've got a lot of training to do." I had been ordered to the training command, the advanced training command, and "I don't know how we're going to do it with not too many people with experience to be instructors." I wasn't speaking of learning how to fly. I was speaking of learning how to fight in the advanced training command, and Jimmy suggested, "You know, I've been talking to Walt Disney, I think he would like to help us." We decided we had to get some training films on tactics and it wouldn't be easy to do because one of the most difficult sort of photography, motion pictures, is aircraft in aerial combat, because the distances are so great, they close and then open up so wide, and so on. It's very hard to -

Q: You couldn't get the camera close enough to what was going on.

Adm. T.: You'd need a camera that had a 180-degree eye, or something like that. It's hard to do. Jimmy's thought was that it should be done in animation, and I agreed.

Q: We were talking about Butch O'Hare while we were having lunch and you mentioned the story about him that you weren't sure you'd put on a tape, so at the risk of not losing it why don't you tell it now and then you can put it in its proper place, if you wish, later.

Adm. T.: Fine. As you may remember, during the early part of the war our antiaircraft fire was not too effective. At least, we fighter pilots looked at it with some disdain. Therefore, we weren't too worried when we had to fly through it or near it or if we thought people were shooting at us. I want to hasten to add, however, that later in the war our antiaircraft fire got to be very good so we had to make certain rules about holding fire when our own planes were approaching because they could be hit.

But, to get back to the South Pacific, shortly after Butch O'Hare had shot down six planes in six minutes, he had finished a combat air patrol and was coming in for a landing. Now, at this time, the Lexington, as the other carriers had done, put small caliber - such as 30 and 50 caliber - machineguns mounted on the catwalks just to assist against close-in attacks, such as a torpedo plane attack, in case enemy aircraft get past some of the large caliber, such as 5-inch and 3-inch, and 1.1 mm., maybe the smaller caliber could get them if they came close enough.

After this battle with the new Japanese Bettys some of the young machine gunners were a little trigger-happy, and when Butch was coming in for a landing in the groove with his wheels down, one of the gunners back on the port quarter opened up on him and fired a long burst before anybody could stop him. Butch saw where the fire was coming from but he came on in and landed and, just to show you the kind of person he was, he got out of his plane and slowly walked back and stood on the flight deck and looked down at this young machine gunner and said, "Son, if you don't stop shooting at me when I've got my wheels down, I'm going to have to report you to the gunnery officer."

Q: He must be quite a human being!

Adm. T.: That's all he said! Of course, the young man was horribly embarrassed, in the first place, but somebody asked Butch about it later and he said, "I don't mind him shooting at me when I don't have my wheels down but it might make me have to take a wave-off and I don't like to take wave-offs."

Q: Quite a guy. Should we continue now with your experience with the Disney Studios?

Adm. T.: Yes, after the Battle of Midway. We were talking about my meeting with Jimmy Flatley and our agreement that we - that one of the things we needed more than anything we could think of for training new pilots was some fighter gunnery and fighter tactics training films, and he suggested I go see Walt Disney which I did and he said that he would be very happy to help the Navy in this manner and he thought that he could do it. So when I reported to my new job in Jacksonville, Florida, as training officer - no, first I was assistant training officer.

Q: What was the name of that command, Admiral?

Adm. T.: Naval Air Operational Training Command. No, Naval Air Advanced Training Command. Later, they changed the name. The mission of this command was to take pilots after they had received their wings and knew how to fly and teach them how to use the weapons, if possible, in the service-type, combat-type aircraft, and we were able to get enough of these to do this training job. In the Navy Department was a man named Captain Arthur W. Radford and I went to see him and he recognized immediately that this was a thing that we had to do because with the pilot-training program expanding tremendously we needed all the training aids we could get. He told me that if I needed any help in this respect not to hesitate to call him on the phone and he would also direct that this list of ten training films be produced and through the various training agencies in the Navy Department and in the field they would have a contract with Walt Disney and, as it turned out, with Warner Brothers also to make some of the live-action portions of the films.

So, I found myself with two jobs. One as training officer on the staff of Rear Admiral A.B. Cook in Jacksonville, and additional duty to design and produce these training films. I didn't realize how much of a job this was going to be until I got into it. Of course, I knew that I was going to have to write down what we were supposed to show on the film, but after a few sessions with the people assigned to the project at Walt Disney's studios in Hollywood, or rather in Burbank, I realized that I was going to have to teach a lot of people almost how to be fighter pilots, whether they ever flew an airplane or not.

Q: In order to make the films?

Adm. T.: In order to make the films, especially the animation films.

Q: What do you mean "animation"? Do you mean a cartoon type?

Adm. T.: Yes, like Mickey Mouse and Donald Duck.

Well, with this project that we called the Jacksonville Project at the Disney studio - that is, it became known as the Jacksonville Project - we went to work. Walt Disney assigned a whole three-story building to the project. I remember a man named Erwin Verity was the Disney studio director of the project and he was extremely cooperative. To make one film they have hundreds of people working on the animation because any figure in an animation film that moves they have to draw thousands of pictures for just a few feet of film. They have experienced artists draw these movements with too much space in between the pictures that he draws so that he won't have to draw twelve of them when a man raises his hand up to scratch his nose, he may only draw two or three.

Then they have a lot of little workers, a lot of them are girls who are just trying to get a start at being an artist and young boys and all kinds of people. They call them "in-betweeners" and these in-betweeners then see the beginning and the end of a motion and they draw the same thing all in between so that the film is not jerky, it looks rather smooth.

So, in order to show what an airplane is doing when it makes an attack or starts an approach, I had to illustrate to them just what it did and what the target was doing and the relative movement, which was a difficult thing to show. I would illustrate this time and time again, and then they would start to put it on paper and if it looked all right, then they could draw the smooth sketch often in color.

Q: You were illustrating with your hands?

Adm. T.: Yes, and sometimes with a little airplane that I stuck between my fingers so that they could see the wings better because it was very important how much bank you had at various times and various places in an approach to a target because it was kind of like an S turn.

Anyway, they all got very enthusiastic and they knew they were helping the war effort. It was a very dedicated and pleasant association, but I felt at times that I had a whole building full of fighter pilots because they got so they were talking the language. That's the way it had to be. Sometimes they would get in arguments with each other about what was right and what was wrong, and they'd always send for me to straighten it out! I would normally spend two weeks in Hollywood and two or three weeks in Jacksonville, and when they got into deep trouble and no one could settle what the next move had to be, they would send me a wire and I would come hiking out.

Q: It's so much more complex than the words say. Making an animation film sounds simple but, as you explain it, it's extremely complicated.

Adm. T.: Yes, and, of course, the important parts of this film couldn't be just faked. You had to show everything because you must not keep anything from the new pilot. He's got to be able to see exactly the position of the plane - the relative position - and what it's doing all the time, whereas in an entertainment film you can just sort of zip it along and it doesn't make any difference if the wing isn't at the right amount of bank or angle, if his nose is too high or too low. This had to be just right because thousands of pilots might get the wrong impression if it were a little bit off. So this was one of the more difficult things.

Then, of course, this animation had to be narrated and I said, "Now, I want a narrator who sounds like he knows what he's talking about, and I don't want him to try to over-dramatize it, I want him to be perfectly matter-of-fact. He's got to be like a school teacher."

Q: So guess who they chose!

Adm. T.: Well, they looked around and did a few takes on some people and Walt Disney didn't like it and I didn't like them either. Finally Walt turned to me and he said, "Well, for heaven's sakes, we've got the man sitting right here who knows how to tell it. You've got to do the narration."

I said, "I'm not a professional narrator, I don't know how to do this."

He said, "You sound better than any of the rest of them to me, and at least you're not going to put emphasis on the wrong things. Just the way you pronounce a word."

We had one little test, for instance, where if you don't start far enough ahead or if you don't turn in soon enough you'll be drawn into a stern chase - a chase from the stern. One narrator says, "If you don't turn in soon enough, you'll be drawn into a <u>stern</u> chase."

Q: A completely different connotation than you intended!

Adm. T.: So we had the Jacksonville Project going on -

Q: And you did do the narrating, then?

Adm. T.: I did all the narrating, finally.

Q: Of twelve films?

Adm. T.: Ten. Some of them we made at Warner Brothers studio, live, on the gun sight and how to use it. The second one was fundamental gunnery approaches, the various kinds of gunnery approaches and how to make them, which would be the overhead, high side, low side, and so forth. Then there was defensive tactics against enemy fighters, offensive tactics against enemy fighters, escort tactics, attacks against enemy bomber formations, combat air patrol, "don't kill your friends" which was the safety film.

Another film was a live thing illustrating typical tactical errors that people might make and why they shouldn't make them and what happens when they do. And I think there might have been a conclusion - I've named about nine -

Q: Yes, you have. How long were these films?

Adm. T.: Oh, thirty to forty minutes. Some of them maybe a little less than that. Some of them may have been twenty minutes.

Q: And how long did it take you to complete all of these?

Adm. T.: It seemed like about ten million hours! I don't know.

Q: All the time you were at Jacksonville, where you were working on them?

Adm. T.: Oh, yes, and in touch with the people who were doing the filming. At one time, I had three films being produced at one time and I was writing as hard as I could on the next two or three. As it progressed along, I would have to be over at Warner Brothers where I had to take part as an instructor to give illustrations to two young students on what was gospel and what wasn't. That was where I played the part of myself. They wanted that.

It took, oh, I guess, four or five months. I'm not sure how long, but I know that at one time before the first film came out, Admiral Cook got a little concerned about my spending this time out in Hollywood, California, when there was serious business to attend to, so he talked to the chief of staff apparently and said, "What is Thach doing out there?"

The chief of staff said, "He's supposed to be making films, although we haven't seen any yet." The Admiral said, "Well, I'd better talk to him." So the chief of staff called me and said, "The Admiral wants to talk to you about maybe you can spend less time out there in Hollywood." The way he said it sounded like they were a little suspicious, maybe I was out there having a good time instead of working. Actually, we worked day and night.

I went to see him and Admiral Cook said, "You've got to get started teaching these new pilots. We've got a lot of new pilots coming and and I want you to go round and teach them all this stuff. You spend a lot of time in Hollywood and I know you're busy when you get back here, but when are you going to go around to the training commands and make these lectures to them?"

I said, "Well, Admiral, I don't think I could ever do it as well as a film because I'm only one person and all the experienced fighter pilots I know agree that this is the way to do it, and it will be standard if we do it by film. It would be almost impossible to do it otherwise."

He said, "Well, I'm very anxious to see the first film." And I said, "I'm trying to get them out just as fast as is humanly possible." He said, "All right. I just wanted to know what was going on. Fine."

I wasn't too happy with that interview because it sounded like he thought I wasn't doing as much of what I should be doing. So, when the first film came out I showed it to him and he was enthralled with it. He said it was terrific, he didn't realize it could be done. I said, "It ain't easy! We had to teach all these young artists to be fighter pilots, and they did a wonderful job. They got into the spirit of the thing."

The Assistant Secretary of the Navy for Air came down and he looked at the next one, the second one that came out, and they were both very enthused about them. After the Admiral had seen the first three or four he was detached and the day he was detached, just before he was leaving, I went to tell him goodbye and we were in his office alone and he said, "You know, I owe you an apology." I said, "I don't think so. Why?" He said:

"Well, I thought you were playing around out there in Hollywood and you couldn't have been since you made all those films. I know nobody out there knew how to do it and you had to do it all. I just want you to know that I owe you an apology. I'm sorry I ever doubted what you were doing."

That made me feel pretty good.

Q: I want to ask you the effectiveness of the films?

Adm. T.: I don't know who can judge the effectiveness of them. The pilots who went through training saw them, but of course that was a captive audience. They had to see them and they used the tactics. I ve heard a number of people say that they saved their lives, which is understandable. You've got to have a plan to fight in the air. You'll do better, even if you have a lousy plan and you're trying to put it into effect. You'll make out better than if you have no plan at all and the enemy is working his plan on you.

So, no matter how good, bad, or poor these films were, they gave them something to try to do.

Q: Were you satisfied?

Adm. T.: Oh, yes, I was completely satisfied in the end. There were many, many times both with the Disney people and the Warner Brothers when I was not satisfied, and one time it came to the point where Warner Brothers' producer insisted that we couldn't produce a certain scene because it would cost so much to get that one scene and he said, "Do you know that would be only about three feet of film for that amount of money? Several thousand dollars for just two or three feet of film." I don't know how many thousands but he named a large figure.

I said, "I don't care how much it costs. I don't care whether it costs a million dollars for those few feet because those were the feet - the three most important feet in the film. When lives are at stake, I don't think it should cost a million dollars, but if it did, I think maybe the lives would be worth it. We're spending a lot more than that on things that I think are not quite as important. That's the way I feel about it."

So he said, "Well, if we make this film the way you want to, it will take an elaborate set-up to get that particular thing, and then when we put the price tag on it, the Navy's going to say, we aren't going to pay that kind of money for this little old film."

I said, "I thought you understood that I had unlimited authority in this film business, these training films."

"Yes," he said, "you told me that." And I said, "Well, it was true."

He said, "But you're not the Navy Department."

And I said, "Well, I'll call up the Navy Department and get Captain Radford on the phone and I want him to talk to you."

So I called him up, luckily right away, and I said, "I want you to talk to the production manager. He's worried about the cost of the film and it's one of the most important and it's a critical portion of the film that shows a pilot how to do it. Of all the things in this film this is, to me, the most important. I told him what you told me, that I had the authority, no matter what it cost." And he said, "This is true. We can't place a price on lives. Is he there?"

I said, "Yes, I want you to talk to him on the phone and tell him."

I didn't hear the rest of the conversation. I just handed the fellow the phone. He turned around and said, "No more problem with me. He told me that whatever you wanted you could have." This was very wonderful to have that kind of support from a fellow who used to be my squadron commander and later became Chairman of the Joint Chiefs of Staff.

Q: I've observed that every experience you've had with people of that caliber that you must have presented your story well enough because never have they turned you down!

Adm. T.: On those important things, no. But I'm sure everybody's been turned down on something.

Q: But I'm speaking of the times when you presented a real problem and presented it well enough, they had recognized the problem and agreed with you. That, I would suspect, was your outstanding contribution during the time you were in Jacksonville. You didn't have time for anything else, did you?

Adm. T.: Yes. During the two weeks out of each month I was there I visited all of the training fields, and we had many of them all throughout Florida, and we had our plans to carry out. We had to work on getting training devices set up and getting the right kind of training devices, and having training devices invented to help attain the kind of performance we had to have from each student. Many of the training devices that were used for a number of years in the Navy and the training devices center came from this - came out of World War II, from this problem. I was working very closely with the training devices people in Washington and at the training devices center.

And, of course, there was the business of watching the syllabus and the scores made by the pilots with various weapons, guns, bombs, torpedoes, and deciding what the scores should be for qualification to build a syllabus with the right amount of time on each weapon to bring them up to as great a proficiency as we could before releasing them to the fleet.

Q: When they left you, they went right into action?

Adm. T.: They went right into combat squadrons. They had learned everything before then except maybe the squadron doctrine of that particular squadron, and if the squadron had gotten new airplanes and the training command didn't have any of them they'd have to check out in the airplanes. But they learned to fight as a team and they learned proficiency with the weapons, and if they didn't meet the standards we set they failed.

And, of course, I used to have to do a lot of liaison with basic training commands. One time I took five jackets - that is the record of a student - over to the chief of basic training and told him that here were five people that he had murdered. He reared back in his chair and said, "What do you mean?" I said, "You didn't do it intentionally but that's the way it turns out. These people had extra time over here a number of times. The instructors wrote in their jackets that they should be discontinued because they were dangerous and would kill themselves. The young men were very personable and they finally got a chance to talk to you, they shed a few tears in your office, and you gave them one more chance, and they got through. Then they came to operational training and we killed them - or they got killed over there because they weren't good enough. We would like for you to tighten up and when more than one instructor says that the man is going to kill himself if he isn't washed out, I think that he shouldn't be given extra time, because almost anybody if given enough extra time can squeak through, but those aren't the kind of people that we want to see in the combat squadrons. We have to be real tough - "

Q: Did it work?

Adm. T.: Yes, it worked. I never had to carry pilots' jackets over there again. They did tighten up. But they didn't realize - you see, before that there wasn't any liaison with the fleet or liaison with the advanced training command, so they didn't know that these people - they didn't hear any more about them. Maybe they got killed, maybe they didn't. They were very busy people. This was just one bit of coordination that had to be done. You've got to have a feedback to know how your product is. It's like having a customer come and tell you that the automobile you sold him is no good and proving it to you, so you make it better.

About the time I was involved in making these films, the Lexington, which had been sunk in the Coral Sea, was reborn and a new Lexington launched in Boston. I had been up in the Navy Department, in the Bureau of Aeronautics, and the OpNav people wanted to have a technical interview with me for the purpose of improving the design of equipment for fighter aircraft, and they did the same thing with other types. I think they had a number of people who had been in combat to come in and be questioned on how they thought the equipment could be improved and the airplane itself, et cetera - a long interview. I criticized a number of things, I hope constructively. At least, they were changed. We had a gunsight that was totally inadequate and the performance of the aircraft wasn't what it should be, too heavy and under-powered, and a number of things of that nature.

The Assistant Chief of Public Relations saw me in the corridor and said, "Why aren't you wearing your decorations? What's the matter? Aren't you proud of them?" I said, "I don't have any decorations. I haven't been awarded anything." Well, he was appalled at how long it was taking to process the recommendations, because it had been several months since I'd been back, and he said, "This is a crying shame." He was really incensed. His name was "Min" Miller, and he was the executive officer of VP-5 when we flew nonstop from San Diego to Coco Solo and we all got struck by lightning.

Q: Oh, yes, I remember.

Adm. T.: Not long after that I got a letter saying that I was invited to attend the launching of the new Lexington and on that occasion some awards would be given. I went to the launching and then after the launching the commandant of the district, the 1st Naval District, had me in his office with newsmen that were available there and made the presentation of the Distinguished Service Medal, my first Navy Cross, and the Gold Star in lieu of a second Navy Cross, and then the press wanted an interview. I saw Noel Gaylor there and I said, "The press wants to talk to me, how about coming in and helping me on it? They'll be interested in what you have to say, I'm sure." So he came in with me. Noel Gaylor had been in my squadron VF-3 although he was not in it in the Battle of Midway because he had gone to VF-2 in the Lex.

They read the citations and began asking me about the Battle of Midway and I told them -

Q: I wanted to ask you about the first Navy Cross, so will you clarify?

Adm. T.: Yes, I forgot. It was my first Navy Cross and the second at the same time. It was quite unusual to have someone get in one presentation two Navy Crosses and the Distinguished Service Medal, and that drew the curiosity of the press. We had a press conference and they asked me about the medals, so I told them, and they said, "Weren't the enemy carriers already hit before our carrier pilots got there?"

I said, "Well, if they were they were repaired again. They showed no damage because they were steaming at high speed into the wind and so forth." Then Noel Gaylor spoke up and said - he explained how difficult it is to hit a ship with high-level, horizontal bombing.

Q: Such as the B-17s would have done?

Adm. T.: Yes, that's the way they bomb. They're designed to do it. This is all right against an area target such as a city but no good against a ship. We had a horizontal bomb sight in our torpedo planes, so that we had the option of horizontal bombing at high altitude - from high altitude - or a torpedo attack made at deck level. Whenever we had a ship target we'd always put the torpedo on it. We gave up horizontal bombing and I think the torpedo planes took the bomb sight out of the planes because they could do better otherwise. This is the sort of thing that Noel and I were trying to explain to these people because we felt the press ought to be a little more aware of what was what. I was well qualified to discuss the problem of horizontal bombing because I had corns on my knees from kneeling over a Norden bombsight and undoubtedly had more experience with that kind of bombsight than any of the bombadiers in the B-17s.

A little of this appeared in the Boston newspapers,

Thach #3 - 303

not much. Anyway, the Washington press corps, of course, read it and they fussed at our chief of information and said, "You had this interview up in Boston and we didn't go up there. We'd like to have an equal chance to have an interview with Lieutenant Commander Thach because it's not a very usual thing that somebody is given three big medals at once. So we want to talk to him." He said, all right.

About a week later I had to go to Washington and had the interview in a room full of Washington correspondents, some very experienced. I was very inexperienced at having press conferences. They asked me to tell them what I saw in the Battle of Midway and I did. With a few illustrations I tried to show why dive-bombing and torpedo attack was the best way to hit a ship, and one of them said, "We understand the B-17s were the ones that really did most of the damage to the Japanese carriers in the Battle of Midway."

I said, "Well, when we arrived over the enemy fleet they were steaming at high speed, not making any smoke, and I didn't think they were damaged. They obviously weren't damaged very much or they wouldn't have been able to do what they were doing." So I thought maybe I could educate these people, too, and so I did some of the same thing we did at Boston to show how the commanding officer of a ship has a bomb sight in reverse with his fire-control system, really a better one than can be carried in an airplane, bigger and more stabilized, so he knows the exact point that the bomb is going to be dropped, or should be released as well as the bombardier because he's tracking him all the way in. All he's got to do is wait until just about the time the bomber gets to that point and then make a 90-degree turn and since the bombs have a long time to fall they're going to fall where the ship was going to be if it had not turned. When the bombs finally get down to the surface of the earth, the ship's over here - quite a distance from the original track - and the bombs fall way up there on the extended line of the former track of the ship but way behind the current track of the ship.

They said, well, now, a lot of ships have been sunk by the B-17s. I said, "No, I don't think so. As a matter of fact, not one major ship has been sunk by horizontal bombing in this whole war, either in the Pacific or the Atlantic." That startled them, as I knew it would, and there is where I fell into the trap. I had this fellow right on my right who was from the Washington Post and he said, "What about the Hiruna? The battleship Hiruna was sunk by Colin Kelley. You're not going to try to take that away from him, are you?"

I said, "Well, gentlemen, I don't want to take anything away from Colin Kelly. He's done more than I have. He gave his life for his country and I haven't done that, and he did everything he could. I know that he deserves an awful lot of credit for his courage and his heroism, but I know my ship recognition and I saw the Hiruna in the Battle of Midway! She was one of the battleships there. Again, I don't want to take anything from Colin Kelly and I'm sure that someone thought the ship was sunk but ships are hard to sink. They don't sink very easily, and the Hiruna apparently got repaired if it was damaged and was back in service."

The next day there were big headlines in the Washington Post, "Lieutenant Commander Thach contradicts the Secretary of War." Other newspapers weren't so harsh. The New York Times didn't mention this at all. Their headline was my answer to a question near the end by one of them who said, What do you think it'll take to win the war out there?" And I had answered "With a couple of dozen aircraft carriers and enough Marines to make a landing we can cut a path across the Pacific Ocean right directly to Japan and make it stick." That was their headline. They said, "New Blueprint for Victory by Lieutenant Commander Thach." I was very happy with that treatment because they emphasized the important thing instead of this unfortunate controversy brought on by the attempt of the Army Air Corps to sell something to the public that simply was not so. Other publications played it various ways. One fellow who used to write a little Wings-type column in Collier's Magazine chastised me severely for being very unsportsmanlike in trying to degrade a man who had given his life for his country and received the highest award.

Later he was in the Navy as a lieutenant and I saw him one time and I said, "I'd like to talk to you." He said, "I know what it's about." I said, "You do?" "Yes, it's about an article I wrote in Collier's Magazine a couple of years ago. I've learned better since then. I was just misled by some Army Air Corps people who convinced me that's what I should do."

"Well," I said, "you haven't retracted it." So he felt very uncomfortable. He is, I think, now the editor of the Navy League magazine, Navy.

Q: He is, now?

Adm. T.: Yes. He relieved Ed Prima, I think. He either is now or he was a year ago.

Q: Did the publicity bother you?

Adm. T.: Naturally that article in Collier's bothered me more than the "contradiction" headline in The Washington Post because I've always felt that if you have the truth on your side you can't very well lose any argument or discussion, even if it's with the Secretary of War, and I didn't think that I was going to have to argue with the Secretary of War.

Q: And did you?

Adm. T.: No. I didn't think I would and I didn't because not only did I see the Hiruna, but later, before this happened, I learned from ONI that they knew the Hiruna wasn't sunk or even damaged. They knew it was operating. They were listening to it talking all the time. They had the call letters of it and they had intelligence on it. There was no question about it. And "Hap" Arnold knew it, but he went over and fussed at Admiral King, I heard later. I don't know what exactly Admiral King said to him, but I heard he said, "Well, maybe we'd better be more careful about what damage is done and what isn't, especially if it concerns ships because ships have a way of sailing round and becoming seen after you think they've sunk, and you and I know it wasn't sunk."

A lot of people said, "Well, you sure cooked your goose," and I said, "Would that bother you?" It didn't really bother me but it made me shall we say "vexed" because these people were so low as to try to trap me in a thing like that. I tried to figure out what else I should have said. When I said no major ship had been sunk by horizontal bombing, I didn't think anybody was going to bring up the Hiruna. I wasn't thinking of the Hiruna. I just knew that that was a fact. Some had been sunk by torpedo planes, a combination of high-level bombing and torpedo planes - at least they were bombed from high level, they also had some fish stuck in their sides and they did sink, but not by horizontal bombing. I don't know what else I could have said to avoid this embarrassment of seeming to degrade a fellow countryman who gave his life for his country.

Q: It certainly wasn't your intent!

Adm. T.: That's the thing that made me very unhappy. Not the fact that I was in trouble, so-called, with the Secretary of War, which obviously I was not.

So that was an interesting little episode which I've regretted happening, but it wasn't my fault. It was the fault of the people who were so lax in their judgment in assessing damage to the enemy that they made a bad mistake, and it caught up with them. It was bound to sooner or later. I just happened to be the unfortunate one that had to do it.

No one in authority in the Navy - some of my contemporaries, classmates, and friends of the same age - kidded me about it and said, "When are you going to Siberia? When are you going to be ordered to - and they'd pick out the funniest places - Adak where I was going to be ordered.

Thach #3 - 309

Q: The funny part of it is that you went to a very fine command, very fine job, from Jacksonville!

Adm. T.: Oh, yes, the best.

Q: At what time did you become commander?

Adm. T.: I made commander while I was at Jacksonville, shortly before I went back to sea. It was within about a year after I was in Jacksonville that I made three stripes, so I was a lieutenant commander a fairly short time. But I was an ensign for four years and a JG for six, and a lieutenant from 1936 to 1941 - five years. I was a pretty old guy when I was a lieutenant and made lieutenant commander, so the fact that I didn't wear three stripes very long didn't bother me!

Q: Then you made captain how soon?

Adm. T.: Before the war was over. Not long before the war was over.

Q: Did you go directly from Jacksonville to work for Admiral Mitscher?

Adm. T.: Yes, in this way. Admiral McCain, who was then

in the Navy Department as chief of the Bureau of Aeronautics - at that time the chief of the Bureau of Aeronautics did a lot of the jobs that the office of the Chief of Naval Operations does today, as far as assigning aviators to jobs and so forth and making decisions. They were more of a combination of Op-05 or office of CNO and the Bureau of Weapons, so it was a more far-reaching job with more responsibility and authority than simply chief of the Bureau of Aeronautics.

Admiral McCain came down to Jacksonville -

Q: Admiral who?

Adm. T.: John Sidney McCain - and I had staff duty and when he was ready to leave he had gone to see the chief, the head of advanced training, and before he got in the airplane he called me over to the side and said, "How would you like to work for me?" I said, "What job, Admiral?" He said, "Well, I don't want you to tell anybody about this, but I'm slated to get three stars and go to the Pacific to relieve Mitscher and we'll work alternately on various campaigns. If you'd like to go, I'd like for you to be my operations officer."

I said, "That's very flattering. I'm delighted. I can think of no better job that I could have." I thought at first he wanted me to come to Washington and work for him, and I didn't want to do that. I was all wound up in this training business and I always loved the training job because I think I have the instinct of a teacher anyway - a school teacher type! If I hadn't been in the Navy, maybe I'd have wound up being a school teacher. My father taught school for eighteen years and my mother taught school for sixteen years, so I come by it naturally.

Anyway, I said, "Have you talked to my boss about it?" He said, "Oh, yes. He'll let you go if I want you." I said, "Admiral, may I ask you a question?" He said, "Sure, Son, shoot."

"Why did you select me? You don't know me. I've never worked for you."

He said, "I'll tell you one reason. I've heard that you're not a yes man, and I don't want any yes men on my staff. I like what you've been doing, too. I'll send a message to your boss. I want to see you in Washington before we go."

So that happened and I went to see him. He said, "I can't get away yet, but I want you to go out ahead of me anyway and start picking out people who should be on my staff. I want you to go out and I'll have you ordered to Admiral Mitscher's staff for temporary duty in the operations department, and you'll go with them on a certain campaign that's about to start. You'll find out where it is when you get there, but you've got to get there pretty soon. I'm going to get orders out for you tonight."

I went back and told Madelyn. Of course, she wasn't too happy at my going to the Pacific again, because we'd only been ashore a little over a year, but she understood.

I got these orders and they gave me No. 1 priority on all aircraft, commercial and otherwise, to get from Jacksonville to Majuro in a very short time - just about as long as you could make quick connections and get going. So the way was really paved. When I got to San Francisco people said there must be some mistake, it says priority one, nothing takes precedence over that. That's usually reserved for people from the White House. I said, "I'm not from the White House, but that's what it says." They said, "Okay, but I never saw anything like this before." They were a little irked because this was true. But John Sidney made it that way and got permission to do so because I couldn't afford to miss getting aboard the Lexington, Admiral Mitscher's flagship, which had just arrived at Majuro. And within a few hours we were underway. I just barely made it. I got there one afternoon and we were on our way early the next morning before daylight.

That was in April 1944. The operation was called Operation Forager and we were going out to soften up the islands of Saipan, Tinian, and Guam preparatory to amphibious invasion of those places that were held by the Japanese at the time.

In that part of the ocean, when you got close to those islands, of course the Japanese had bases that were within range with some of the long-range land-based aircraft, not within range of enemy fighters, at the time I'm thinking of, but at night or just at dusk the Japanese would come out and bother the task force, mostly with what we called snoopers, search planes, and then every so often a torpedo attack by the twin-engined land-based aircraft that had enough range to reach us.

I remember one night - I think it was shortly before the Marianas Turkey Shoot - we'd had a few snoopers during the late afternoon and at just about dusk you could see on the horizon a number of airplanes milling around. They'd picked exactly the right time so that it would be to their greatest advantage to see the ships, not quite dark, but it was hard to see them in the fading dusk, and they came in with these new type aircraft which we later called Fran. They seemed to be very high speed, quite streamlined, twin engine, torpedo bomber types, a similar type to the Betty but newer and with more speed.

Obviously an attack was forming up. I was on the flag bridge, looking, at the time, and here these things came in all of a sudden, very low, on a torpedo attack. The Lexington combed a couple of torpedoes. I remember looking over the side and seeing the torpedo wake - it just looked like a few feet beside the Lexington. You had to look almost straight down to see the wake. Well, the skipper did a good job of combing that one. Another one came in, dropped its torpedo, and the skipper did a little jog and straightened out again. It went on the left side, but the airplane was coming straight on in, and right over the bow, low, and it looked like it might crash into the bridge or right in the middle of the flight deck. I remember all of the guns up forward opened up and looked like they were hitting it. There was a *Time Life* correspondent or photographer - he was mainly a very professional and expert photographer. Later he took some of the best aerial shots of the Blue Angels I've ever seen. He was there, standing right by me on the bridge. I saw this Fran coming and I knew it was going to come pretty close, and I nudged him and said, "Ed - his name was Ed Eyerman - it looks like you're going to get a good picture." He had a little Leica camera hanging around his neck on a string.

This airplane came right down the center line, over the bow, and it seemed like we had to lift our chins up to let the left wing go by. By that time, the AA fire had gotten to him and he was beginning to flame. You could see the silhouette of the two pilots sitting in the front, in the flames from the starboard engine, as it came right down the flight deck. Everybody thought, especially since it was beginning to burn, that it was going to plough right into all the airplanes parked on the after part of the flight deck. But it just cleared them. He pulled up a little bit to clear the last few wing tips that were folded up, and went into the water with a big splash and flame, right astern of the ship.

I turned to Ed Eyerman and I said, "Ed, did you get that picture?" He looked at me with a perfectly straight face and said, "No. I couldn't lift this heavy camera."

Q: That must have been a devastating experience! I would have thought they would have wanted to hit the planes - the Japanese?

Adm. T.: No. I think that he was not a suicide type. He wanted to survive and maybe get back, but the plane just burned off the wing and he went in. You see, this was just a follow-through from his torpedo attack. He came in real close and the skipper of the ship just turned right toward him which made him fly right up the flight deck. He couldn't make a tight enough turn to get away from it, but he just kept away from the bridge and he kept above the wing tips that were sticking up in the air. Then his wing burned off and in he went, just astern of the ship.

Q: Who was the skipper of the Lexington?

Adm. T.: We were able to recover a man from that airplane.

Q: You were?

Adm. T.: Yes, and he wasn't wounded very badly. He was in the rear and he was a radioman type. He had some cuts and bruises on him. I saw him and he was a very fine-looking young man, slender, and very well built, athletic type, and he looked quite intelligent which I'm sure he was. He was treated by the doctors and was given some food and later transferred to prisoner of war status and questioned, of course, by the intelligence people to get as much information of their operations as he would know, which probably wouldn't be very much.

Interview #4 with Admiral John S. Thach, U.S. Navy (Retired)

Place: His home in Coronado, California

Date: January 9, 1971

Subject: Biography

By: Etta Belle Kitchen

Q: We were speaking of the date when you reported to Majuro. Would you want to clarify that date?

Adm. T.: Yes. I think it must have been about 5 or 6 June because I believe that Task Force 58 left Majuro on 6 June to go to the operation of softening up Saipan, Tinian, and Guam for re-taking.

Q: Did you go immediately into a job or were you going on a make-learn trip at this point?

Adm. T.: I was assigned as special assistant to the Chief of Staff on Admiral Mitscher's staff, and Arleigh Burke was chief of staff.

Burke gave me special projects to work up such as a plan for the next exercise and so forth, and of course I was mainly observing what was going on.

Q: Do you remember at what time you did relieve the air operations officer - I should say the operations officer?

Thach #4 - 318

Adm. T.: Well, when I left Mitscher's staff and went right with McCain.

Q: Oh, so all the time you were on Mitscher's staff you were —

Adm. T.: Yes.

Q: — special assistant to the chief of staff?

Adm. T.: I think that's what they called me. I'm not really sure I had a title, but that's not important. I was working directly under Arleigh Burke and with the operations officer. Everything he did I watched and sometimes helped him.

Q: It was to learn, wasn't it?

Adm. T.: Well, not really. It was mainly to observe. After all, I knew as much if not more about carrier operations as anyone on Mitscher's staff. McCain one time said, "I want to get you out there as soon as I can, then you watch and see everything they do and be sure and make a note on any mistakes they make." So I did.

Q: Did you ever operate as a fighter pilot after this?

Adm. T.: No, not in a combat squadron. I was too senior for that. I was a commander when I went back out to the Pacific Fleet.

Q: Can you identify the last time you ever did act as a fighter pilot?

Adm. T.: You mean in combat?

Q: Yes.

Adm. T.: The Battle of Midway.

Q: Inasmuch as you were with Mitscher early in June, that was a precursor of the Battle of the Philippine Sea?

Adm. T.: Right.

Q: Which is history and I know you participated in that. I guess the first subtitle of the Battle of the Philippine Sea was the Marianas Turkey Shoot?

Adm. T.: Yes, I think that would be about right. You see, the location of the Japanese carrier task force was not known to Mitscher at the time of the Marianas Turkey Shoot.

Q: Was or was not?

Adm. T.: Was not. Let's put it this way. The location wasn't known well enough to throw a strike. We had some reports from the submarine flying fish of a task force clearing San Bernardino Strait earlier, that it had moved out and was headed in our direction. That's about all we knew at that time. I spent quite a bit of time in the combat information center, specially the first part of this, and my first suggestion was to strike everything below except fighters and simply run fighters through the deck because it was obvious that there was something big going to happen.

Q: When you say it was obvious that something big was going to happen, can you amplify that?

Adm. T.: Yes. Numerous reports that, for instance, airplanes were being fed into Guam and to some of the other islands from the Philippines or somewhere and extra snoopers all around. You get a feeling that something's going to happen and that there's going to be an attack. So it came and we simply - of course we had submarines and patrol aircraft out at distances from the task force and had pretty good warning of this large strike force of enemy airplanes coming. When they were first picked up they were high and there were so many of them they showed up a long way away on the radars. So all the dive bombers and torpedo planes were ordered to be put below on the hangar deck and all the fighters on the flight deck and we simply kept running them through to refuel and launch again to have the maximum in the air at the time the brunt of the enemy attack came in. Not very many got anywhere near the carriers. Our fighters really had a field day.

I remember one dive bomber that I saw - I think he was the closest that came to the carriers - I believe it was the aircraft carrier Cabot. He came in from medium altitude and dove on the Cabot, and it was the most amazing thing. The Cabot apparently didn't see this airplane soon enough and only one twin 40-mm on the Cabot opened up and it fired two bursts - actually a total of four rounds of ammunition, boom, boom, a twin mount - and split this airplane wide open and it missed, splashing near the Cabot. That was the one enemy airplane I saw that day and yet there were, I believe, more than 400 shot down.

Q: Where were you?

Adm. T.: I was on the bridge of the Lexington.

Q: You were on the bridge so you could get a view of everything?

Adm. T.: Well, I was on the bridge some of the time and some of the time I was in the combat information center depending on what was happening and where.

Q: Can you tell, when you see the approaching group on the screen, the kind of plane it is?

Adm. S.: No. In those days we could say it was a large group or a small group or maybe one or two aircraft. Now, you can tell a little better. And, of course, we had our own little signal that showed on the radar, our IFF, Interrogation Friend or Foe is what it stood for. The enemy didn't have that, so you could distinguish that way. It wasn't perfect but it worked pretty well most of the time but you couldn't depend on it absolutely. For one thing, sometimes the pilot would forget to turn it on, then he'd look like an enemy! Also, the enemy aircraft could trail our returning strikes and get in underneath or near them and that would prevent them from looking like a separate airplane with no IFF.

Q: Did the Japs ever cause any damage by doing that?

Adm. T.: Oh, yes. Sometimes the kamikazes came in that way. More about that later. So we had a real big day and then of course the job was to find the enemy task force. A submarine had seen them and a patrol aircraft, PBY, had made a contact report - a very good contact report - to his base. In other words, it didn't get to Admiral Mitscher, it didn't get through. The patrol plane pilot thought it had, but it didn't. That was a very unfortunate thing that happened. It teaches you the lesson that if you've got vital information, whoever has it must keep sending it and sending it out in every possible way he can on as many different frequencies, if it's going by radio. We seem to have to learn this lesson over and over.

Q: It was a terribly tragic error. It would have saved hundreds of miles of steaming because of not knowing exactly where the enemy fleet was.

Adm. T.: Well, not as tragic an error as the one Spruance made later. We could have saved a lot of airplanes if we had done what Arleigh Burke and I wanted to do that night, the night before we finally made the attack on the Japanese.

Q: You're going to tell me what you wanted to do, of course?

Adm. T.: Here was the situation. Admiral Spruance, who was the Fifth Fleet commander and his job was to take these islands, had amphibious forces there ready to go in and the operation was all set up and moving. We knew approximately the distance that the Japanese fleet was. We knew they would come in to throw their strike at maximum range and then withdraw a little bit to keep away from our search planes from Task Force 58. The wind was blowing from the direction of Saipan from the

East, the prevailing wind, and away from the direction of the enemy. I talked to Arleigh Burke very urgently to tell him that we would never catch those people if we didn't run toward them, especially since the prevailing wind was such that when we launched and recovered aircraft we would have to be going away from them. So that night I wanted to run all night long toward them, and that's what I thought, of course, Mitscher would do and that's what Mitscher thought he would do, too. But Admiral Spruance vetoed that idea. He said the job of the carrier task force is to protect this amphibious landing and stay right there near Saipan.

This was a case, in my opinion, of being overcautious and coupled with a lack of understanding that an aircraft carrier doesn't protect an amphibious force by being within sight of it or within gun range of it. It will do better to go out and find the enemy and hit him because we had such a wide span of search operations that nothing could do an end run around us and get to the amphibs. But that's what Spruance was worried about. He was afraid they'd do an end run and they'd get in between us and the amphibious force and somehow we couldn't catch them. They'd already spent most of their strike capability. They had very little left except the ships and, in effect, they were relatively harmless because they had lost control of the air.

Q: Had the airfields been rendered helpless as well?

Adm. T.: By that time, yes. We'd burned many aircraft on their fields. Some as they were landing, some as they were taking off, and some of the fields. So we had done the softening-up job, although on the day of the Marianas Turkey Shoot they were feeding more into there just down the hopper to be killed but they didn't realize it.

All night long Arleigh Burke and I sat up writing messages for Mitscher to send to Spruance to try to get him to let us run toward the enemy so that the next day we could afford to run into the wind which would be away from the enemy and toward Saipan, launch a strike and we'd be close enough to them to be within our combat radius.

Q: Who was advising Spruance? Do you know?

Adm. T.: I don't know. Captain Moore, another non-aviator, was his chief of staff. In Mitscher's several messages was some good advice and incontrovertible argument in favor of running toward the enemy that night. Anyway, he was very adamant about it. He wouldn't give in to logic. Mitscher sent two messages - maybe three. We wrote dozens of them, some stronger than others, and finally we wrote one that said, "You can have my job if you won't let me run toward the enemy." Mitscher wouldn't send that one! But I would have done it, I'm sure. Arleigh Burke would have, too. Arleigh Burke would have sent it because he understood this situation. So the next morning we sent fighters

Thach #4 - 326

and scouts with belly tanks instead of bombs on them for long searches. Finally, an F-6F that stretched its search pattern a little bit saw them. There was some question about whether we could carry bombs and still get there and get back.

Q: How many miles away were they at that time?

Adm. T.: At that time, they were over 350 miles away. That figure seems to stick in my mind. After a lot of consideration, Mitscher decided he had to throw the strike because they might get away, so we did. You see, the search had to be made, then the search planes finally got back. Mitscher wanted to be sure he knew what was there and what the search plane saw, and that took most of the morning. So it was in the middle afternoon before he finally sent the strike and, having stayed so close to Guam all night long instead of running toward the enemy, it became a very questionable thing as to whether aircraft with bombs could get there and back.

Well, they didn't get back before dark. I believe the Hiyo was sunk, the Zuikaku, Chiyoda and Junyo were hit and damaged and a tanker was sunk. At that time so many of the pilots weren't night-qualified for this. We'd expanded so fast, they ran them through to get them out. Some of the pilots were night-qualified. Being night-qualified is a kind of nebulous thing. If you can land aboard a carrier - I used to say, "If you know how to land aboard a carrier, why can't you do it at night if you can fly the airplane at night."

Q: If you can see it?

Adm. T.: You can see it easily. You can see the landing signal officer's wands, you never see the flight deck itself. At least you never used to. I think you should be able to and later I strongly recommended that we light up the flight deck like the runway of a commercial airport, because with the advent of radar any enemy that doesn't see you on the radar before he can see those lights is not very much to worry about anyway, if he can't do better than that!

But we turned on the lights and the worst thing about it was pointed out by Ralph Weymouth, the dive-bomber skipper on the Lexington when he finally got aboard, was that you couldn't tell one carrier from another and you couldn't find your own because you couldn't read the numbers, and all carriers at night look alike, what little you can see of them, even though the lights look alike, what little you can see of them, even though the lights are on, some lights would dazzle your eyes and the risk of collision with other aircraft milling around was quite high.

It wouldn't be difficult to find one and land aboard it, if you knew where it was, but with a large number of aircraft carriers in the same formation, three or four in each task groups and the task groups very close together, and all these strike planes returning and milling around, it was quite difficult. As a matter of fact, it's surprising that any aircraft got aboard his own carrier. That wasn't too important, the important thing was to get aboard any carrier and that was the objective. The reason Mitscher turned on the lights was because he knew they were very short of gas and, being at night, they didn't have much time to fool around.

The traffic patterns were overlapping and people having near collisions, according to the dive-bomber skipper that finally got aboard the Lexington, and the worst thing about the whole day's operation was trying to dodge your own airplanes in the dark going every which way right over the task force trying to find their own carrier. Of course, once a pilot gets down to where he knows he can make only one or two more circles, he'll go in and land aboard any carrier. Some carriers got filled up full and others weren't quite so full, and a number of them, of course, had to land in the water. I've forgotten the number.

Q: Can you tell me the actual procedure? Do you keep in touch with the airplanes from your own carrier and say "Jo, here's the Lexington. Come back." How do you do that?

Adm. T.: You don't do it! This situation wasn't a normal sort of a situation.

Q: But you have constant contact with all your planes?

Adm. T.: No. Most of the time you will want to maintain radio silence to prevent the enemy from getting a radio bearing fix on your location. When they come back, you identify them as being friendly, then you give them a signal to come in to the landing pattern and come on in.

Q: Can you say, "We're the Lexington, we're the third one from some direction"?

Adm. T.: Well -

Q: Can you try to tell them where you are and which one is the Lexington?

Adm. T.: There was too much urgent conversation necessary at the time, such as how low certain planes were on gas and to let them get in first, such things as that. In those days the landing signal officer didn't do much talking to the planes, somebody else did if it was necessary to talk to them.

Q: I'm sure it was complete chaos at the time. Is that putting it too strong?

Adm. T.: Yes, it's a little too strong.

Thach #4 - 330

Q: How would you describe it?

Adm. T.: Well, it was a situation where all aircraft were faced with not being able to get aboard because they didn't have enough gasoline to make one more turn around and approach to the carriers. That was the thing that made it tense and urgent. At the same time there were a lot of near collisions because people were trying to get aboard their own carriers instead of just landing aboard any carrier. Of course, if all of them tried to get aboard one carrier, that wouldn't be any good because it couldn't take them.

Q: Did the carriers stay in the same formation that the planes left from? Relative to the other carriers?

Adm. T.: Yes, but to stay in the wind the <u>Lexington</u> might be north of another carrier and remain north of it, regardless of what course she was going on. But it was even difficult to tell which task group you were over.

Q: Let alone which carrier!

Adm. T.: Yes, let alone which carrier, although there were certain little homing devices in the airplanes, a bird dog, a little instrument with a needle. The carrier would emanate on a certain frequency and if this thing was working real well, you'd get a homing course, but by the time you got over the task group it was going in all directions.

Q: Oh, I see. There was nothing that said, "This is your carrier"?

Adm. T.: No, it wasn't that easy, not that precise - a little more difficult.

Q: I'd like to picture you during that time and what you were doing, and your reactions?

Adm. T.: Well, I certainly agreed with Admiral Mitscher turning on the lights when it came to that point. It was not my original idea at all, but I agreed with it. I kept thinking what a shame. We didn't have to have this happen, if we'd done the right thing last night. That was the thing that kept sticking in my craw. I hope I'll never be faced with another situation like that. Any damage done to Ozawa's large task force by our pilots was not because of anything Admiral Spruance did but in spite of what he did. That was, I think, one of the things that Admiral McCain was talking about when he told me to go out there and make notes on whatever mistakes are made, because he wasn't about to make them.

Q: What were you doing during this time?

Adm. T.: I was mainly observing, not having been given any responsibility, but Arleigh Burke would always get my advice on any problem or question that came up.

Q: Were you still on the bridge?

Adm. T.: I was between the bridge and the CIC, mostly on the bridge.

Q: Morison makes the statement that during the Marianas Turkey Shoot the brain work of the carriers' CIC in tracking the Japanese was to a large extent responsible for the success of the Marianas Turkey Shoot?

Adm. T.: There's some question about that. To some extent yes, but tracking this large formation was the easiest job the CICs had. The whole organization of combat information and fighter direction communications and the fact that we were not hampered by having to operate any other type of aircraft at the time was part of the success picture. You can launch a fighter pilot off in a hurry - and actually we completed this business of putting other types down in the hangar decks after the strike had been seen on radar. We had time enough to do it, not very much but time enough, and get more fighters in the air, so that the first fighters that were vectored out, they just kept vectoring them out in groups, towards the enemy large formation, just fed them in there. Also, don't forget that success in this battle was, in the final analysis, due to the fighter pilots ability to shoot and hit! Then, the first ones to intercept that were already on combat air patrol ran out of ammunition and they came back and landed aboard, were reloaded, and actually got back in the air. I don't know whether they got back in the fight or not, but they did get back in the air. I think some of them actually did get two separate combat flights that day, which is amazing, all in one strike. But of course there were airplanes attempting to come from the other islands. I definitely remember one pilot reporting that a group of six enemy planes had come in when they attempted to land at Guam and that they had burned them all and he said, "Now there are no more active airplanes on Guam." Then we sent some more fighters over there, and here was another group coming in, so they were bringing them in all the time.

It was a kind of all-day affair with the enemy fields on those islands.

Q: The whole thing lasted approximately eight hours.

Adm. T.: Yes, I think so. So that was the story as I saw it, turning on the lights because they had to be turned on.

Q: During the Marianas affair, would you like to comment on the training that our pilots had compared to the training that the Japanese had at the same time? Did you feel our pilots were well trained?

Adm. T.: Oh, yes, I think relatively speaking they were well trained. I never thought that any pilot was well trained enough, me or anyone else! You always feel that you should have some more training, and I had the conviction at one time that if you really could have a squadron kept together long enough and could train them well enough, you could take maybe twelve fighters and, no matter how many enemy there were, if these people made no mistakes, you never would have to lose a man. You'd always make no mistakes, keep in superb condition and come out without losing anyone, and that was my goal. I didn't see any excuse for anybody getting killed, if you could train them to handle every situation in combat and never miss with the weapons.

I think it's well recognized that the first team of the Japanese air forces of all Japanese pilots in any force, land-based or otherwise, the real cream were the ones who attacked Pearl Harbor and the same ones in the Battle of Midway and the Coral Sea Battle - those three battles. So many of them were lost during those latter actions that they didn't have too many real experienced fighter pilots left. They had some experienced torpedo plane pilots because a lot of the torpedo planes, the Bettys and the Frans, were not in action in the Coral Sea battle or the Battle of Midway or the attack on Pearl Harbor.

The ones who were at Pearl Harbor didn't sustain very many losses. They were highly successful, so they survived to fight again.

Q: Did you ever talk to any of the pilots who had had the advantage of the training films that you developed?

Adm. T.: Oh, yes, many. As a matter of fact, all of the fighter pilots of the Army Air Corps as well as the Navy and Marines used them in training as standard doctrine. Even today people I meet or maybe recognize me come up and say, "I remember you because I've looked at your training films so often." Some of them come up and say, "I wanted to meet you because you saved my life." Very flattering!

Q: Satisfying, surely.

Adm. T.: I think the Japanese training command broke down as the war went on, and by this time they were putting people out there that were not as well trained. Some were very good, but not enough. And they kept their experienced people in combat so long that too many of them were lost. We brought our people who'd had a certain amount of experience back to the training commands to teach the others. The Japanese apparently couldn't manage that kind of large-scale system of pilot training and they didn't have as many hours. And, of course, they were beginning to hurt as far as gasoline was concerned.

Around the middle of July the amphibious landing on Guam took place. This was very well organized. The Marines and amphibious forces. I remember attending a number of conferences with the Marine officers and the amphibious commander on the detailed plan of close air support. Again, I'll say that the pattern naturally runs this way - the Japanese did it as well as we. When you make an amphibious landing, you go in first with your carriers, way ahead of time - maybe a month, maybe several weeks, at least a week - before anybody else is anywhere near, and you do everything you can to wipe out completely any air opposition within range of where the landing is to take place. Then this becomes more intense. After you've got control there and you know there are no aircraft available to the enemy in the vicinity, you start working on the landing beaches and defensive positions that the enemy may have. And then finally, there are the D-day early strikes, and then the H-hour strikes, when the first wave hits the beach. H-hour strikes go right up to that point and then stop hitting the defensive positions on the beaches just the moment that the first amphibious craft hit the beach.

Then, of course, the close air support phase, the plan of the ground forces, how much land and what progress they plan to make, so that the air support may walk along ahead of the advance forces that have landed. Then there's this close air support, which means only one thing to me, and that is air support on the call and direction of the people on the ground. They know what's hurting them, they know that a gun emplacement over here on x or a is the one that they want you to knock out right at the moment. Earlier it doesn't make any difference to them. Later it may not make any difference to them. But now they want that one knocked out because it's got them pinned down and it's hurting them. And so they must control the airplanes. This is the principle on which Navy and Marine close air support has been based from the beginning.

Q: And where are these airplanes at the time they're called for? Are they orbiting in an air pattern?

Adm. T.: Oh, yes. Close air support must immediately have airplanes available. This is the reason I made this point, available to the close air support controllers on the ground, who are probably aviators who know the plan and what the ground forces do, and they direct the airplanes and they have them available. You keep close air support aircraft on station, continuously, ready to be called.

Q: How far away would they be?

Adm. T.: They might be sitting right over the head of the controller, or they'd be in the vicinity so that in a matter of seconds they're in his hands and he's in communication with them from the time they check in. They check in with him and they belong to him then until they have to go or he lets them go.

Q: And they're relieved by another group?

Adm. T.: Yes, they're relieved by another group. This system was followed through by the Navy and Marine Corps on through Korea, et cetera.

Q: I read something that indicated to me that, using that pattern that you just described started with the Marianas.

Adm. T.: It may have. It might very well have because that was, I guess, maybe the first amphibious landing where we had - well, no, I won't say that - where we had air opposition because there was air opposition before. I don't know whether it started there or not. I don't remember when it started. I know the Japanese certainly did it, they did it in the very beginning of the war when they took one-sixth of the earth's surface in six months. That's how they did it.

I want to talk more about this close air support when we get to the Korean War. There, I think, there were particular incidents that emphasize what the Navy and Marine Corps mean when they say close air support. But the Guam operation went off with great precision and almost perfection. Guam was well defended, but it just worked like clockwork - we had enough by then to do this. We could keep aircraft available all over the place for any purpose that was needed and of course they remained there until the beaches were secured and all opposition near the beaches had gone, and then for any advance across the island close air support was available, but it wasn't needed in such great numbers then, so most of the carriers could leave, maybe all but one.

There was something else in my head, but I forgot it while I was talking!

Q: I wanted to ask you if you had wished that you might be in an airplane during some of these operations?

Adm. T.: Oh, yes, a number of times, especially the Marianas Turkey Shoot, and also the close air support at Guam. It was going just according to plan and was a beautiful operation as far as team work, clockwork, and expertise were concerned. We really looked professional.

Q: I think I'll make a comment here to remind you that when you see your manuscript maybe in the meantime you'll remember the incident relating to close air support at Guam and you can insert it here, if it comes to mind.

Adm. T.: Yes.

Later, much later, I did plan to lead a strike - well, I'll tell you about that, when the time comes.

Q: We're talking now, I think, of round about July of 1944. Did the task group then go back to Majuro after the Marianas?

Adm. T.: After the Guam operation the task force, I believe, went back to Eniwetok and I departed and went back to Pearl Harbor and met Admiral McCain when he came out from Washington.

Q: Did you know what date that was, approximately?

Adm. T.: It was I think in August 1944. I got back there before he came out. He had directed me to select a staff and, at the time, I said, "Admiral, are you telling me to pick out your chief of staff?" and he said, "No, he'll be an admiral." I said, "Well, I could make some recommendations." He laughed and he said, "All right."

Q: Did you?

Adm. T.: Yes. I made one but - I recommended Captain Duckworth but that was against the rules. The chief of staff had to be a non-aviator. McCain was an aviator, his chief of staff had to be a non-aviator, preferably one who understood destroyer and cruiser operations and such things as that. I interviewed people mostly at Pearl Harbor and I went over various lists of people that I knew and knew their talents.

Q: Were you still a commander?

Adm. T.: Yes, I was a commander. I interviewed several very interesting people I'd never seen before and never heard of but they wanted to get on the staff in some capacity. They'd heard about it and they came to see me. One of them was a fellow by the name of Albert M. Grafmueller, who was a young lieutenant, and I had him tell me about what he had been doing all his life, what his background was. He said he had a greeting card business in New York City, and I asked him about its capacity, what amount of business he did, when he started, and was he the owner, and so forth. He said, yes, and told me what he'd done, and he'd apparently been very successful. Then he said, "I don't know why you're asking me about the greeting card business. I don't know what good that will do me in helping to fight a war." And I said, "Regardless of the business, you went out on your own and you started a business and this shows that you know how to get something done."

We needed someone on the staff in the capacity of a logistics planning and arranging for getting various replenishments and working up a requirements list for the big replenishment forces which come out. We would have to keep track of all the requests from other ships, what they needed and what was available from the replenishment forces, divide it up and direct where it would go. This was a big job.

Q: Complicated, too!

Adm. T.: A big job where you take about a hundred ships and all of them needing different things - one a dozen cans of beans and another one 150 cans of spinach, another one four pilots and six airplanes of different types, another one so much 50-caliber ammunition. The battleships might need 16-inch shells, and so forth. So it was everything from bullets to beans.

So I told him I would take him. I took him really because he wanted to go so bad and I was sure that whatever job he was given he would break his neck trying to do it well, and he did. He did a wonderful job.

Another one was an expert in ordnance we got on the staff. He was a postgraduate in weapons and he had a master's degree in science. He was very well educated, and he had been in the ordnance test business.

Q: A Reserve officer?

Adm. T.: No, a regular, I believe. Commander J. H. Hean - he was a lieutenant commander when we got him.

And another one was an expert - a fighter director. I had wanted to have a force fighter director, not to do the intricate job of making intercepts with fighters against enemy planes, but to control the patterns, the plans, and augmentation of fighters to meet any sudden change in the situation in the air.

Q: To have overall control?

Adm. T.: Yes, overall control of each fighter director aboard the ships.

Q: That had not been the case?

Adm. T.: No, we hadn't had a force fighter director. We were getting to it. It was going to be obvious. I mean it was already obvious, and the fighter director aboard the flagship was more or less acting that way, except he didn't have the name yet or the real authority I wanted to give him. I wanted to make it formal. Then we got a communicator.

Q: How large a staff did he eventually have?

Adm. T.: Counting all the communicators who had to do a lot of decoding, about thirty.

Q: And you selected all of them?

Adm. T.: All except the communicators. I selected the communications officer, but all the young communicators were right out of school and you just asked for them in blocks.

Another one was a young intelligence officer by the name of Thacher Longstreth. He was an interesting person. I knew him as a ship's air intelligence officer before, so I knew his capabilities. He became one of the greatest authorities on the Japanese ships and aircraft, I think, of anyone I know. And even today he can remember a Japanese merchant ship - he could recognize it and maybe call its name. He did this on many occasions. One time we got a photograph from a strike of a Japanese merchant ship - medium sized, I think about 8,000 tons - and he said, "Well, that's a new one on me. I don't know this ship. Wait a minute! Look what they did to the old Fujo Maru." They'd changed the superstructure a little bit and fooled him. But you didn't fool him for long because after looking at the photograph a while and talking about it, it dawned on him what that ship was, and, sure enough, this had happened.

So he was an extremely valuable young man and he studied real hard on this subject, knew it very well, he was a good interrogator, interrogating returning pilots who'd had combat or been out on a strike. He was about 6 feet 4 inches and had a pair of shoulders on him that you wouldn't believe, and a very thin waist line. He would do 80 pushups before breakfast. I remember one time sitting in one of the clubs - he was sitting down in an overstuffed chair and a fellow came along and tripped on his feet. Well, Thacher Longstreth didn't look like much sitting down in a chair. He wore glasses and had kind of a meek-looking expression although he had a strong face, and this fellow turned around and looked at this little squirt and said, "Look, get your feet out of the way or I'll break 'em off." And Thacher said, "I'm sorry."

"You've got to be more than sorry, you've got to get those feet back under that chair." This fellow had had a couple too many, I think, and was belligerent. Thacher Longstreth started to get up and it took him a long time because he was so tall and had such wide shoulders. He finally stood on his feet and looked down at this fellow and said, "I apologized once and that's all I'm going to do.

The fellow said, "Okay, okay." and hurried away.

He was the most deceptive individual because he liked to lounge way down low in a chair and he looked like he was sort of a little shrimp when he was sitting down, but not when he got up!

He had a very successful tour on the staff. He stayed with us till the very end, and he - well, I hope I'll remember when I get to the time.

Another one was a man by the name of Don Thorburn. I met him at the Disney Studios in Hollywood. He was writing the weather films for the training of aerologists and training of aviators - an aviator's got to know something about weather, how to read a map, and so forth - and this was aerology sense pamphlets and he was writing them. He wasn't an aerologist himself but he was a great writer, especially for this sort of instruction because his background was that he was an executive in the head office of J. Walter Thompson in New York. I guess J. Walter Thompson Company has been known for many years as one of the largest and most successful advertising agencies. So Thorburn grew up on advertising writing which has to be very concise and to the point - the punch line - so he was very good at that.

I got the idea that maybe he could write a pamphlet to accompany each one of my fighter films, so I made arrangements for him to be ordered to duty on my team.

Q: That was when you were at Disney?

Adm. T.: Yes. He did a good job, too.

Q: What did he do on the staff? What did you select him for on Admiral McCain's staff?

Adm. T.: I selected him to be the public relations officer, or press relations, you might say, because we always had war correspondents aboard in every operation and somebody who

Thach #4 - 347

understood them and could be a good thing for them, and so we wouldn't get too bad a press!

These people that I've mentioned, especially the ones with purely civilian backgrounds that had come into the Navy just because they wanted to do something, each one of them was extremely eager to get out into the combat zone. I like people who have that attitude, and it turned out that each one of them did an outstanding job.

Admiral McCain arrived and I went over the list of people I'd selected and told him about them, and he said fine. Then he told me who his chief of staff was going to be, Rear Admiral Wilder D. Baker, who is living in San Diego now.

Q: He was one of my bosses at one time.

Adm. T.: He was commandant of the Eleventh Naval District, I think. So away we went with our new staff.

Q: What dates are we talking about? Would this be September?

Adm. T.: Yes, or the latter part of August. Yes, August. McCain took command of Task Group 38.1 under Mitscher.

Q: Would that have been 38.1 or 58.1?

Adm. T.: No, 38 or 58, it doesn't make any difference. It

was the same thing. I guess it probably was 58 if Spruance was still - Spruance had the Fifth Fleet and Halsey the Third Fleet. When Spruance was there it was 58.1 and when Halsey was there it was 38.1. So, it was .1.

Q: Did you tell me what his flagship was?

Adm. T.: The USS Wasp. Then 2 September, I think, we left Eniwetok and went to the operation at Palau and Peleliu. The landing on Palau was, as I remember, fairly routine. Peleliu was a different matter. Peleliu had a very extensive defenses dug in caves in the sides of hills and, although the landing wasn't too difficult, getting inland against the network of defenses was one of the toughest things up to that point. The Marines kept describing each new one that they discovered, new system of caves in the side of a hill with disappearing guns the Japanese could bring out and then pull them back in, and the Marines couldn't seem to reduce them.

Since we were doing the close air support job, they said when they were going to assault this hill, and I went to Admiral McCain and said, "Instead of just sending the usual number of strikes in to support the Marines in their effort to take this hill (which had gotten the name of Bloody Nose Hill), let's send a big group and just pulverize the place." And he said it sounded like a good idea because they were in caves.

I think they asked for eight aircraft and I sent forty-eight, and they were overjoyed. They didn't think we could spare them for some reason. They didn't know enough to ask for them. That would be a strike of forty and then we'd do it again, and we just poured the stuff in there, including rockets and bombs, machine gun bullets, and everything we could throw at these holes in the side of the hill, and they took the hill.

There's a little Japanese flag over there in that drawer that the Marines sent to me because they appreciated those aircraft, and it's a flag that they took off of Bloody Nose Hill.

Q: Before we go on, I think it's interesting that Admiral McCain was a Task Group commander instead of immediately taking over from Mitscher.

Adm. T.: This was the way Admiral McCain wanted it. I think he could have. It was sort of a process of relieving, just going on a couple of campaigns and then having been a part of this with not quite so much responsibility, he would be better able to do the job when he took over.

Q: It's reasonable, but it's kind of unusual, too, isn't it?

Adm. T.: Well, yes, because McCain was a vice admiral and a vice admiral in command of a task group - usually a rear admiral

Thach #4 - 350

is in command of a task group. He was senior to Mitscher. But I think it was all right. I got a little impatient toward the end because, specially when the kamikazes started coming, I felt that McCain had been at this make-learn business long enough.

Q: Can you describe the difference in the personalities of Mitscher and McCain?

Adm. T.: Like night and day! Quite different, yes. Mitscher was a taciturn individual. He never had too much to say, and he wasn't one who would have a conference and solicit opinions from other people. He was an old-time aviator, he had his own convictions and he didn't see the need to hear from anybody else much. Basically, I think there is no question he was very good. I would far rather work for McCain or Halsey than Mitscher.

Q: Personality or competence?

Adm. T.: Well, personality, and it was hard to change Mitscher's mind if you thought he was doing something that he could have done better. He wouldn't change his mind. He'd say what he was going to do and if somebody came up with maybe wanting a modification or something different, he wouldn't listen. Of course, I may be too critical of him. I might be influenced by a thing that happened sometime back, or maybe he was! Maybe both of us. I've mentioned earlier in the interviews about one of my aircraft in the Battle of Midway with a fused master gun switch came in and landed, the gun went off and killed some of the people in his ship, the Hornet, and he strongly recommended that they put a cut-out switch into the system of lowering the hook, so that when the hook was lowered you couldn't fire the guns. There'd be another opening in the circuit. The Navy Department asked me about it when I was back there, and I said I would be dead set against it because I felt it was more important for the pilot to be sure to have his guns and it was just another switch to go wrong, and if you got dirt in it and it failed to work just when he was going to shoot down a torpedo plane, that would sink the ship. I thought the ship was more important, and I did think that this very rare situation of a bullet going through the master switch and fusing - it wouldn't happen often enough, maybe never again or once in a million times, to make this worthwhile.

Q: And Admiral McCain was much easier to work with?

Adm. T.: Oh, yes, far easier. He often said, "I like to talk to the people who are actually doing it. For instance, if I want to learn how to tie a bowline on a bite I'll go to the bo'sun's mate, not my chief of staff."

And he liked to talk to the pilots who returned from

strikes. I was delighted with this because I would pick the ones that had the most significant experiences and bring them up in droves to the flag bridge and go into the admiral's cabin and he'd sit around and give them a cup of coffee and listen to them say what they saw and what they did, and then he always said, "Do you think we're doing the right thing?" He'd ask them, young JGs.

Q: Why not? They're the guys –

Adm. T.: Absolutely.

Q: I'm sure they liked it, too?

Adm. T.: Oh, they loved it, terrific. Something new to them. And this was good. He was a very human individual and a very modest and thinking of his own experience and knowledge. He never quit learning. In other words, he didn't have complete and abiding faith in his own judgment, and I don't think any-one should.

Q: Well, you've made the distinction very clear.

Adm. T.: Of course, working under Mitscher, we broke our necks to be sure that we did everything exactly as it was planned. We didn't try to go off on our own in any way and we got some particular "Well dones" from the task force commander to Task Group 58.1 - to commander Task Group 58.1. I know that Arleigh Burke wrote them but nevertheless Mitscher did send them.

Q: Your relationship with Arleigh Burke sounds very fine?

Adm. T.: Oh, yes, it has been for years. I didn't know Arleigh Burke in the early days of the war when he had a destroyer squadron and did such an outstanding job. Arleigh Burke was a destroyer sailor and we were aviators, and we found that we had a great deal in common. He and I used to sit and talk and he said, "You know, fighting destroyers is very much like fighting fighters, I think." And I said, "You're right, I'm sure it is." He understood the use of air power and the fact that it could have a broad range, it wasn't just like sitting behind the turret pumping a gun in gun range. He understood the situation. He knew the timing, and the fact that you had to think ahead and run downwind if you want to be in the same place when you've finished landing aboard. You've got to get downwind for a little while.

Q: Takes time!

Adm. T.: It takes time. There was no question about his feeling that night that we wanted to run downwind which, incidentally, was toward the enemy, because we knew that the next day the prevailing wind would come up and we'd have to run - well, Arleigh Burke knew this just as well as any aviator ever knew it. I really appreciated his understanding of that. He's a very smart man, and a very wonderful friend, too.

So, then we went on to Morotai. There wasn't too much opposition at Morotai to the strikes to more or less try to see what reaction we would get - that was the idea. One of the interesting events that happened - one of the pilots was shot down and landed in a harbor with narrow little crooked channels entering the harbor. We had what we called "rescue submarines" on station. Each pilot in his briefing just before taking off for a strike would be given the position that the rescue submarines would be, so if he was in trouble or hit he would stretch everything to try to get to the vicinity of the submarines, and he had a special channel he could tell the submarines where he was going in the water, or if he had to parachute, where he was, before leaving the airplane.

Well, this pilot was downed in the harbor and he'd got into his little rubber rowboat and the wind was blowing onto the beach, and there were enemy on the beach. Apparently they didn't have any boats handy, they didn't come out to get him. They were just standing there waiting for him. Art Downing was flying an F-6F fighter - Lieutenant Art Downing. We got the message this plane was going down and he want over there and looked at it. Then he talked to the submarines, which of course were out in the ocean, and he said, "You can get in and get him." And the submarine skipper said, "If I can get through the channel." Art Downing says, "I'll get you through the channel. I will con you through the channel." The submarine skipper was apparently a similar type to Art Downing because he said, "All right. Come on. We're going to get this man."

So the submarine started in. He didn't have any chart of this channel. So Art Downing flying in his fighter would tell him so many degrees right, now you've got a sharp turn coming to the left," and he just coached him right into the channel.

Q: Submerged all the time?

Adm. T.: Conning tower up. No, not submerged - all the time the wind was blowing this poor little raft with the pilot in it closer towards the beach.

By the time the submarine got in there, they were shooting at him with machine guns from the beach. The submarine got in there and went between the beach and the pilot drifting down and picked him up, and Art Downing coached him back out again. As soon as the submarine got clear he called Downing and he said, "I don't know whether you noticed it or not, but there were two Japanese planes flying above you. I didn't want to tell you about it because I was afraid you'd leave me in the harbor!"

Art Downing said, "I saw them, but I figured that they were too curious about what you were doing to bother me." And that evidently was accurate.

Q: Isn't that peculiar!

Adm. T.: I don't know why. Art had seen these enemy airplanes over his head and had to coach this submarine through the channel. That was hairy!

Q: I've never heard that story before. Is it known?

Adm. T.: Not very well. It's known to Thacher Longstreth and Jimmy Thach and Art Downing and all the people in the submarine. I don't even remember the name of the pilot to whom this happened.

Q: Do you remember the name of the submarine?

Adm. T.: No. I wish I did. We sent a big "Well done" to the submarine, no less.

Q: I'm sure. That's a wonderful story.

Adm. T.: Art Downing later became a fighter ace. He shot down more than five airplanes. I saw him not long ago at a fighter aces convention.

Well, to get on with it, we went in later to Davao and Mindanao and there wasn't much there.

Q: This is all before Leyte?

Adm. T.: Yes. There wasn't much at Mindanao - a few airplanes but not much activity and not much going on.

MacArthur wanted to hit - I think he wanted to take Talaud and Sarangani Islands. By this time, Halsey was back out there. I don't remember the day he came, but it was the Third Fleet then. Halsey talked him out of that. Halsey wanted to go up and hit Leyte and Negros, Iloilo, Cebu, and so forth, which we did.

There was an aviator shot down on Leyte and recovered very quickly, but in the meantime - I mean within a matter of weeks - a young fighter pilot from Hornet, and he was passed from one native group to another who were Filipinos on our side, and got out in a hurry. He came back and gave us some very fine intelligence on the fact that there weren't very many Japanese on Leyte. Everybody thought they must be pretty well loaded with enemy there, but they weren't. That plus the fact that we saw very little at Mindanao is probably what gave Halsey some ammunition to convince MacArthur that we didn't have to go into Mindanao. Mindanao is a huge land area, a large island, and Halsey wanted to go into Leyte and bypass

Mindanao. MacArthur didn't understand this business of bypassing as much as Halsey did. He wanted to work his way slowly up the island chain, which was a kind of useless thing if you could go right ahead and take Leyte. Then he was finally convinced.

There's a little island called Macao and we noticed that there were training operations going on there. So there wasn't too much at the time the decision was made to go into Leyte, not too much on the beach.

Q: What do you mean "there wasn't too much on the beach"?

Adm. T.: Well, for example, they didn't have large armies.

Q: Oh, not too much defense?

Adm. T.: Yes, not too much defense. And although they had an awful lot of airplanes on Luzon and some of the other islands there wasn't too much to prevent an amphibious invasion. We knew we could take care of the airplanes.

We're getting into October now and the decision had been made to go into Leyte, of course, plans worked out and people were underway for the operation. We hit Okinawa and really got a jackpot of airplanes. I think the enemy didn't expect us to hit up that far. This was the beginning of our period of softening-up for the landing at Leyte, by going in and wiping out as many enemy aircraft as we could way up the Ryukyu Island chain.

Q: They hit Formosa and Okinawa at the same time, didn't they?

Adm. T.: Yes. We went up and hit Okinawa and had a jackpot full of airplanes.

Q: I think those dates are October 10th, 11th and 12th.

Adm. T.: Yes, October 10th at Okinawa. Then we came on down and hit Formosa and got another jackpot of airplanes. So we were starting at the upper end of the island chain to wipe out as many airplanes as we possibly could and come on down into Luzon.

Q: This is the entire task force?

Adm. T.: Yes, the entire task force, Task Force 38.

Q: And McCain was still 38.1?

Adm. T.: Yes.

When we went in and hit Formosa we got pretty good reaction. In the afternoon when the intelligence boys got the photographs from the strike on Formosa, always a lot more airplanes show up on the photographs than the pilots see. The Japanese were very good at camouflage. They would even hide planes sometimes five miles away from a field in the woods. But the photographs showed there were quite a number of torpedo planes, Frans and Bettys, and Thacher Longstreth came to me and said, "I think we can expect a pretty husky attack along with torpedo planes." So I said, "I wouldn't argue against that. We'd better be ready, at least in our task group." So we sent an intelligence-type message pointing out the numbers of aircraft that we'd seen and types and so forth, and indicated that we were sure that these aircraft would be involved in any attack.

Q: That went to Mitscher?

Adm. T.: Yes. Of course, I wasn't saying anything different than he did at the time.

Q: Before we get into this, I should have asked you before, but I'd like to pinpoint what your responsibilities were under Admiral McCain. You talked about what you did with Admiral Mitscher and Admiral Burke, but now that you are in operations with Admiral McCain, can you describe, say, a day, what you did, your responsibilities, your quarters? I'd like to get a picture of you.

Adm. T: I was the operations officer, which meant that I was operations officer for any operation at any time, air, and so forth, and had the responsibility of planning the air strikes, deciding the formation of the ships, how they would be disposed, and, in a way, conducting the operations, watching it and changing it, if necessary, which sometimes you had to do.

Q: How long would it take you to plan an operation?

Adm. T.: That depends. You see, there would be an operations plan put out by Commander, Third Fleet, and then based on that plan which would show the general objective, what the objective is, then the task force commander would put out his operation order - of course, Halsey would have an operation order, too, operation plan and an operation order, so would Mitscher - and then based on that, the task group commander would put out his schedule of his operation order. So it was my job to write that operation order, plan it, and direct it.

Q: How long would that take?

Adm. T.: I don't remember! It would depend on whether it was a brief thing. If it's something like the Leyte invasion, then it might take - with the task group operations officer - anywhere from five hours or ten hours to three days. If it's a quick thing, a dispatch, why, in a matter of thirty minutes or an hour you could get a dispatch op order out.

Q: And where were your quarters on the ship?

Adm. T.: Down below the hangar deck. It was the policy to spread the staff around and not to put them all in one area in case a bomb hit that and the whole staff would be gone.

Q: Were you by yourself?

Adm. T.: Yes. On a normal day I would be up about 3:00 or 3:15 a.m. and look at the weather and get any last-minute information and see whether we wanted to give it to the pilots or not, get the first strike off.

Q: Every day did the pilots go out?

Adm. T.: Well, if you're back away any raids -

Q: No, but I mean when you're out in the area?

Adm. T.: Oh, yes. We did something every day. One day we hit Okinawa, and the next day Formosa, and the next day Luzon.
  Then, by the time the first strike got off, I would get some breakfast.

Q: Did you watch them go?

Adm. T.: Yes.

Q: You'd be on the bridge?

Adm. T.: I'd be on the bridge because if you run into some sudden change I had to be right there by the phone to change it. Just about thirty seconds before launch of the whole task force, one time, of a thousand airplanes, I had to stop it all.

Q: Was that at Okinawa?

Adm. T.: No, that was up around Hokkaido later in the war.

Q: Just so you don't forget that!

Adm. T.: No, I won't. My fingers feel wet!

Q: Just thinking about it?

Adm. T.: Yes.

Q: So you would be there watching them take off on the first strike?

Adm. T.: And then once they all got in the air and were on

their way to the target, I would have time to get some breakfast because there'd be nothing happening. Usually enemy planes hadn't been able to know where we were, they hadn't been able to find us, they'd have to search before they found us. So this was the beginning of a pretty quiet time. Right after breakfast I'd check to see what reports there were from the target area, whether they were running into big opposition, did they see any strikes coming out toward us, and so forth and so on, all the data that we had up to that point.

Q: And you were on the bridge then, getting that information?

Adm. T.: Yes, and then about nine o'clock I'd go to bed - 9:00 a.m.. I'd go and take a nap. Sometimes I'd just get settled on my pillow and the admiral would send for me! Of course, I was up at 3:00 a.m. and having gone to bed sometimes as late as midnight, so you had to get your sleep piecemeal.

After my nap the first strike would have gotten back - if I got the nap, sometimes I didn't at all, didn't even think of it. And then you'd get photographs, wet, and look at them and make any changes you needed to for the second, third, and so forth strikes. This was the routine throughout the day. Of course, any enemy aircraft, whether or not to augment the combat air patrols, and there was the routine of the daily fueling of destroyers and so forth.

Q: Did you talk to the pilots?

Adm. T.: Oh, yes. I always talked with some of them, the strike leader, if he had anything worth talking about.

Q: After every strike they always knew that they were going to talk with you?

Adm. T.: Yes, more so because Admiral McCain was so interested in them personally and I wanted to be sure I didn't miss any good experience that might be helpful to Admiral McCain. The day would wear on and you'd get your last strikes coming back and by that time we'd be smoothing out the flight schedule and operations for the next day, and looking at the latest intelligence information to kind of place the strikes in the right place and the right numbers.

Q: Did you have an office?

Adm. T.: Yes.

Q: Where was it?

Adm. T.: It was right under the flight deck, about the middle of the ship.

Q: So you were between your living quarters and your office

and the bridge and flight deck all the time?

Adm. T.: Yes.

Q: You've given a graphic picture of the day.

Adm. T.: In the evening usually, having been there all day, there'd be some snooper that had come out so we'd figure on how we were going to operate against this snooper. Of course, at that time we didn't have - we didn't launch night fighters. We didn't have any night fighters. Yes, we did - I beg your pardon. I'm going too far back. At this time we did have night fighters.

Admiral Mitscher wasn't too enthusiastic about having night fighters. He thought maybe the risk of getting on and off and what they would do for the task group wasn't enough to make it worthwhile, and he felt that the enemy weren't going to attack us at night, in complete darkness. He didn't think they had that capability, and he'd rather rely on his antiaircraft fire at night against any snoopers that got too close.

I'm going back a little bit now to before Mitscher left. Mitscher's still -

Q: Mitscher's still with you?

Adm. T.: Yes, he hadn't left yet. Anyway, when I was with

Mitscher in the Lexington, one night they had a snooper and he'd show up on the radar about 100 miles away, and he started coming in and coming in. Then he would turn a little bit and you could tell, well, he's picked up another group of our ships. Then he'd come on. You could just see from the radar picture what was going on in his mind. He was trying to see if he'd left out anybody. He'd go around and look and then start in again. He finally was headed right directly over the Lexington and those fighter directors were pretty clever, I might say crafty, because they wouldn't put a fighter on him, they kept holding him off, saying "Wait." He said, "I think I see him. Can I go on and shoot him?" Hold it! They were in touch with Mitscher's operations officer and the operations officer wanted to get the airplane right over the Lexington before he shot it down! He wanted to convince Mitscher that night-fighting was a good thing. Well, this actually happened. This airplane got overhead and I got out a pair of binoculars and looked at him, but it just was almost overhead and the operations officer got Mitscher and said, I've got something out here to show you. There's an enemy snooper we're going to get, we hope."

Apparently they released the fighter and he'd gone in by this time and I was looking. I said, "The enemy plane's shooting at the fighter before the fighter starts shooting at him," because they had an officer along and he'd seen the fighter hanging back there. But apparently they didn't hit the pilot, but the fighter shot him and the snooper made a great big ball of fire. So Mitscher was a little more favorable to night-fighting after that!

Q: Well, we want to go back to Formosa. I interrupted you. You said that your intelligence man had told you that there was to be a big fight on Formosa and I distracted you by having you describe your duties, or your day. So we should return to that.

Adm. T.: Of course, every day wasn't exactly the same, but in order to get all the information that was available from one day's operation order, which we sent out by dispatch, took quite a while, and we would keep trying to get this thing out early enough so that most of the pilots always wanted to stay up and get it as soon as it came to them, came to their ship. They really didn't need it until briefing the next morning before taking off, but they liked it to get a little ahead of the game. And, of course, the briefings, as the war got more complicated, took longer and I got worried about the pilots not getting enough sleep. So we'd try real hard to get something out by dinner time, the operation order for the next day, but sometimes we didn't get it out until midnight.

Q: What time did they have to get up in the morning?

Thach #4 - 369

Adm. T.: They'd get up about the same time I did, around 3 o'clock.

Q: Oh, my.

Adm. T.: In order to have a pre-dawn launch. Not all of them but some of them would. We'd call the ones that had to go.

We hadn't by any means gotten all the planes on Formosa and, sure enough, here came a big strike at us. It was mostly shot down. They were using, and it was the first time I had seen the Japanese do it, antiradar devices.

Q: Jamming, you mean?

Adm. T.: Yes, snow, throwing out these little ribbons of foil, a big ball of them would appear. It would cause a clouded area on the radar scope, One name for this stuff was "window" another was "chaff".

Q: Throw them out from the planes?

Adm. T.: Yes, and they did some pretty tricky things, far more sophisticated than I thought they would be at that time. They would come in with several groups headed towards the task group, drop some "window" and split and so forth. Half of them would come in high while the others would dive down to low altitude.

Well, in the late afternoon, just before dusk - it was clear enough to see them - here came some Bettys and Frans, and they didn't mill around outside getting organized, they came right smack on in, real low, so low that they'd have to pull up a little bit to go over a destroyer and then flatten down inside of the destroyer screen, right low on the water, and drop a torpedo, which they did and hit the Canberra and the Houston, both of them. Well, they hit the Canberra on the first attack, and we moved a detachment of destroyers to stay with the Canberra, and then the Houston got in the same slot position in the formation as the Canberra had been, and the next time they hit the Houston.

Q: They were following the same tactics?

Adm. T.: Yes. So here we had two crippled cruisers on our hands, and there was some question about whether they should abandon ship and so forth. Anyway, they both got hit in very vulnerable places, the engine room, and they were dead in the water. So Mitscher told McCain to stay with them and he would arrange to get a tow. We were to protect them and they were going to be towed out. Mitscher took the other task groups and got the hell out of there leaving McCain with Task Group 38.1 alone to do this job. They finally got a tow hooked up to them, each one. Of course, before the tow tugs got there, big seagoing tugs, another ship took one of them in tow. What a wonderful opportunity for the Japanese to annihilate one whole task group. We were there for several days and the Japanese threw everything they could get mustered at us, and, as I was saying, they did some very tricky things. They would come in sometimes high and sometimes low, and they'd come in and throw out a bunch of chaff, antiradar - it makes a blip on the screen. Of course, it stays still once it's out of the airplane, but it's confusing to operators and it masks anything that's moving in that vicinity through it. They would start up high and come drifting down. In those days radar had what we called "nulls" where if an airplane was flying at the same level of altitude all the time it would go through these various distances and angles that you could see on the radar and then it would disappear. Although it was still there it wouldn't show on the radar for a little while because it was in a null.

Q: That's a valley or something?

Adm. T.: Like a narrow band.

Q: Like a space between two TV channels, or something like that?

Adm. T.: Yes, something like that. That's one way they got in with these torpedo planes. But the length of time that we were there, I've forgotten how many days, the Japanese were coming out looking at this thing. They had evidence that they had hit two cruisers and they were stopped, so they thought - or must have thought - if we were foolish enough to stay there they'd keep working on us and gradually eliminate us. But the fighter directors and the fighters on both the Essex-class carriers and the cruiser-type carriers did a magnificent job of stopping the attacks before they got in to work on the main body.

Remember, this was now just one task group.

Q: I was going to ask you, had the others left?

Adm. T.: Yes, the others had left and left McCain there. Mitscher told McCain to stay there and try to get the cruisers out if he could, and they went on away.

Q: Did that leave just one carrier?

Adm. T.: No. It left, let's see, the Wasp and the Hornet and the Cowpens, and the Monterey. If left four carriers.

Q: How long were you there, before you got moving?

Adm. T.: It was about eight hours, I think, before they got the two rigged. I've forgotten whether it was the Houston or the Canberra, but they came very close to abandoning that ship. The captain thought maybe he should abandon at one point, but later it was decided he didn't have to, although I believe they did take some people off. And as this was a very slow process, we lost our high-speed mobility and just had to try to keep between any attacks that the Japanese sent out and the tows that were making this slow progress. We just had to sort of run in circles and stay there.

Q: You said earlier and I'm not sure the tape picked it up that you were making a speed of two knots.

Adm. T.: Yes, that's what the speed was the first day or so of towing. Later, I think they were able to work up to three knots. Just whizzing along!

Q: So you were within reach of Japanese air power for how many days?

Adm. T.: Several. I wish I could remember the dates exactly and the days we were there, maybe four at a time. In a situation like that and in other situations similar, unless you are striking, day and night doesn't mean very much and you sort of lose track of how many days. I just don't remember. I think I never did remember.

Q: But you were under constant attack?

Adm. T.: Not constant, but frequent, and this was a very clear illustration of the capability then of a task group to defend itself against conventional attack. Halsey and Mitscher both sent McCain a big "Well Done."

Q: You're credited with planning those air operations and you received a Silver Star medal for them and it states that you directed the defensive air operations against numerous large-scale enemy air attacks when mobility was denied by the necessity to protect two crippled cruisers being towed at a speed of three knots, it says, until you were out of range of enemy air.

Adm. T.: Well, this was my job. I not only planned what we were doing in the way of protection but very closely conducted it with the talent we had in the fighter directors who really did a fantastic job. There were times when we thought, well, this is a bad spot to be in, maybe we whould have left the cruisers there -

Q: Were there no other hits after those?

Adm. T.: No other hits after those.

Q: It's incredible, isn't it?

Adm. T.: Yes, it is.

Q: I shouldn't say it that way. It is the result of excellent planning and execution of defense!

Adm. T.: Well, it worked. As we began to get a better idea of what we could do against such tactics -

Q: Was it a new method you used?

Adm. T.: Well, almost every time you confront a situation, if you haven't been in that situation, what you do to combat it is new. It was a matter of placing fighters on combat air patrol in the right numbers at the right altitudes, because I kept some low, and some at medium altitude, and some high, and at various places. We wouldn't send everybody out at the first inkling of an attack coming in. We would hold some back in a good tactical position to either augment, if the battle were not going well or if they were getting loose and getting through, or to send out quickly if there were another strike coming in from a little different direction.

Q: Were there two levels of planes in the air any time there was a strike?

Adm. T.: Yes. So it was in a way like the Marianas Turkey

Shoot. Of course, we weren't doing any striking ourselves, so we could put all our effort and use all the deck space for fighter operations for defense. There's no use in keeping fighters on the hangar deck for tomorrow if you might get hit today. You want to be sure you don't get hit. This is the principle on which we operated.

Q: I would think that the whole atmosphere of the group would have been enormously improved by seeing what could be done?

Adm. T.: It was. It gave us a tremendous lift, because it was doubtful it we could get away with it and everybody knew it.

Q: You were almost immobile and yet you were able to withstand raid after raid of attack.

Adm. T.: Right, but we had the advantage of knowing that they were obviously coming. We were set for them and prepared. We weren't caught napping, we were ready for them when they came. They were sending in these groups, none of them were very large groups, but they kept coming, hoping that some of them could get through, of course. But we were able to use the principle of concentration of force and put enough fighters on each group and with enough backup and not have them all occupied and leave unopposed somebody else coming in. So it worked.

Q: That was remarkable. You make it sound easy but I know it was because of the intelligent and skillful planning.

Adm. T.: About this time, two new airplanes of the Japanese showed themselves. One of them was called the George and was a much higher-speed fighter than the so-called Zero. Another one - I forget what day it was, but it was right about this time, either while we were off Formosa or a little bit later - an airplane appeared overhead, it was picked up by the radars, and it was at very high altitude, higher than we could get any of our fighters to get it, and it turned out to be a Myrt. This airplane was well above 40,000 feet, and with our fighters loaded with ammunition and gasoline, we couldn't reach it, and it just flew around over the top of us completely immune. This gave us pause to think about it - what did this portend? It reminded me of reading about Genghis Kahn when he swept across Asia out of Mongolia moving toward Cathay. He would send a high-speed scout on a horse and I remember in the book it told about when people saw this advance scout of Genghis Kahn appear over a ridge and stand there motionless for a moment studying the city or the town or the terrain and then like a flash disappear, it wouldn't be long before something devastating was coming. I thought of that when this Myrt appeared overhead and looked down on us and we couldn't get at him!

Q: Where did the name Myrt come from? Do you know?

Adm. T.: I don't know. Just like George. The Defense Department decided what names we would call them. The name is phonetic and you wouldn't mistake it for something else.

Q: I wondered if you named them yourselves.

Adm. T.: No, we didn't. Of course, most of the time when you first encountered an airplane, if we hadn't had a name for it, when we first saw the Bettys some people thought it was some other old airplane, but it wasn't, it was a new one, and later they gave it a name. They didn't know how to talk about them in correspondence.

Q: Did they get out great numbers of these high-altitude - ?

Adm. T.: Fortunately, no, they didn't. On the other hand, this airplane could do us no damage physically. The only thing it could do was to be a scout because it couldn't hit us with a bomb dropping it from up there. It wouldn't carry a bomb at that altitude, anyway. So even if it did drop a bomb, it would be just like anything else bombing from high altitude, it couldn't hit anything. And what other harm could it do to us? It wasn't a case of reporting our position for other aircraft to attack because everybody on both sides already knew where we were.

Q: Psychological, probably.

Adm. T.: Psychologically, it was bad! It surprised us. They didn't get too many of those built.

Q: How long were you underway with the two cruisers?

Adm. T.: As I remember, it was about five or six days before they got out of danger and were given a couple of destroyer escorts, or some destroyer escorts, to protect them against submarines, and away they went.

Q: And you joined Admiral Halsey?

Adm. T.: Yes. Speaking of Admiral Halsey, on the 20th - oh, before we get to that. Then we joined Task Force 38. It was off Luzon. There were quite a large number of airfields in the Philippines, over fifty of various kinds on Luzon alone, where Japanese airplanes were basing or had based or could base. Not big, complete air base complexes, but fields where they could operate. So we were trying to take a look at all of these and catch anything on them and wipe it out with the idea of working on the whole line of aircraft that they might be feeding down into the Philippines.

So on the 17th of October the amphibious force went into Leyte, and we had had the usual pre-landing strikes and D-day

Thach #4 - 380

and H-hour strikes and close air support. A few days later, Admiral McCain's task group 38.1 was directed to withdraw and refuel and go to Ulithi. We started back east and a large force, including Japanese aircraft carriers, was discovered up north and by this time we had finished fueling and were directed to search to the north and slightly west - search a wedge - to the north of our position, which was done. Our scouts discovered part of this force and reported it, and we were directed to take the scouts back aboard, continue on to Ulithi, and the other task groups were to go ahead and attack it, which they did.

But just about this time and long before our scouts got back - we had two squadrons of dive bombers searching - we heard urgent messages coming from the vicinity of Leyte. It seemed that all hell had broken loose among our poor little escort carriers who were there to continue the air support. They were being shot at by battleships. Before we were recalled, McCain decided that we shouldn't go to Ulithi and we headed at high speed back toward Leyte.

Q: Even before you were recalled, he was on his way?

Adm. T.: We never got the recall till late that night, after we'd thrown a strike, so this is what I want to point out - that he made the decision that we certainly should be recalled and if we hadn't gotten a recall message that didn't make much difference to him. He knew what to do.

Q: This was as a result of getting the messages of the needs?

Adm. T.: Yes, intercepting these messages. The air was just full of them, and we couldn't get any message through. We wanted to ask where they were and if Tacloban was still in our hands - we had some information of where they were at the moment - but we were going to go in and hit them because we were closer than the rest of the task force -

Q: At that time.

Adm. T.: - at that time - but we still had to get our scouts aboard and the prevailing wind was from the northeast. So we did something that I think even a lot of experienced officers who operated aircraft carriers would hardly believe - in later years I've heard people say that you couldn't do it - we made a speed of advance of thirty knots downwind. In other words, our point option did move thirty knots downwind, and at the same time we took those planes aboard. Now, how do you do this?

I decided that instead of turning the whole task group around, when any carrier had as many as six planes, or more to take aboard, (these scouts come back at different times)

<u>she</u> would make thirty-three knots and gradually punch out, bulge the screen out and get a little bit ahead, and then start the landing pattern with the planes flying a landing pattern to come upwind, which would be over the bows of the ships. Then when they're all set in a good landing pattern and you know you're going to get the first one aboard as you hit the wind line, make a quick turn back and come right back through the formation and get those six planes aboard before getting too far astern and have to whip around and come back and catch up.

Fortunately, we didn't have any battleships with us. We just had cruisers in that task group and they could make thirty knots. The battleships couldn't quite make that much. The carriers could make thirty-three. So until we got all those planes back aboard this is what we did. Each carrier whenever it got some of its airplanes back overhead, would bulge out front, making thirty-three knots, whip around into the wind and take them aboard. I described this to the carriers very carefully because I didn't want to turn that whole task group around but I wanted them to make thirty knots because we had an agonizing decision to make in another respect.

We'd had torpedoes on the torpedo planes because torpedoes sink ships, as I think I've said many times, and we wanted to get close enough so that they could carry their torpedoes. They didn't have the combat radius with a torpedo that they had with a few bombs. We decided finally that we weren't going to get close enough to launch these torpedoes and so, reluctantly, I called the task group and said I was very sorry but we had to change and put on bombs because we were going to send a strike as soon as they could change and get ready. And obviously there was a lot of disappointment in my voice because Admiral Artie Doyle, who was then Captain Doyle and in command of the Hornet, spoke up right away and said, "Don't worry. We understand. We'll get it done right now." He was right with it. He knew what was going through my mind and the horrible decision we were having to make and all the time this screaming coming from Leyte -

Q: What you did was enable the task group to proceed at top speed and you still made the turn with the carriers without impeding the forward movement of the whole task group?

Adm. T.: Exactly.

Q: And that hadn't been done before?

Adm. T.: No, and it hasn't been done since that I know of! At least not to make 30 knots downwind while landing two squadrons aboard. But they were able to keep that thirty-knot speed of advance for the whole task group, although when the carriers were taking planes aboard they were going in the opposite direction.

Q: That was a very tricky maneuver, wasn't it?

Adm. T.: It was, and the pilots had to be on the ball, too. They were instructed in the air what we were going to do, and the minute that a carrier got into the wind it wanted to see a plane at the cut -

Q: Did you say they were instructed in the air?

Adm. T.: Yes. We didn't want to waste too much time. We just told them what we were going to do. We told the carriers skippers not to turn back just because they saw an airplane on the horizon, but to have him ready to land aboard so that the moment the carrier got into the wind we got a cut signal. That's what I wanted - the cut signal the minute the carrier was in the wind, close enough to the wind for the airplane to land, and then take the next one and the next one aboard. By the time six or eight had landed, they'd be through the task group and about to get left too far behind and have to catch up. This was the situation.

All the time I was beating our communicators over the head, saying "Do something to find out whether Tacloban is in our hands or not." We didn't know. There was some doubt about whether we still held Tacloban because the Japanese were moving in in various forms, both on the ground and by sea - there were all kinds of reports flying around about a big movement of Japanese toward Leyte.

We got the bombs on and we threw the strike. I knew it was going to be touch and go that some probably wouldn't have enough fuel to get there and get back, and some of them didn't, but they did land at Tacloban and we didn't lose too many - but why did Admiral Kurita turn around and go back through the strait? He had everything going his way. He was chewing up the escort carriers and the aircraft carrier pilots - the ones in the air - had expended their ammunition on him and then kept on making simulated torpedo runs on the battleships when they didn't have a thing left, but they tried to keep him worried, anyway, so he wouldn't shoot as straight! But he did turn around and start back. Why? Many historians have wondered about this.

Well, I believe that at the time that he had indication or saw this strike coming he had communications intelligence on it, because otherwise he had no reason to turn around and run away from a very successful battle he was fighting. Later, in his interrogation after the war, he was asked why he turned back and he explained that he saw this large strike coming from he didn't know where, and that's the reason that he turned back. He had indications of where Halsey and Mitscher were. He thought the whole task group was up there, and he didn't know about McCain. As a matter of fact, neither did Halsey and Mitscher know what McCain was doing at the time.

Admiral Kurita's chief of staff, in his interrogation

after the war, said the same thing. So we have two Japanese officers who were there explaining why they turned back and I think if there is any mystery left about this it should be cleared up.

Q: Two questions: How far were you away when you started your strike? Do you recall the miles?

Adm. T.: I don't remember exactly. It was changing all the time, but it was about 400 miles.

Q: And how many planes were you able to put in the air?

Adm. T.: We flew everything that we could get going - four deckloads, which would probably be about 150 airplanes.

Q: I'm sure that made a sizeable impression on the Japanese!

Adm. T.: Oh, yes.

Q: In one of my reference books, I noticed a phrase that said, "McCain launched his planes from such a distance that they did no damage." Would you comment on that?

Adm. T.: Well, they didn't sink any of those ships that were shooting at the escort carriers - by the time our strike got there Kurita was going back through the straits, but they did catch some of the ships and attack them. I'm a little appalled at the phrase "did no damage" because at least they must have prevented a lot more damage to our escort carriers, because that strike was the reason Kurita turned back.

Now, why were we in a situation like that? I know that an awful lot has been written about whether or not Halsey should have gone north and it is questioned whether he should have. Some people say that Japanese Admiral Ozawa was acting as bait and wanted to be found. But Ozawa had at least two aircraft carriers. In my opinion, Halsey should have looked ahead further than the landings at Leyte. He was looking, I believe, far ahead and whenever you know where two enemy carriers are - two or more - and you have the power to sink them or damage them, that is what you should do, I believe, because what would have happened if he hadn't? Sometime later maybe those carriers in a surprise move would have done far more damage than it turned out was received by the American forces. Not too much damage was done. Actually, more damage was done to the Japanese because Halsey went north than was done to the American ships, and anybody who was brought up in aircraft carriers would know what they were capable of. When you find two and you can reach them, they are the high-speed mobile air bases and extremely dangerous and they should be put out if at all possible. If I were Halsey and had the whole thing to do over again, even knowing what's been written

in all the books, I'd still go after those carriers. I think
he did exactly right, and I think that sooner or later if
people really look at it and weigh the thing they'll see
that he did. There's a little calculated risk in everything,
but in my opinion he certainly should have gone after those
carriers.

Q: And how much damage did he do to Ozawa's force?

Adm. T.: He practically wiped it out. They were then no
longer any threat. I doubt if Kurita could have done much
more damage if he hadn't turned back because Halsey also knew
that Task Group 38.1 was not too far away, it was in the
vicinity, and I think it wasn't too much of a calculated risk.
It's interesting, though to note that at the time we were
attacking the ships - I guess it was a sister ship of the
Yamato, the Mushashi, again Lieutenant Art Downing was going
on a strike against these ships and he asked Lieutenant Commander House - I guess it was Herschel House - if he had an
opportunity to attack a ship like the Yamato where would
he put his bombs. And he said, "I'd put it right behind
the forwardturret." That's exactly where Downing's hit went
on the battleship that I think was a sister ship of the Yamato,
the Mushashi, I believe. So this is another interesting little
item on Art Downing.

After this campaign, as far as the carriers were concerned,

the Leyte Gulf thing drew to a close and the Japanese were trapped in the Surigao Strait and annihilated by a very expert ambush, McCain relieved Mitscher on October 30, 1944.

Oh, before that, the first kamikaze hit an escort carrier on the 25th of October and this was obviously an intended suicide attack because it didn't inadvertently crash into the ship, it was not damaged, it just came in. We were becoming quite concerned, of course, about this very effective method of hitting our carriers. It wouldn't have been worthwhile on any other target in the world. There's no use in diving into part of a factory, for example, or an antiaircraft installation, the surprise isn't big enough. So the Japanese hit upon the idea of the Divine Wind which is, I believe, the definition of "kamikaze," and gathered together some of their most patriotic individuals and formed the Kamikaze Corps.

This was a weapon for all practical purposes far ahead of its time. It was actually a guided missile before we had any such things as guided missiles. It was guided by a human brain, human eyes and hands, and even better than a guided missile, it could look, digest the information, and change course and avoid damage and get to the target. So we had to do something about this. I'd been thinking about this from the time I heard of the first kamikaze. Later, you know, they built a thing called a Baka Bomb. It was a small, very compact airplane powered with four rockets - this is way back in the middle of World War II, rocket-powered airplanes.

Q: Who is "they"?

Adm. T.: The Japanese. We didn't even have any jet combat airplanes then and they were going to rockets. They had four rockets and they could set them off all at once or set them off in series, and this airplane could make around 500 miles an hour, so it had to be carried fairly close to the target before they were released. Some Betty-type bombers were re-configured and fitted to carry this Baka Bomb with the pilot in it in the cockpit and drop it and then the pilot would set off the rockets and go swooshing away toward our ships. They would bring the Baka airplane to within range so that by the time the fuel ran out the pilot would be right at his target.

Q: And they were kamikazes, too?

Adm. T.: Yes, there was no other purpose for it.

Q: He had expended all his fuel by the time he got there?

Adm. T.: Yes, usually, but even if he hadn't he still would dive right into the ship. The only thing with these little airplanes, I learned later from destroyers, was that after they got to full speed it was hard for them to turn, in case they weren't headed just right and hadn't read the destroyer well enough, they would try to turn and wouldn't quite make it and would go over the fantail and miss the destroyer. So again, this was something that was very serious and I had decided that we might take a page out of past experience with football teams and so forth and devised some training practices as a defensive measure against Japanese suicide planes.

I'd just like to read the first paragraph of this exercise order. It was from Commander, Task Force 38, to each one of the task group commanders, the four task group commanders, 1, 2, 3, and 4:

> Training exercise for defense against enemy suicide attack groups. Exercise Moose Trap.

Why Moose Trap? Well, I asked my wife every time she wrote me a letter to please enclose some of the comic strips and especially Little Abner, so she'd send these Little Abner strips to me and there was a little series about a moose trap which I thought was very funny, so I named this exercise Moose Trap. It was phonetic and everybody could understand it and there was nothing else like it. We said:

> The most successful football teams obtained the formations and trick plays used by their opponents and duplicate them to get at the first team in practice until a satisfactory defense is perfected. Exercise Moose Trap is designed to do just that. The task groups commanders will whenever the opportunity presents itself or can be made, conduct one

or more of the parts of this training exercise and report results.

And the idea was to try to discover the disposition and size of our combat air patrols. So we would have these Moose Trap exercises and designate one squadron or two squadrons to send planes out and come in as a kamikaze may approach, riding down the nulls of the radar and coming in high and low and so forth. Some of the kamikazes came in in pairs and one of them would come in high and draw a lot of fire, and the other would come low over the water and bust right into the side of the ship while the other one dove right straight down onto the flight deck.

So we needed to have not just a good air defense. We had to have a complete airtight defense. Not one airplane must get through because usually the kamikazes would hit. Not always, but often. This was one of the first orders that we put out.

Q: I notice that's dated 11 November 1944.

Adm. T.: Yes, it was just after McCain took over.

Q: He took over on the 1st of November.

Adm. T.: Yes. So we did this. I don't think that Admiral Mitscher practiced this. He liked to depend on AA fire and the fighters, but I don't remember whether he ever adopted this or not later on. I know that he didn't adopt it right away because when he had command of the task force up around Okinawa quite a few carriers got hit by kamikazes, including an old dear friend of mine in the USS Saratoga, which I hated to see happen. But this turned out to be successful.

With this we developed putting combat air patrol over the pickets - we put out a pair of destroyers quite a distance from the force in the direction that our own strikes would be coming back and in the direction that enemy strikes might be made on us.

Q: How was that successful? How did it work in becoming successful?

Adm. T.: Well, it worked this way. First, we couldn't just go on defense and stop striking, so we put out destroyers and called them in one place Tom Cat and in the other one Watch Dog. Admiral McCain thought of those names. He wanted to call them that. He never would explain why, but that was all right with us. We were delighted.

The idea was to put a good fighter director in a destroyer and give him eight airplanes - eight fighters - in addition to the combat air patrol that we'd have over the carriers, put him way out fifty miles or so. And we would require that the returning strikes would make a turn over that Watch Dog picket, who would be off set, say, a little bit to the right of the course that they'd come back, and then the carrier task groups in groups more or less perpendicular to the line of the turn so that aircraft could beat in around behind them and come in after going over the picket and checking out over the picket. The reason we wanted them to check out was to get de-loused - we used the term "delousing" for pilots who after making a strike would get tired on the way back and they didn't look back under their tails to see whether there's a kamikaze tucked under there, and quite often there was. But to make them circle over the outlying picket before coming on in to the task group, the fighters would look them over and de-louse them of any enemy planes that were tucked in under there hiding under their IFF.

We also had a "fair game" area where you'd normally come from enemy fields toward the carrier, any airplane out there was fair game, and you'd send fighters out and shoot it down, no matter what it was, even if it was our own airplane. And we told the pilots that they were just likely to get shot at if they didn't come back and de-louse themselves over the picket. This left the area clear and if a kamikaze was coming out, or any attack was coming straight out like they usually do, we'd pick him up very much quicker. So that worked.

Then we'd stack the combat air patrol up over each task group, and I kept the task groups together close enough so that they would have mutual support, unlike the Battle of

Midway when we got too far away.

Q: I know you commented on that at the time.

Adm. T.: And with this mutual support and the pickets, and then for the night attacks or dusk attacks where we had to have most of our fighters back, we'd send out - we devised some things called jack patrols. They would go out in a direction toward the enemy in a fan-shaped sector and look over and search that sector low to see if they could see on the horizon any torpedo planes coming out because they had the habit of coming out and waiting to attack just at dusk. If they could catch them out there in formation they could break them up or shoot them down before they got set to attack. And this happened a few times. We got quite successful with these jack patrols because the enemy figured that we'd be taking everybody aboard before sunset - or most people, all except night fighters - and they wouldn't expect they'd be coming in low or below the radar. The night fighters at high altitude who were already up there wouldn't see them. But the jack patrols would pick them up visually and then alert everybody and go in and fight them. That way we reduced almost to nothing the dusk torpedo attacks.

Why did we call them "jack patrol"? Well, Lieutenant Commander McInnis, who was by that time the force fighter director, asked me why I wanted to call them "jack patrol," and I said, "I have a son named Jack and I'd just like one little thing named for him during this war!" So he said, "I'll buy that." He was looking for the name to describe what they did, but this is something that you really shouldn't do. That's the reason you should call something by a name that's remote from its mission. Instead of calling a night fighter a "black widow" - that's too obvious.

Q: Did this prove to be successful in combating the kamikazes' attacks?

Adm. T.: Yes. In the last two months of the war - I'm getting a little ahead of my story but I might as well say it now before I forget it - not one carrier was hit by anything. We did have an air defense. In the last two months of the war when we were roaming up and down the Japanese coast, where there were many aircraft, and it wasn't because they didn't try, we shot down 130 airplanes attempting to get to the carriers. They did hit some destroyer pickets, but the last two months of the war not one carrier was hit by a kamikaze or anything else.

Q: Where was the task group when you put out Operation Moose Trap?

Adm. T.: We had just finished up the Leyte operation and were

Thach #4 - 397

on our way back to replenish and get ready for the next operation.

Q: You went back to - ?

Adm. T.: We had to go back to Leyte several times. There seemed to be a little public relations battle going on between the Army Air Corps, General Kenney's outfit that went in to Leyte, and the Navy. Although I think just one side was doing any fighting in this public relations battle and that was General Kenney's outfit, or his public relations officer. I was very unhappy to see the tone of a dispatch released to the news media and they had pretty good channels to news media published all over, that said, "Now that the best pilots in the world, the real professionals, are here at Leyte, the Leyte forces don't have anything to worry about anymore." Those were practically the words of the message. Well, it was a left-handed slap that anybody else was second best, that we who had established control of the air in that area and anxious to get on with the war and leave it - we didn't want to go back there - we wanted to go to other new places where there were bigger jackpots than the airplanes they had around there, but we were unfortunate - because this is the kind of thing that makes the other side do something that really shouldn't be done, too, and make a dirty crack against the Army Air Forces, which shouldn't have been done but probably was. It was a bad thing. You'd think that there were two wars going on, one between us and the Japanese and the other one, but I suppose that they felt that they hadn't gotten in on much and now that they were there they wanted to make a good thing out of it. That, in my opinion, was not the way to do it.

Anyway, I mentioned that only to show that the Navy didn't have to reply to a thing like that because later actions showed - actions speak louder than words.

Q: You had to go back to Leyte at least twice, didn't you?

Adm. T.: Three times, as I remember, MacArthur called us back. In fact, almost like yelling, Help! And this is the way it was, because the few airplanes that the Japanese sent in there the Army pilots couldn't seem to handle them. One of the reasons, I think, was because they got bogged down in the mud at Tacloban and their guns wouldn't work and their planes got stuck deeper in the mud, they couldn't even fly them.

Q: They had difficulty in establishing new airfields, as they had expected to do, I think, with far less trouble?

Adm. T.: Yes, no question about it. But it was an entirely different environment than a nice clean hangar deck where you have all your shops and big tools, too, like lathes, and any big machine shops where you can make anything, close, tight-knit repair and maintenance facilities for the airplanes. There's just no comparison between trying to base in a forward area environment on land and the advantages you have in being aboard an aircraft carrier. Just the dust alone, even if there's no mud. Dust gets into all the equipment and the guns and so forth. Then if it's cold weather, why, the mechanics' fingers are hard to handle. There are a lot of things that make them less efficient and they have a tough life. So they turned out to be not as effective as they wanted to be, and they had to call us back.

So they called us back and we would work over the airfields, then they'd say, okay, now you can go on your way again. So we'd go away to hit something else, go out and replenish, and they'd yell for help again. This went on a whole month, as I remember.

Q: I have the figure that you were operating steadily for eighty-four days - by the end of November?

Adm. T.: Yes, well, all of it wasn't as serious as going back to Leyte.

Q: No, but the task force had been at sea for eighty-four days.

Adm. T.: Oh, yes, we could have stayed at sea indefinitely -

perhaps a year. We had a big replenishment group that would come out and give you everything from bullets to beans, replace pilots, replace airplanes, everything except providing wives which people wanted more than anything else!

Q: I would have thought that the nerves of all the people involved would have been at the breaking point at the end of eighty-four days?

Adm. T.: Oh, no. No, just looking for bigger places to hit.

Q: They had the right kind of man when they had you, I'm sure.

Adm. T.: Well, the pilots could be rotated, but they were still full of all kinds of spunk and morale was real high. If you're successful in what you're doing, you don't have as much trouble with morale as if you're sitting doing nothing or resting too much or if you're defeated. Even in defeat your morale doesn't have to be low. That's not really a measure of morale. Low morale is when you're worried about breaking down from within. An enemy can completely annihilate you and the last man may still have the highest morale that you can imagine.

One thing that MacArthur did that I guess came from a conference with his Army Air Corps people there was to draw a line just north of a place called Legaspi, an east-west line, and said, "Now, when the Navy is back here the carriers will take care of the enemy air north of the line and the Army Air Corps everything south of the line. So don't attach anything south of the line and the Air Corps won't attack anything north of the line." This would have been all right except that one, we never believed in lines that restrict our operations when the carrier task forces had this great mobility and can hit something that might do some good, we ought to be able to hit something that might do some good, we ought to be able to hit it, no matter who else is hitting it. And, as it turned out, we went in there several times and got hit by kamikazes, one of the carriers, and this was bad.

We had developed another system against the kamikaze which was in addition to Moose Trap training for the defense - I developed another system for offense which we called the three-strike system. Is there time to explain this?

Q: Yes.

Adm. T.: Up until this time strikes were sent in by deck-loads; a carrier with its air group and two deck-loads sent in half of the group that was going to strike. It would go in and come back, and they'd send in the other half. Well, inasmuch as kamikazes could come from any airfield, any of those many airfields in the Philippines - and I think there were as many as eighty, counting all the small little strips that they could hide Kamikases on- I figured out that we had to keep them covered a little better, in fact a lot better. So I worked out a system of dividing the air group into three strikes and called it the "three-strike system."

I have a little notebook here that I resurrected. I had it when I first did this and it says, "Offense to spoil kamikaze raids on the task force, three-strike system, will provide a holey blanket over enemy known operational airfields - a holey blanket, but only small holes, I hope." The reason I say "small holes" is that we couldn't keep airplanes over every field all day long. If we could that would be great, but we came very close to doing it, and this is how it happened.

Let's just take a typical time period. Say, we'd launch the first at 6:00 a.m. - I called the strikes A, B, and C. Launch A with bombs and B with no bombs - launch them both together, two-thirds of your strength. They'd take off at six o'clock, en route to the target about an hour and fifteen minutes. So they'd arrive over the target, both A and B, at 7:15. The reason for sending that much strength on the first was because we weren't sure how much they'd been able to feed in during the night and what opposition they would find. So we'd double our strength for the first strike, so that A and B both could fight them. Then A would depart at 7:30. It was only over the target fifteen minutes. B would remain there. Then at eight o'clock C would take off, and then at 8:35 A would land and re-arm.

Now at 9:20 strike C would arrive over the target, but at

9:10 strike B would have departed. Now that's only a ten-minute gap between the departure of one strike and the arrival of the next one, and we would split these people up and cover all the airfields and just watch them. And many times they'd see airplanes being towed out from under the trees just as they arrived. They had been uncovered for ten minutes - they'd try to get this airplane out and get it on the field and here would come the next strike.

Q: When they were over the fields were they just circling or would they actually bomb?

Adm. T.: Well, if they saw anything worth bombing, they would bomb. B had no bombs so they could stay there longer, but they had their rockets -

Q: But they weren't just flying around, they would either strafe or bomb, whichever one was necessary, depending on what they saw on the ground?

Adm. T.: Or just flying around if they didn't see anything worth wasting ammunition on. In other words, a combat air patrol over the enemy to prevent them from taking off. And so on down. Then, as I said, strike B departed the target at 9:10 and strike C arrived at 9:20. Then at ten o'clock, A, having been re-armed would take off again. Then at 10:45

Thach #4 - 404

B would land. Of course, we had to ccordinate this so that we wouldn't have to stay in the wind all the time. It was a very complex thing. A at 11:20 would arrive over the target the second time, and at 11:10 C would have departed. And so on all through the day, so that you'd have a kind of a roof over the target - one of the people on the staff said, "I think we ought to call it the Thatched Roof"!

Q: This was your own development.

Adm. T.: Yes. This is called the blanket attack system.

Q: Can you tell me how many carriers you had? Were there fifteen?

Adm. T.: Around fifteen and sometimes sixteen or seventeen. For instance, here are 38.1, .2, .3, and .4.

Q: I was just figuring sixteen times three meant there were 48 groups that you were dealing with, and you say fifty different airfields?

Adm. T.: Yes, at least. The pilots had to be good and they had to get back on time to provide for the right coordination. We had to give a little extra attention to running downwind at the right time because you just couldn't be in the wind either launching or landing all the time. But you gained a little bit because they were smaller strikes than a whole deckload. So you lost a little bit because you were throwing more different strikes and they were landing and taking off at different times and closer together, but you gained some because they were smaller groups, and coming from all the different carriers by the time they got over their targets they made quite a force.

This worked, this blanket.

Q: That word sounds so simple and you well deserved your Legion of Merit, certainly. But until you explain it, as you have, it's not possible for a layman, I don't believe, to understand the complexity of what was involved. Your citation speaks of directing a 1,000-plane air attack against over 100 enemy airfields in the Philippines.

Adm. T.: Yes, in the whole Philippines there were over 100. In the area where we were I'd say there were about eighty.

Anyway, MacArthur drew this line -

Q: Can I ask you how long this went on?

Adm. T.: For the rest of the war.

Q: Oh!

Adm. T.: Sure, the kamikazes were trying to get at us for

the rest of the war. Later I recommended strongly that Jimmy Flatley take the job of operations officer for Mitscher. I got to Arleigh Burke and told him how good Jimmy Flatley was. Also Jimmy and I thought a lot alike and it was easier to relieve when we rotated so we were able to meet a few times and agree on the task force instructions. Finally it got so they were doing pretty much the same thing - we were both doing the same thing. We learned from each other. But it was some time before this was accepted, quite some time, by Mitscher himself. Jimmy Flatley finally talked him into it.

MacArthur drew this line, I said, and the line went just north of Legaspi. Well, one time one of our carriers was hit, one of the Essex class, and had its flight deck out of action, burning. They finally put it out but the airplanes couldn't land aboard in all those flames and there wasn't room for them on the other carriers, so we caught them en route and told them to go back and land in the Philippines - I forget the Air Force base. It wasn't Tacloban, it was somewhere else. They did, and they flew over Legaspi and saw all these airplanes. They landed at this base because they didn't have anywhere else to go and they talked to the squadron commanders there, and Air Corps operations officers, and told them about these airplanes, and they said, "They're not bothering anybody, are they?" or some such remark. So the Navy pilot said, "Well, that's the reason we're here. We got hit by a kamikaze and we think maybe it came from Legaspi. We're not permitted to hit it and we would like for you to hit it." They said, "All right, we'll take off tomorrow morning and we'll give you some bombs and you can go with us." This was fine, so they loaded some bombs on the Navy planes as well as the Air Force planes, and they said, "You lead us up there and show us these airplanes."

So away they went. They flew pretty high, but the Navy airplanes always liked to fly lower. They said, "We don't see any." Of course, you couldn't see them from that altitude. The torpedo planes were going in and winding around the trees and picking out an airplane and dropping a little bomb on it, and one of the strike leaders of the Army planes said, "We'd better get up higher. There's a lot of antiaircraft going off down there." They couldn't even see our torpedo planes either.

Q: But they could see the "antiaircraft"!

Adm. T.: That got straightened out and they all went in and got quite a few of the airplanes and some photographs. Well, we finally made room for them on other aircraft carriers and got them back. So we sent a blistering message on the basis of this. We argued against this line in the first place but we didn't get to MacArthur and he was the one who did it.

Halsey immediately saw the problem and he argued with MacArthur against the line, too. He finally told MacArthur that when his carriers were called in to do a job they had the right to protect themselves and to hit any airfield that was within range because the kamikazes were undoubtedly coming from airfields that had not been properly attacked such as Legaspi. He didn't argue anymore. He just told him, and we didn't hear anymore about it.

Q: That was the end of that!

Adm. T.: Yes. Of course, we felt the best way we could protect our position in the Philippines and our troops there that had landed ashore was to cut off the Japanese air power that was continuously feeding down from the homeland through Formosa and Luzon into the Leyte area. So for the rest of December 1944 - November and December - we worked on Luzon and, using this blanket method of striking, rolled up quite an impressive total of aircraft destroyed, some in the air but mostly on the ground. All of this to wear down and get a good big attrition against enemy land-based air power because now that Halsey had done the right thing enemy carriers were no longer a threat. There just weren't any operating on the high seas.

So we would go from Formosa to Luzon, spend quite a few days in a certain position off Luzon where we could strike all the fields including the northern tip of Luzon and clear back down to and including Legaspi and other fields in that vicinity, all at the same time. This involved the indirect support of - and some direct support - of the landings on Mindoro after softening them up, but in the first part of January we went up to Formosa again and northern Luzon and finally took the whole fleet into the Yellow Sea in order to cut off any possible threat from that area to the Lingayen area to support the Lingayen landings.

This sortie into the South China Sea was amazing in the number of ships and aircraft that were destroyed with very few losses of our own. There was one antiaircraft position on the southern tip of Formosa and we finally gave this character a nickname. Anyway, he shot down a few of our airplanes every time we attacked that area. This fellow apparently had had enough practice so he knew how to hit aircraft. So we decided to take him seriously. We had to send in a good heavy strike - eight airplanes - on him and wipe him out. Even so, we lost two planes doing that. But it was important to get him and also to get the lookout. We began to suspect that they had a radar. We knew that we were going into the South China Sea and we would go through probably the Bashi channel and they might know about it too soon, so we were doing everything we could to clear that area out as well as catch all their airplanes that were feeding down from the Japanese homeland.

I think before getting into the actual operations in the South China Sea - well, is this a good place to stop?

Q: Yes.

Interview #5 with Admiral John S. Thach, U.S. Navy (Retired)

Place: His home in Coronado, California

Date: 13 March 1971

Subject: Biography

By: Etta Belle Kitchen

Q: We have several interesting things to start with today, Admiral. Do you want to tell me the name of the man on the tip of Formosa that you have remembered since our last interview?

Adm. T.: Yes. We gave him a nickname. Actually, it was an antiaircraft battery, and we called him Pistol Pete because he got so good, and we began to wonder if he had some new fire-control system. We weren't sure because he was so accurate.

The reason for going into the South China Sea was very apparent to all of us. The invasion of Luzon from the Lingayen Gulf was planned and unless we made sure that there's not going to be any stiff opposition to that invasion, they'd be taking a risk that would be serious and utterly unnecessary. So it was a natural place for Halsey to take his Third Fleet, and so he did. He was really, I think, rather hoping that remnants, you might say, of the Japanese Navy, some down at Singapore and some at Brunei Bay in the southern Philippines, might join forces from the homeland that we knew were still intact to form a last-ditch attack on the mass of transports and amphibious forces that would be at Lingayen. In the event that the Japanese decided to do that, he was hoping to intercept them in the South China Sea. Of course, the very presence of this large American force in the South China Sea might discourage them and apparently it did - it either did or they just didn't have enough left to make any opposition at all and it would have been really a suicidal venture.

Q: Those operations lasted how long?

Adm. T.: In the South China Sea?

Q: Yes.

Adm. T.: Well, we did some preparation ahead of time on Luzon - well, to answer your question, we went through the Bashi Channel on the 9th of January and came out Balintang Channel on the 20th of January. But before that, on the 3rd of January, we started striking. We planned to hit Formosa on the 3rd and 4th, which we did - Formosa and the Formosa area. The weather is always stinking at that time of the year (January) in that part of the world, as it is in many other places. On the 3rd we had to discontinue striking in the early afternoon because the weather got so bad. On the 4th we struck Formosa again and we were in position between Formosa and Luzon where we could in one day's run strike either one or the other. It was very important that we reduce as much as possible the enemy air opposition on Luzon in preparation for the Lingayen Gulf landing, and on Formosa which was the main staging base for aircraft down from the homeland. So we tried to do a real good job on that, also to knock out any seagoing transports, any kind of ships, which was also done.

So on the 3rd and 4th we hit Formosa and on the 6th and 7th back to Luzon, and then on the 9th Formosa again and the night of the 9th we slipped right through the Bashi Channel. This preparation may have aided us in getting into the South China Sea undetected by the enemy.

Q: Were the patrols over the enemy airfields still being maintained?

Adm. T.: Yes. This was the way we operated, our policy.

Q: You described the detail of it previously and it was very interesting, but I'm interested to know whether from then on that policy then was adopted by both task forces, by Admiral Spruance as well as Admiral Halsey? Or was that just when Admiral Halsey was in charge?

I think I'll ask you that question again, Admiral, when we get up to the point where Admiral Spruance is relieved by Admiral Halsey off Okinawa. It might be put in more appropriately. But I do think it's interesting.

Tell me the different titles that they called this operation that you worked out. I know it was under different names by different people. You told me someone wanted to call it the Thatched Roof. Is that right?

Adm. T.: Well, yes, somebody did! We called it the blanket attack system. It was a three-strike system instead of having each carrier throw half of its airplanes and then the other half, as I described earlier.

Q: Other books refer to it as The Big Blue Blanket. Does that mean the same thing?

Adm. T.: That means the same thing.

Q: And then I notice here that - and I want to refer to an article in The Saturday Evening Post dated July 1945 by Vice Admiral McCain in which he attributes to you the successful tactics that were worked out. What did he call that?

Adm. T.: He called it the Constant Cap - constant combat air patrol - over enemy airfields. The reason he did that for publication during the war he didn't want to call it by its right name because we used that name in dispatches and it might help them break down that information during the war. So that's the reason he called it the Constant Cap.

Q: Do you want to comment further on the article while we're talking about it, Admiral? Are there any points that you might want to bring out?

Adm. T.: I think that the significant figures, as a result of using this system, show that we forced the deterioration of the enemy's ability to put planes in the air. As you know, this was the age of the kamikaze and I've described that before - a guided missile guided by human hands. So we had to do everything we could to be sure that they didn't get enough in the air to be able to penetrate the task force defense and kamikaze the carriers.

Well, on the 3rd of January against Formosa we caught and destroyed or damaged 204 airplanes on the ground and only 27 in the air. But then on the very next day, you'll see that on the 4th we caught 82 on the ground and our fighters in the air shot down only 3. This evidence seemed to pile up when we went back to Luzon on January the 6th. We had a two-day strike there, and on January the 6th again not a single Japanese plane came within many miles of the task force and we had a good day on shipping as well as aircraft on the fields, and again this interesting disproportion of aircraft caught on the ground versus the ones that we tangled with in the air. They had 160 on the ground on the 6th and only four lonesome Jap airplanes in the air.

Q: Did you believe that that was the solution to the kamikaze attacks?

Adm. T.: Yes, that was part of it. That and our Moose Trap exercise that we trained in defense of the task force.

On the 9th we struck Formosa again and caught 103 on the ground and caught only 5 in the air and shot those down. So, as a result of this, they were getting more or less flat on their backs. It was partly due to the really shock effect of a carrier task force strike. If you put yourself in the position of the enemy, although he had hundreds of airfields within range, what can he do? He may have thousands of airplanes, which he did on Luzon alone. They may know that one day we're going to strike and come in over all their airfields, but do they know exactly what hour? No, or even what day. Can they get all their planes in the air and keep them there? If they did, they might do it at the wrong time, then they'd be out of gas just about the time - they'd be landing just about the time we arrived because we didn't arrive at the same time every day. We tried to vary this pattern. That alone makes it very difficult for them to be ready for an attack.

Also, can you fully man all your antiaircraft batteries continuously, twenty-four hours or all the daylight hours? No, you can't, not unless you have some pretty good intelligence. You can do it for a short time but people just can't stay on complete alert all the time. Then the fact that we had worked out this three-strike blanket system so that their fields weren't left alone except for a short gap between strikes and then another short gap between the late afternoon and before dark.

On the 5th of January we were able to do something about closing that gap. The <u>Enterprise</u> and <u>Independence</u> joined with Admiral Mat Gardner and we designated him Task Group 38.5 as the night operations group, and they would operate at night and not in the daytime. So we had something going for us. They would handle all the night combat air patrols, the night hecklers who would go over the target, and we formed a new little gimmick called "zippers" to help close that gap between the time the daylight strikes left the target and darkness. So, again, they couldn't have very much time to get organized, get their planes going, and come out and find out where we were, because they never knew exactly where we were, although some of the kamikazes, as you know, did tag on to our returning strikes as a kind of a tail-end Charley and find their way back with us, but we cured that again with the Moose Trap business of having a clear sector where our planes were not allowed to be and where the enemy would normally come in on a direct line and where these Tom Cat destroyers with their combat air patrol could de-louse the returning strikes.

Q: You mentioned that before, yes.

Adm. T.: So it's a combination of those things, I think, that helped, although they were still trying to hit us and did have some success later, as I've pointed out.

But we went through the channel on the night of the 9th.

Q: Shall we now proceed with the South China Sea operation?

Adm. T.: Yes, but I think we must keep in mind that here was an area - well, some people call it a kind of a dirty sea because it's full of reefs and little submerged islands and you had to be real careful with your navigation where you went, especially with a large force like that that covered miles of territory. And it was surrounded by enemy land mass where they had airfields that could launch aircraft to come at us from practically all directions. There was no friendly land surrounding us at all. Some people might look at this as though we walked into a trap. Sure, it could have been a trap had the Japanese been stronger but we felt they were getting weaker and it was certainly a reasonable risk to take, even if some ships had been damaged, which they weren't.

Anyway, the entry was so successful and I think partly because we prepared and gave the treatment to the adjoining land masses going in that we went almost a thousand miles down toward Indochina before the enemy even knew that we were in the China Sea. We were plagued with bad weather. Sometimes we had difficulty fueling and the pilots flew in some of the worst and lowest ceilings that we had sent strikes up to that point, and they did a magnificent job. When they'd go into a place and attack enemy airfields, the pilots had a difficult time in actually seeing aircraft if the enemy was trying to hide them.

Thacher Longstreth, the staff intelligence officer requested permission to be dropped behind the lines in China. In addition to finding out what the Japanese were doing, he wanted to investigate the propaganda that stated "the Chinese Communists were not really communists - they were peaceful agrarian farmers." Thacher did not believe that. However, much to my relief Admiral McCain would not approve of him doing such a thing.

About this time the Japanese started doing a far better job than previously of camouflaging their aircraft. They were pretty good at it from the beginning, but they would not only paint the aircraft a mottled color - the color of the background - but hide them in all kinds of places, in villages and wooded areas, sometimes four or five miles from the field where they were based. But this, in a way, worked a little disadvantage because it would take them longer to haul them all the way back to the field to take off and strike, if they wanted to. But the Japanese were also beginning to suffer at this time from a shortage of experienced pilots, in fact, maybe a shortage of pilots, period. The training command must have broken down because it seemed they did not replenish pilots as fast as they had been shot down in the air, and we got the impression that they were trying to conserve pilots. This may have been part of their game of hiding aircraft so far from the field, if they didn't have enough pilots really to fly them and perhaps they were saving for the defense of their homeland.

But all of this entered into our estimate of the situation and made the risk less than it would have been in an earlier day when they had more power.

On the 12th of January, the first day, we hit an area of about 300 miles along the Indochina coast, the Saigon River and Camranh Bay, about 180 miles north of Saigon, Quinhon, which is another 120 miles north of Camranh. This was a highly successful day's work. We caught four different convoys in addition to the shipping that was attacked in the harbors, and the tonnages on that one day alone came to about 127,000 tons of enemy ships sunk and an additional 70,000 tons damaged and some of those, obviously, were put out of action. This was a total of 197,000 tons and I think this was an all-time record for one day's strike by fleet carriers, or maybe most anything else.

Another interesting thing is that the strike - we expected a counterattack, of course, once they knew we were in there, but again enjoyed this element of surprise that a fast carrier task force has, they didn't expect to be hit. They weren't ready to counter-strike at us and nothing happened. We weren't attacked at all. As I mentioned before, the navigators - and in every ship, you know, the navigators do their navigation even though they're in a task group or a task force - turned in their estimated positions to the task group commander and the task group commander to the task force commander and the task force commander says where he thinks the flagship is, and the fleet commander can agree with him or not, depending on his navigator.

So all this time we were in the South China Sea the weather was so bad that there was no opportunity to get a sun sight or a star sight to get a fix, so it was all done by very good dead reckoning. I say "good" because we didn't run onto any of those reefs. And in this same bad weather on January 15th we hit Canton and Hong Kong and caught some more planes and additional shipping. On the 16th we went back to the same area, Canton, Hong Kong, and also struck Hainan Island in the Tonkin Gulf area.

Q: Did you want to go back the second time?

Adm. T.: No, I was about to say I didn't want to send those pilots back to Hong Kong that second day. The ships that were in there were no real threat and Hong Kong is a place where they were anchored between high rises of ground which made a natural flak trap and the AA set up on the land could combine with AA fire from the ships and, in order to hit the ships that were in a kind of a gorge, you had to go in one way and come out the other way, or vice versa. So they could set up a real good flak trap, which they did. But we didn't prevail. The order from Admiral Nimitz, CinCPacFlt, relayed through was that shipping had to be first priority. So we had to go back again and we lost twenty-two pilots. I thought that was too much of a price to pay for going back to that place when we'd found out that it was a flak trap the day before.

Q: Did the order actually come from Nimitz to do that?

Adm. T.: Oh, yes.

Q: Admiral Halsey didn't make the decision himself, it actually came from CinCPac?

Adm. T.: Yes, it came from CinCPac. There were other things that happened later that I think were taking too much detail out of the hands of the task force commanders there on the spot and doing the job, but I'll get into that later when I refer to a situation where we addressed ourselves to that in an official action report.

Well, all in all, as far as knocking out shipping and aircraft, this was a highly successful sortie into the South China Sea and it absolutely assured that the amphibious forces going into Lingayen would not have any stiff opposition. In terms of the aircraft destroyed, our pilots put out of action 1,283 enemy aircraft in the various fields, including those on Luzon and Indochina, and the Hong Kong area. And they either sunk or beached - probably sunk - 100,000 tons of Japanese shipping. This to a great degree helped cut the Japanese supply route from the south up to the home islands. As I mentioned earlier, our submarines had been working on this supply line so it was pretty badly depleted in the first place. With 600,000 more tons of it gone, this was quite a blow to the enemy. And if you want to consider the past three months, November, December, and January, with 485 planes shot down and 1,072 destroyed on the ground with 310 probably destroyed and 971 damaged, for a grand total of 2,962 planes, that's quite a large portion of production that any country can produce in that length of time.

Then there were the merchant ships and cruisers and destroyers that were knocked out - merchantmen of all categories - 289 ships amounting to 995,000 tons. Cruisers and destroyers 101 ships - these were combat ships - 147,400 tons, and then small craft probably amounted to 20 tons, and the small craft the Japanese used very effectively carrying small things. Some people felt that it wasn't too worthwhile to hit these small vessels, but each one of them carried some cargo and some of it was vital.

You add all that up in tons of ships and you've got 1,162,500 tons in the past three months.

We lost 155 officer pilots and 96 enlisted men in the aircraft crews. And how many ships did we lose? None. No successful attack on ships. So I think it was a very worthwhile sortie into the South China Sea.

Q: That's an interesting and a pertinent summary. There's a publication called The Fast Carriers by C. Reynolds in which he implies that it was not of much value and I think you've well answered that. I don't want to get away from the fact that this is your biography, but there's one item also which he mentions relating to Admiral McCain and Admiral Halsey's relationship implying that Halsey was irritated by Admiral McCain and bypassed him, particularly referring to the night of January 11th when he indicates that a task group was taken away from him.

Adm. T.: What?

Adm. T.: He refers to Admiral Halsey bypassing Admiral McCain and gave Sherman command of tasks groups 38.1 and 38.3 and Bogan led the nighttime approach of task groups 38.2 and 38.5.

Adm. T.: Well, I can tell you this. Halsey never took a task group away from McCain -

Q: Do I misread it when I say that?

Adm. T.: On the 11th of January, I think you said - well, I have the records right here and in view of that it would be in order to set the record straight. I would like to read just exactly what went on that day. This was a day designated for fueling the task force. It was the day before we struck Indochina and the weather was pretty bad so each task group had difficulty fueling and the tankers couldn't get to all of them at once. They would go to one task group and as soon as they'd finished they would come over to another one. Some task groups would have more tankers at one time than another task group would have refueling them. So, this is what happened.

We always told the task group commanders to take charge and re-fuel their groups, rather than holding them to a task force course or speed of advance. Now, we were anxious to get on down on the 12th, the day we planned to strike and did, because no one knew - we had no searches down the South China Sea - no one knew what was there. We didn't know whether there were a few cruisers or battleships on their way up to try to make a raid and clobber the amphibious forces at Camranh Bay. So it was very urgent that we get something down there to search as soon as possible, and Halsey and McCain discussed this, and it was decided that whatever task group finished fueling first would start high-tailing it on down there and get going, and we'd tell the others to join as soon as they could. And this is exactly what happened at 1430. Task group 38.2 was finished and ordered to proceed independently to tomorrow's launching position off Indochina, while Task Group 38.1 and 38.3, which had not completed fueling, were directed to follow keeping close up as much as possible. In other words, to catch up and have us together again, and join 38.2 at the earliest possible time.

So at 1500 38.2 departed from the fueling area at 23 knots.

If you call that having Halsey irritated with McCain, which he was not - I remember it perfectly, the plan worked out just as discussed and he didn't take anything away from him. He wasn't unhappy about it at all.

Q: And he wasn't bypassing -

Adm. T.: He wasn't bypassing anyone. They were both performing their normal functions.

Q: Then you did leave the South China Sea by the Balintang Channel?

Adm. T.: Yes, we came out throwing punches. We came out on the 21st. The 21st of January was one of those rare bad days. In the first place, we were still working on shipping as the primary target - I won't say we were still working on shipping as the primary target because in the South China Sea air and shipping we considered of equal priority. As long as there was no air opposition, we'd put more on the ships and vice versa.

But on this day there was more intelligence on more ships in the Formosa area and we had to get them and there was some indication, which turned out to be wrong, that there was something in the Philippines that we hadn't cleaned up. So, on the 21st, the first bad thing that happened was that at eleven minutes after noon the Langley reported being hit by a bomb, which penetrated and exploded on the second deck. We were in the process then of attempting to top off destroyers, so we stopped that.

Then at 12:15 it was indicated by the linking destroyers between 38.2 and 38.3 that the Ticonderoga was hit, and the destroyer Maddocks was on a strike picket station and she was hit at 1:15. Obviously the enemy was able to penetrate and get through.

About 1328, just after finishing lunch, I thought I would go to my operations office, which is just under the flight deck, in the middle of the flight deck. I had another jacket there I wanted to get because I had no idea when I'd be able to get back down again, but I decided for some reason that, no, I wouldn't do it, I'd go on up on the bridge. I thought of something I wanted to do up there, and also whenever I got into my operations office down there it was hard to break away. That is where we did a lot of detailed planning and putting intelligence together and deciding what fields were the ones to strike, and putting together operations orders for oncoming operations. I went back up to flag plot and looked over the situation there. It looked all right. Then I went out on the wing of the bridge where there's armor plate that comes up about a foot below a man's shoulder, and I was standing there watching the planes - the strikes - return and I decided I wanted a cigarette. So I ducked down behind the armor plate to get out of the wind and light the cigarette and, boom - a huge explosion. An officer standing on one side of me had his shoulder blown off and the other one had shrapnel go right through his head. I looked back at the bulkhead, there was a narrow kind of a passageway on the wing of the bridge in an <u>Essex</u>-class carrier, a regular bulkhead, about three feet behind where I was standing and you couldn't put your hand any place there that wouldn't have several big chunks of shrapnel sticking in the side of the bulkhead which would have had to go through my head to get there.

A bomb had hung up in a torpedo plane, hung on the rack apparently, and was half loose and when it landed aboard it undoubtedly fell loose but the bomb bay was closed. It wasn't on the wing, it was I think a 1,000-pound bomb or 500, in the bomb bay - apparently was just resting in the bomb bay, and when he taxied out of the arresting gear and folded his wings and opened his bomb bay to be rearmed, this bomb fell out just that few feet, right on the fuse, and let go. It killed about 34 people.

Q: What was the ship?

Adm. T.: The Hancock, Admiral McCain's flagship. I could look down the hole in the deck and see my operations office - that's where it was. So something told me not to go in there! I didn't and also the cigarette saved my life -

Q: I remember you have told several incidents where you said you just were lucky.

Adm. T.: Well, I just had a hunch about not going into the operations office. I never felt too safe with planes landing right over my head with just a fairly thin - it's not armor-plated - deck, it's a fairly thin flight deck, because there had been cases where - well, there was another case earlier where a fighter folded its wings and apparently in the process of folding contact was made or something, or the wings got back and the guns would be pointing straight down, instead of forward. See, the wing rotates as it comes back. A couple of machine guns went off, 50 caliber, and went right down through the deck and into the flag secretary's office and punched holes into his new operation order that he was just about to distribute! So it wasn't a very healthy place to be when planes were landing. Those were rare occasions, but they still did happen. You say I had a hunch, but maybe it was experience that kept me from going there at the time.

Q: But the bending down to get the cigarette was sheer miracle!

Adm. T.: Yes, I sure bent down at the right time! Anyway, we had a pretty bad day that day.

The Hancock was not put out of action. It was a very short time before they had run patchwork material across that bomb hole in the flight deck and the ship was operational again. They could have taxied around it, but it was fixed up very quickly so the Hancock didn't miss any strikes. The Ticonderoga, I believe it was, did have to go back to Ulithi to get some emergency repairs, or they sent her back to Ulithi. Her main job for the moment was over. The Lingayen Gulf landing was a success and we were out of the South China Sea.

I'm going to refer later to the circumstance which existed when those two ships were hit. We left some fields uncovered in order to carry out the directive of first priority on the shipping, on merchant ships or whatever other ships we could find.

Q: Do you mean you're going to relate to that in connection with the too-detailed directions for operations from high authority?

Adm. T.: Yes.

Q: So you're almost ready to leave the war area, at least the forward area, at this point aren't you? And go back to Pearl Harbor?

Adm. T.: Yes.

Q: If we are, before we do that, I wanted to ask you - I don't want to cut off any part of that story, but if you are ready -

Adm. T.: Let me just check a minute to be sure I haven't left anything out. I think that's about enough on the South China Sea. It was a very fascinating experience. I mentioned that we didn't have any star sights, but when we started to come out the Balintang Channel showed up right where we expected it to be and we came through.

Q: We have omitted, and maybe it's okay to omit it, the typhoon Cobra during December. I know that the typhoon itself and probably all of the aspects of it have been well reported - in fact whole books have been written about the typhoon itself. I wonder, since you went through it, if you have any personal observations that should be put in your biography?

Adm. T.: Typhoons are pretty bad things in any event, but when you don't know where they're going they can get even worse. I would like to say in the first place that this typhoon did one of the things that a typhoon sometimes does very rarely, it did a loop in its course - it did a little loop. So at the time of this loop it was very difficult to determine what track the typhoon was really on.

Q: Were you aware of everything that was going on at the time? Was your job such that permitted or required you to know all of the aspects of the maneuvering at the time?

Adm. T.: No. That was pretty much in the hands of Admiral Halsey and his staff and the weathermen all round the Pacific had a hand in it. I was aware but I had no authority to say, do this or do that. I was in on it with our aerologist, Admiral McCain's staff aerologist, on the estimate of what the track was and the recommendation that Admiral McCain sent to Admiral Halsey of what course the fleet should pursue in order to minimize the damage or avoid the typhoon.

Q: Did Admiral McCain advise Admiral Halsey?

Adm. T.: Yes, and sent information to CinCPac, Admiral Nimitz. Well, Admiral Nimitz with his weathermen estimated what track we should take to avoid the typhoon. He put out what he thought should be done, but it was finally up to Admiral Halsey to decide when we had different recommendations. Admiral Halsey thought we should go in a direction about $90°$

from the one that Admiral Nimitz recommended, and Admiral McCain was about 180° different from Nimitz and 90° away from the direction that Halsey wanted to go.

Q: Did you participate in Admiral McCain's recommendation?

Adm. T.: Yes.

Q: I'm interested because this man again in Fast Carriers speaks of McCain being of no value at all!

Adm. T.: Apparently he's been listening to someone who had, shall we say, a sour grapes attitude on the part that McCain was playing in the war.

Q: I don't want to get into Admiral McCain's biography either but - I think it's interesting.

Adm. T.: No, but there was no better commander that I have ever known than John Sidney McCain. He would listen to people. He wasn't adamant. He wasn't argumentative, and when his boss, Halsey, told him to do something he'd do it. Sometimes we would make recommendations that Halsey change his direction, and I know that sometimes Halsey wanted to but he had orders from Nimitz and so he didn't. Other times he took it upon himself to do so.

Q: I didn't want to pursue the thing but apparently that's a whole lot of story about the typhoon and I was interested because you almost get the implication that he had asked him for advice and didn't get any!

Adm. T.: Oh, yes, he got a definite course. Of course, this is Monday morning quarterbacking now, but had we gone on the course that McCain recommended we wouldn't have come as close to the eye of the hurricane.

Q: Which was you, in effect, because you helped make the estimate.

Adm. T.: No, I don't think that I had so much to do with making that estimate. We looked at the maps and listened to a long exposition by the aerologist, who's the expert in that business, and discussed the pros and cons, and if you are going to get caught by the typhoon what course you should be on, all the considerations we could think of, and then came to a course that we thought would be better than any other, and made that recommendation to Halsey. Halsey got that one and he got one from Nimitz, which was $180°$ different. He considered all of these and it was discussion back and forth. Finally he decided what course he was going on and which he went. That was his prerogative. The man sitting ashore back in Pearl Harbor certainly should not tell him, right 20 degrees rudder, and certainly shouldn't tell him what course to go on, when he's the man on the spot. In other words, the buck passes up to the fleet commander at sea. If, for any reason, Halsey had been somewhere else, say, with a bombardment group and not in the same part of the ocean as McCain, it would have been McCain's job to finally decide. But McCain only recommended, and Nimitz actually recommended to Halsey and Halsey said, no, I'm not going to take either one of those courses, I'm going this way, and everybody said he was better than some of the fighter directors at intercepting when he intercepted the typhoon, instead of an enemy fighter, but that was kind of poor joke, I thought.

Anyway, there's one more thing I must say about the loss of those four destroyers - I believe it was four. It was urgent that they get refueled, especially if we were going to have a long siege of bad weather and those typhoons cover a large area and you can't get out of them if you once hit them. So it was very gravely desired to get all the destroyers fueled. These four had emptied ballast water and they were very light and riding very high and were far more topheavy than in any other condition, and they were caught suddenly by a rapidly increasing wind and couldn't get the water back in and couldn't get fuel. They were ordered to do this but couldn't do it. That's the reason they were lost. Other destroyers of a similar type that were properly ballasted - or maybe had already refueled or weren't going to refuel quite so soon - didn't pump out the water and weren't going to until later were fortunate and these four were very unfortunate.

Q: Where were you?

Adm. T.: In the Hancock.

Q: But were you right in the eye of the storm?

Adm. T.: No. We didn't catch exactly the eye, this task group. You see, the task groups covered quite a large area - fifty miles, about a 50 mile front we had.

Q: What was Admiral McCain's reaction to the loss of those destroyers?

Adm. T.: Well, it was just like the loss of anything else. He felt it very personally. Whenever a pilot was lost it was not just a sad thing but it seemed like a personal loss to him and it took a lot out of him, anything like that.

Q: Now we're on our way back to Pearl. Right?

Adm. T.: After these two carriers were hit on the 21st of January, Admiral McCain requested permission from Com Third Fleet to attack airfields instead of shipping and harbors.

Permission was granted and Com Task Force 38 directed that all flights concentrate on enemy airfields with aircraft as the first priority target.

Q: How long had you had your other priority of shipping? Do you recall?

Adm. T.: I don't recall, but I think it was that one day.

Q: In any case it was at the time when the ships were hit?

Adm. T.: Yes. We had shipping as the first-priority target and so we had to put - to be sure you got every ship you saw, and this took away from getting airplanes on the field and undoubtedly left some not well enough covered and the enemy slipped through.

Q: That's a startling example of what happened when you didn't keep them covered, isn't it?

Adm. T.: When we didn't work that blanket system. By this time we felt that the enemy's ships, including his navy, were really no longer a threat, but the aircraft obviously were a threat. That was just painfully apparent.

So now we go to Ulithi.

Q: Ulithi or Pearl?

Adm. T.: We went to Ulithi and then went from there to Pearl, and Admiral McCain and I came on back to the United States.

Q: I have a date of January 25th for Admiral Halsey being relieved by Admiral Spruance.

Adm. T.: Yes, and McCain was relieved by Mitscher. Then Admiral McCain went back to Washington, D.C. and he took me with him. We went to see Admiral Ernie King, who was ComInch, and it was a very pleasant visit. I didn't think Admiral McCain would take me into Admiral King's office with him but he did and I was very pleased that he would do that. I thought they'd probably want to talk about something that only they were cleared to discuss. But they had a good conversation. Admiral King had a great admiration for Admiral McCain. I knew and, of course, Admiral McCain knew that there were other officers who wanted very much to have that prize job of Commander Fast Carrier Task Force. Mitscher and McCain were alternating and there was a lot of talk started such as "wasn't it about time somebody else had a chance to do that." And McCain didn't want - because, you see, he'd had this experience and he was a good fighter. This was where he wanted to be and he felt that to give somebody else the job totally inexperienced in that sort of thing would be like changing to an inexperienced horse in the middle of a race - or in midstream, so to speak. Admiral King indicated, not directly but by what he said concerning the future plans, that he wasn't about to relieve Admiral McCain.

Q: Was that part of the conversation when you were with them?

Adm. T.: Yes.

Q: That's extremely interesting.

Adm. T.: It was a very cordial visit and pleasant and, at the same time, serious because they were talking about the job to be done from now on.

Q: I'm impelled to refer again to Clark Reynolds' book, at the risk of seeming to talk more about Admiral King, but it refers to you, because he states again that "Slew McCain was nothing more than a deputy to Halsey. He never enjoyed tactical command in any crucial situation and relied heavily on his operations officer, Jimmy Thach, for tactical innovations."

Adm. T.: This is not at all true. Talk about McCain not being given - he had tactical command _all_ the time. The fleet commander had overall command but we (Admiral McCain) gave the tactical orders to the task force. This sounds like more sniping at McCain and it just isn't true, furthermore, remember, the time off Formosa, talk about a critical tactical situation, when we had those two damaged cruisers and they left McCain up there to protect them and get them out, just one task group against - right near Formosa, between Formosa and Luzon, where they could hit us from all angles and they did their best. McCain certainly had a responsible job then - I mean it was a critical situation.

Furthermore, all during the Philippines campaign McCain had tactical command. Apparently this young man did a lot of looking up references but he didn't do his research into how a fleet and a task force operate. The tactical commander always when he puts out a signal or a dispatch for an operation he includes the fleet commander as one of the information addressees. In other words, he informs the fleet commander what he's planning, which direction he's going to go, and so forth. There's a continual exchange all the time between them. Halsey was wonderful as a fleet commander, the best, as far as I'm concerned, and I experienced it under both Spruance and Halsey.

As I related earlier, this business about having to turn on the lights, that would never have happened if Halsey had been there, because Halsey had a better appreciation of the fact that you should run toward the enemy when you're going to have to run into the wind away from him the next day and you'd get too far away.

Thach #5 - 440

Q: You're speaking about the Marianas?

Adm. T.: Yes, when Mitscher had to turn on all the lights. Also, there were things that came from Halsey that you would prefer that he'd done it a little differently and if they were serious enough McCain wrote out a long message describing why and often Halsey would change, once he understood what was in our minds, and sometimes Halsey would want to change the target because he would get intelligence, maybe from CinCPac or maybe from somewhere else, on what looked like a good target - maybe the night before we were going to strike and send all these 1,000 airplanes in, and if you change a significant number of airplanes from one place to another, it affects everything else. You might uncover a field that you were going to cover.

Admiral McCain and I went over one time to Admiral Halsey's flagship to describe what had been happening, that if he wanted to re-designate the priority of targets, please do it early, don't wait till the last few hours because the pilots have to start getting briefed about where they're going in the morning, and if he changes it at midnight this just causes one heck of a problem. We went over to explain that to him. He understood and told his staff, "Now, look, we'll do no more of this last-minute changing. We can handle a late change, for example, if there's something like the sudden appearance of a threat, of course, we're flexible - but just because some intelligence tells you that there may be a better target than one of the many that you're hitting, don't do a change too late because it hurts the pilots. They have to stay up longer and get up sooner and so on." And so he didn't do it any more. We had disagreements with him, this was one of them, but he changed.

Q: Obviously they had a relationship which —

Adm. T.: Oh, marvelous rapport. I have photographs of them when they didn't know they were being taken, and they were just wonderful close friends. You know, you don't make sort of kidding remarks when you're having a fight with somebody, you're serious. You're not friendly enough to make light of certain things and do a little kidding job. Well, Halsey was doing that with McCain and McCain back to him sometimes, and they'd laugh about it. They were very friendly and very cordial, and every time I went over there there was no inkling that there was not perfectly wonderful rapport between Halsey and McCain.

I just wish people who write books would do a little better research.

Q: It's interesting, however, and I'd like your comment on the fact that he did rely heavily on you. Do you want to amplify that? Or comment on it?

Adm. T.: Well, I was a fairly experienced aviator by that time and he picked me for a job that he should rely heavily on. As a flag officer in tactical command of a task group or a task force, I relied heavily on my operations officer, just as he did on me, because he should be kept free to consider things of greater strategy than some of the details that I had to get into, and I never did anything concerning policy or of great significance without his approval.

Q: But he did give you, as I read our conversation, a great deal of latitude to put into effect the things that you wanted to do?

Adm. T.: He did, and I had no proof that they would work, except what I thought was logic.

Q: I thought there were several things in your career, especially in this part of your career, that were interesting and it seemed to me that - extraordinary in that you are innovative and creative and to have the opportunity to implement them that Admiral McCain gave you, and further -

Adm. T.: Just lucky, I guess!

Q: No, and the third one was that you not only implemented them but you would send the strike. You not only had the authority to put them into operation, but you did in fact carry them out, which is kind of unusual, it would appear to me, in a position such as yours.

Adm. T.: Well, I think the best solution to problems comes from people who are doing them. And remember a long time ago I said Admiral McCain was wonderful, he said if I wanted to learn how to tie a bowline on a bight, I will ask a bo'sun's mate. He relied on people who were doing the things and who'd had the experience. Yet it all had to make sense to him. I wanted to do some things - and I'll tell you about one of them later - that he didn't let me do. Now I realize that he was right.

Q: Also, you've told me that you would actually send a strike?

Adm. T.: Oh, yes, and I would hold them if - one morning, well, I'll get into this later when we're up off Hokkaido.

Q: That is kind of unique, is it not, that first you were in a position where you didn't have so much rank but you had the ideas, you had the authority to carry them out, and you in fact did do it, not just say somebody else do it? That was a unique combination of circumstances.

Adm. T.: Well, I considered that was my job and Admiral McCain agreed, and when something happened suddenly such as times when we were just about ready to launch all these airplanes before daylight, absolutely black, and I would get some information, maybe the aerologist would tell me the spread is getting down to nothing and conditions are right for fog, I'd stop launch, tell all these task group commanders to hold everything until further notice. Then I'd run in and tell Admiral McCain what I'd done, and he said, "Okay, if it looks dangerous to you, I don't want to do it."

Q: I think it's interesting, too, that story about Admiral King, that he indicated in your presence that he had no intention of replacing him.

Adm. T.: Yes, I thought that was interesting. I didn't expect to hear that. I didn't expect him to replace him with somebody else, but I didn't think he'd talk about it in front of me, but they did.

Q: They both must have had high regard for you.

Adm. T.: Well, you know, Ernie King treated me like a father, like he was my father, when I flew this seaplane to Panama, and then McCain certainly treated me like a very close member of his family.

Thach #5 - 445

Q: That's wonderful. How long were you gone on leave?

Adm. T.: We just went on leave a fairly short time. We went to Washington and I never consider going to Washington being on leave!

Q: Oh, no. I'll rephrase it and say, how long were you gone from the Pacific?

Adm. T.: We came back in - at the end of June. We came back from the United States after a week. I don't remember how long we were in the U.S.. Those times are kind of vague because not much was going on. I liked it better when we were in the Pacific. I think I did have a week's leave and then we went back to Pearl Harbor, that hole in the ground, to start planning the next series of events.

Q: My dates show that Admiral Halsey relieved Admiral Spruance 26-27 May of 1945. Do you have any recollection of that particular event?

Adm. T.: No, that would be the same time that Admiral McCain relieved Admiral Mitscher and the staff shifted. Except this, that Jimmy Flatley was the operations officer for Admiral Mitscher, my counterpart with Admiral Mitscher, and we, of course, have been very close all our Navy lives, and this was a very fortunate thing because we knew how each other was thinking, we worked very well together, very closely, and whenever he discovered something that he thought would be useful to us he passed it to me immediately, whether I was at Pearl Harbor or where, and he was on the line, and I did the same thing. Of course, when we actually made a change of command and McCain relieved Mitscher, why, we would take their entire reports and study them carefully and any changes that they had made in the task force instructions and we would do likewise, although there were some little differences in the task force instructions - operating instructions - because of the difference between Mitscher and McCain. Mitscher wasn't very quick to pick up a new idea, a new untried idea, for a solution to a problem such as the kamikazes.

Q: I was going to ask you about your comment - maybe it's appropriate here - that the kamikazes seem to have been somewhat controlled by your strategy in the Philippines, and yet the toll from kamikazes was just overwhelming at Okinawa, and I wondered if Admiral Mitscher could not use the same strategy or tactics that had been developed by the Third Fleet? Or do you know?

Adm. T.: To a degree but not as much as we did, and I don't remember hearing of him practicing this Moose Trap business, although I think that Jimmy Flatley did persuade him to go to the three-strike system when they were striking an area. But there he was in more of a defensive position at Okinawa and the Moose Trap disposition would have helped him a lot, I think, but he didn't use it the way that we did. I know from talking with Jimmy Flatley that he was all in favor of it and little by little he would attempt to persuade Mitscher, but Mitscher was reluctant to take up new ideas, just as he was in the night fighter business. He was frankly dragging his feet on accepting night fighters. He was an old-time aviator and in my opinion he figured that he had the experience within himself and he never took to new ideas or wasn't able to recognize them as well as McCain.

Q: Were there so many more fields in the Okinawa area that it wouldn't have been practical to have the blanket?

Adm. T.: There were fewer number of fields in the Okinawa area. Furthermore, any place in the world is practical to do it, as far as you can reach and wherever you attack. You can use this and should if you want to keep the enemy from getting off the field and coming out and attacking you. He did put out the destroyer pickets to give them warning, but I think part of the reason he got hit pretty badly was because he was prevented from using mobility. He was pretty much attached to the beach by edict from higher authority. However, all the more reason to use Moosetrap and the Blue Blanket.

Q: Admiral Halsey had to do that, too, for a while, didn't he?

Adm. T.: For a while, but I have a little note in my notebook that says "are we going to be tied to Okinawa forever" with an exclamation point. That I put in after we'd been there only a week, but we were all chomping at the bit, including Halsey, to get away from there and to keep the enemy from hurting us by attacking him rather than being on a defensive position. We wanted to utilize all of the basic fantastic things that the fast carrier task force has and should be exploited. When they are exploited, we usually don't get hurt. We must pay attention to the basic principles of warfare. If you have mobility and don't use it you're likely to get hurt. But if you violate a principle of warfare, such as keeping a task force tied in one spot, it puts it in the same category as land-based air. You know where it is so you can plan to hit it next week. But when the carriers were operated the way they should be operated you can't do that. We didn't want to be in the category of land-based air because they're too easy to knock over.

Q: When Halsey was detached from Okinawa he did move freely up and down the coast of Japan, didn't he?

Adm. T.: Absolutely. We got loose and did a much better job on the enemy. Before we get into that, I might mention that while we were in Leyte Gulf - this was between the time we were freed from Okinawa and went back up to hit the main islands of Japan - Admiral McCain went to Manila and called on General MacArthur and he took me with him. We also had an appointment to see Commodore W. A. Sullivan, who is now retired Rear Admiral Sullivan living in La Jolla, I believe. Sullivan was doing the job of salvaging all those sunken ships in Manila Harbor and he did the same thing in Europe. He had a fantastic ability and technique for doing this so, of course, Admiral McCain was anxious to see Manila Harbor because we'd attacked ships in it so often and we'd made this and other harbors in the Philippines, some of the smaller ones, so crowded with sunken ships that you couldn't get anything but a small craft in there. That's one of the things that worked to our advantage in the Lingayen Gulf - they hadn't had anything very big in some of those small harbors. Of course, Manila Harbor was a large one and it was pretty crowded underneath the surface along the piers, and he was very anxious to spend most of the day with Commodore Sullivan, but we had this appointment to call on MacArthur.

So I went to MacArthur's office with him at the specific time that he was going to call on him. General MacArthur kept Vice Admiral McCain cooling his heels in an outer office for a full forty-five minutes. It seemed like longer than that to me but I'm sure it was at least forty-five minutes, and the more this went on the madder I got, and I mentioned it to

McCain. I said, "What's he trying to do to you, keeping you sitting out here? This is not right at all." He said, "Maybe he's got something very important. Maybe he's talking to Washington or something." Well, I don't think he was. Nobody came out of his office, and McCain finally went in. McCain, I think, wanted to take me in there but by then he was so irked that he just walked in himself. That, I thought, was a thing that should never be done - to keep a task force commander who had helped MacArthur so much and saved him in the Leyte business when MacArthur had to ask for us to come back three or four times, and the first time he'd seen him, he shouldn't have kept him waiting that long. I've been in positions where I had a lot of things hot on the fire going and I wouldn't keep any officer waiting if he had an appointment with me. If he was a lieutenant or a lieutenant commander and I couldn't see him right away I would usually walk out, shake hands with him real quick, and say, "I've got something real hot. I'm going to have to delay but I'll be with you as soon as I can. I want to apologize for not keeping the appointment." He didn't do that. He just let him sit there for forty-five minutes. But, of course, MacArthur felt that everybody was quite a few notches beneath him, so he was, I understand, prone to do this.

Well, I railed about this all the way over to see Sullivan and McCain finally just laughed at me. He said, "You can't afford to let things like that affect your actions." He was afraid I was going to open my mouth and tell somebody about it.

Anyway, we went to see Sullivan. We had to delay seeing him and in the meantime I had called and said that McCain was being held up in MacArthur's office. Sullivan understood. It was fantastic what Sullivan had discovered. He knew that ships had been sunk alongside a pier so he raised one, and then he discovered a ship right directly underneath it and so he raised that one, and then, believe it or not, he told us he discovered a third one in the same place underneath that one. This third one was an old galleon of some sort that had been sunk I don't know who many years before, and his divers found some pieces of eight - Spanish pieces of eight - and Commodore Sullivan gave Admiral McCain two or three of these and Admiral McCain gave me one, which I still have.

Q: Oh, that's wonderful.

Adm. T.: I never thought I'd see a piece of eight! In more places than one the ships were two and three deep, and the harbor was quite cleared up.

Well, we flew on back and landed - flew back in a seaplane and landed at Leyte Gulf, then got the task force underway for the raids on the home islands of Japan. When we got into the Ryukyus, Kyushu, we discovered a new type of Japanese fighter in there. I forget what we called it at the time. Not only that, the Japanese pilots were far more aggressive than any we'd seen since the early days at the Battle of Midway and such, and their aircraft had certain performance advantages over our Corsair and F-6F. So they shot down a few of our pilots. This was an interesting thing and we wondered how many of these they had. Also, it seemed to be an indication that now that you hit their homeland, why, they were going to use the best pilots they had to try to keep you off.

We'd had some trouble - as I mentioned before, they camouflaged airplanes and hid them and couldn't get them off the ground. They were doing this in such a way that, for example, they would take a damaged aircraft that was all shot up anyway and was no more use and put it in a prominent place near the field along with some maybe dummy aircraft and mass antiaircraft fire around it as a flak trap. I didn't like the idea of our just going down and getting the flak traps. Most of the time the photograph would show that this was a damaged aircraft and you could avoid it, but the Japanese hadn't been coming up into the air and we knew we could get them better by fighting in the air than - and we'd take fewer losses - than we would lose if we had to go down continuously to low altitude for strafing a field with aircraft in the bushes.

So I viewed this new development with mixed feelings. In the first place, I was glad to see that they were finally coming up and wanting to fight, but I was a little concerned because our pilots had gotten into some bad habits and when they saw a Jap airplane they'd head for it head-on with no tactical formation that was very good for fighting and they would try to beat each other to the kill, and that's when they fell into this trap and some of them got hurt. Well, I decided about that time that maybe I'd better lead a fighter strike and I planned it good. I got this group commander all set and I picked out the area we'd go and the targets, hoping that we'd get them up into the air again and I'd take a better look at these things (the new Japanese fighters) and hopefully learn something about their performance. I figured that I was maybe a little more experienced observer than some of the people that had been going. I got this thing all planned and everything then I went to Admiral McCain and told him what I wanted to do. He said, not only no, but hell no! He said, "You're restricted to this task force." And he kind of laughed when he said that.

I said, "I thought maybe I could learn something for us that we need to know."

He said, "I know you're just itching to get in a fight because you haven't been in one in a long time." And I said, "That, I'll admit, is true." But he said, "I'll tell you why you can't go. You know too much. You have highly secret information that none of these pilots have and if you were shot down over Japan and they picked you up, there are ways of making people talk and they'd find out what you knew. So, as much as I'd like to do it, I just cannot permit you to go on a strike."

I understood this but I was sort of disappointed.

Q: Had you been on a fighter strike since Midway?

Adm. T.: No, not since I'd been in a squadron.

Q: That's what I thought. Well, it would have been dangerous anyway.

Adm. T.: Well -

Q: I would think that keeping in practice would be very effective?

Adm. T.: True, but I had flown the various types off and on and had quite a bit of experience and knew that I could do it. It might have been a bad idea, no matter. Maybe it would have been too risky. I failed to get that one across to my boss.

Q: Is that the incident when you said that you - he almost always approved the things you did, but one he didn't?

Adm. T.: That's the one he didn't.

We began to reach much further into the Japanese homeland and were able on one occasion to go clear across and hit the ships in the harbors on the Sea of Japan. One place I remember, Mazaru on the west coast of Honshu, and there were some good targets in there. You see, those west coast targets on the Sea of Japan and some of the places in the inland sea were about the only places left where shipping could come in and they could get any supplies from the China coast, which they were doing all the time, although the supplying was getting weaker and weaker, as I pointed out, and we felt that except for those targets we shouldn't concentrate too much on shipping.

One thing happened in one of the attacks on ships at Mazaru. Two of our pilots were shot down and they bailed out and got into a rubber boat in the water. So there were two row boats in the water. They got a little distance away from the shoreline, but there they were, and we didn't have any submarines anywhere close so we managed to get a big boat, a PBY, and decided to send it with an escort right across Japan, the poor old lumbering PBY, over into this harbor and pick up those two pilots. The PBY crew was anxious to go. They came from the nearest place they could and they were escorted all the way across. By the time they got there, they had to land in two different places. The first pilot they saw and picked him up, but the second one, they had to take off and look for him and finally found him but when they landed there they were being shot at - the rubber boat was being shot at from the shore, it had drifted. But they picked him up and made a second takeoff. By that time they'd used up most of their jato (jet assisted take off rockets) and they started back.

We knew it was going to be dark by the time they got back to the east coast of Japan. Also the PBY had flown quite a long distance to get up there in the first place and he reported that he wasn't going to have enough gas to get back to his base. We gave him our position and said he'd have enough gas to get to us. He said, yes, I think I can make that, so we said, "You come to this task force and we'll take care of you." So he did, but he got there around 9:30 or 10:00 p.m.. Fortunately, the sea wasn't too rough. I designated four destroyers to get in a line into the wind and shine their searchlights out on the starboard bow to kind of light a water runway for him and turn on their lights so that he could use them as a help in his depth perception to land on the water in the ocean, and I directed the destroyers to pick up not only the downed pilots but the whole crew and sink the PBY, which they did.

Then I went to Admiral McCain and we talked about it, and he said, "Don't you think the pilot ought to be recommended for a Navy Cross?" And I said, "That's just what I was thinking of." This young man was an Army Air Corps pilot. The Navy had given them some PBYs and he was in the Army Air Corps rescue outfit, yet he had come all the way out there to rescue two of our people, knowing full well they weren't going to get back. He wasn't sure where he was going to go but he was going to pick up those people and get back as far as he could. He was ready to land in the ocean anywhere just so he wasn't on Japan. We brought him back to the task force and the recommendation went in and was acted on very rapidly and he received his Navy Cross, which I felt very good about.

Q: I've never heard that story before. It's the kind of thing that would happen in the movies, but you'd be sure it couldn't really happen.

Adm. T.: Well, a lot of things happen. Like I've said often, "This doesn't happen in true life, it only happens in the movies," and yet it was happening! Truth is sometimes stranger than fiction.

Q: It only happened in the Navy!

Adm. T.: We had some seaplane tenders that would go from place to place as we took over islands and territories and he came from one of those way down south and it took him a long time to get there, we were hoping that the pilots would still be in their rubber boats and not captured, but apparently they weren't seen until just about the time he got the second one because they did land not right in the harbor but out a little bit, but one of them obviously landed closer to the beach than the other one. But there were ships and shore batteries firing at them and at the PBY all the time he was in there picking up the pilot and after he took off.

Q: How many were in his crew?

Adm. T.: Oh, I'd think about six. A PBY crew in the Navy would have a little different number than in the Air Force because they flew different missions. But I'd imagine there were at least six - they might have had eight crew in there because they'd want a man for each gun, but they wouldn't have a bomb sight in it, so they wouldn't need a bombardeer.

Q: Did you ever know?

Adm. T.: I knew it then at the time. I've tried very hard to remember.

Q: If it should happen to come to you, as sometimes happens, please be sure to add it to the manuscript, as I know you will.

Adm. T.: Yes.

During this period off the home islands we stayed so long some of the pilots got very familiar, especially with the area in Honshu and around Tokyo that they felt they ought to vote in the next election! But the area up in Hokkaido hadn't been touched very much and they had some choice airfields up there and had been relatively free from any air attack, so we decided we'd go up there and make a sweep. One of the main reasons we need to go up there was because - you remember the baka bomb which was a rocket type airplane designed for the kamikazes' special attack corps - the baka airplane, rocket-powered, was designed so that it had to be carried underneath the wing of a Betty or some large plane. We knew there were Bettys that carried them. Although, I don't know of a case where a carrier was hit by a baka bomb but some of our destroyers had, but being rocket-powered it naturally doesn't have conventional fuel - the rocket doesn't last too long - they had about four rockets in the tail of this thing to propel it when it dropped off the airplane and they could cut them in all at once or they could come in in sequence to go further but maybe not quite so fast.

At any rate, the Bettys would have to bring the baka bombs, say, within sight of a target, of the task force, before they would release them and hope they could get there before they ran out of rocket fuel, but they went over 400 or 500 miles an hour. I don't know its exact speed but it was a very streamlined little job and was rocket-powered so it must have come pretty close to the speed of sound - underneath it, subsonic, of course, but fast. Well, we learned that at the field in Hokkaido where they had these Bettys they were specially configured to carry the baka and where they did some training, and we wanted to hit that, which we did and hit a jackpot of Betty bombers and burned most of them.

Then we did a similar blanket treatment to all the fields up there. We also caught these train ferries between Honshu and Hokkaido and destroyed a number of those. I think we just about cut that ferry line. Working on transportation is, to me, a far quicker way to deny the enemy the ability to produce something. In fact, if you can cut his transportation by hitting trains, trucks, boats, ships, and anything that moves, the antiaircraft batteries are going to run out of ammunition because they aren't going to carry them by hand for miles and miles, so it helps you all the way round. This is one of the reasons we hit the train ferries.

We ran into an interesting circumstance of weather up there. The further north you go the worse the weather is, although it was getting to be summertime there was a lot of heavy fog and so on in that area. And about this time a typhoon was coming. We had a pretty good track of this typhoon and decided that instead of running as far away from it as we could we would stick around pretty close to the coast of Japan and wait and determined whether it was going to curve in and hit the coast or whether it was going to come up where we were and we would dodge it one way or another. This might seem strange after the unfortunate experience we had with the previous typhoon, but if the military men are going to use the weather to their advantage they've got to have enough courage to do something when they are in a position to have real good reports on the progress of the typhoon, which we were. It was coming right up a line where we had stations that would report it and we could tell each day and each hour what its track was. So we decided to use this typhoon and we couldn't go too far away and if it did curve in, as is normal, and hit somewhere on the islands, we'd let the typhoon hit and we'd go in right behind it and hit them again. This is the way it worked out. This was a rather classic use of the weather to work on the enemy and they weren't ready for us. It was, you might say, rather a dull day as far as enemy aircraft in the air were concerned because they didn't think we could be so close on the heels of the typhoon.

Q: You spoke of water temperature being used to advantage off Hokkaido. Is that the same thing?

Adm. T.: No. This was another use of weather information to operate and take advantage of the weather situation - or rather, prevent the weather from hurting you when it was maybe covering the enemy.

INDEX

to

Volume I

Reminiscences of Admiral John S. Thach
U. S. Navy (Retired)

AERIAL GUNNER: Thach comments on certain techniques to employ, p. 54-6;

ALEUTIANS: p. 86-7; Thach's adventures in the island chain, (June-July 1935), p. 86 ff;

ARNOLD, Rear Admiral Murr Edward: Air Officer of YORKTOWN - briefs air groups before Midway, p. 227-8; p. 235;

B-17s: how they figured in Battle of Midway - Thach's meeting with press in Boston and Washington, D.C., p. 301 ff;

BAKA BOMB: p. 389-90; p. 459-60;

BAUGHMAN, Commodore Cortlant C.: skipper of USS CINCINNATI (1936), p. 96 ff; story of Baughman and towing of a sleeve for firing from ship, p. 102-4; the Ollie Bomb, p. 104-5; p. 108;

BETTY: the first sketch of this Japanese bomber of WWII, p. 198-9; destruction of planes on field in Hokkaido - planes configured to carry baka bombs, p. 459-60;

BOEING AIRCRAFT: early plane types, p. 59-60;

BOGAN, VADM GERALD: p. 11p. p. 34; p. 37; p. 49; p. 50;

BRETT, Capt. James Henry Jr.: in command of torpedo planes from LEXINGTON, p. 202 ff; his use of glider plane knowledge to get his planes over the Owen Stanley range, p. 204-6;

BROWN, Admiral Charles R. (Cat.): p. 166; p. 168;

BURKE, Admiral Arleigh A.: Thach assigned as special assistant to Burke who was Chief of Staff to Mitscher, p. 317 ff; p. 325-6; p. 353;

BURROUGHS, Everett: gunnery officer - staff of Adm. Halsey, p. 164-5;

USS CABOT: p. 321;

USS CALIFORNIA: p. 30;

USS CANBERRA: cruiser hit by Japanese torpedo plane out from Formosa, p. 370; p. 373;

CANTON, China: air attacks on during South China Sea Operation, p. 420-1;

CAST RECOVERY METHOD: p. 105-7;

CATAPULT TAKE-OFFS: p. 107-8;

USS CINCINNATI: p. 96 ff; p. 109;

CLOSE AIR SUPPORT: Thach's comments on value of, p. 336-8;

COCO SOLO, Canal Zone: p. 78-93; p. 109 ff;

COOK, Rear Admiral A. B.: Commanded Naval Air Advanced Training Command, Pensacola (1942), p. 285; p. 292-4;

DIBB, Lt. Ram: wingman for Thach in VF-3 at Battle of Midway, p. 247; p. 250; p. 269;

DISNEY, Walt: his cooperation in developing animated training films for the Navy at Jacksonville, Florida, p. 284 ff; detailed process of making the films for Jacksonville, p. 286-9;

DOWNING, Lt. Art: guides SS to rescue of pilot in Morotai harbor, p. 354-5; p. 388;

DOYLE, Admiral Arthur (Artie): p. 383;

DUCKWORTH, VADM Herbert Spencer (Ducky): p. 40; p. 48-49; p. 52-3; air officer on LEXINGTON, p. 199-200;

EMILY: a Japanese patrol plane in WWII, p. 187-8; p. 192;

USS ENTERPRISE: VF-3 goes aboard, p. 158-9; Battle of Midway, p. 226 ff;

FELT, Admiral H. D. (Don): p. 133; p. 145;

FISHER, Bubbles: fighter pilot with VF-6, p. 44-5;

FITCH, Admiral Aubrey Wray: in command of carrier division - SARATOGA is flagship, p. 175; his attitude towards order to withdraw from Wake Island area, p. 176; p. 209;

FLETCHER, Admiral Frank Jack: Commander, Task Force 17 in Battle of Midway, p. 226 ff;

FLATLEY, Vice Admiral James Henry Jr. (Jimmy): p. 156; p. 212-213; p. 282; his idea for use of animated films for training purposes, p. 282; p. 284-5; Thach recommends him as Operations Officer to Mitscher when Mitscher returns to command of Fast Carriers, p. 406; ease in making transition from Mitscher to McCain because of close friendship of Flatley and Thach, p. 445-7;

FORMOSA: air attack on in preparation for Leyte Gulf landing, p. 359; Japanese torpedo plane attack on the CANBERRA and HOUSTON, p. 370-1; attacks on in preparation for Linguayan and Luzon landings, p. 410-11;

FRAN: name given Japanese Torpedo bomber (version of the earlier EMILY) p. 313-4;

USS GANNET: BIRD class tender, p. 87;

GAYLOR, Admiral Noel A.M.: p. 192-3; 205-6; p. 301-2;

GEORGE: name given a high speed Japanese fighter that appeared late in 1944, p. 377;

GRAFMUELLER, Lt. Albert M.: in charge of logistics planning on staff of Admiral McCain, p. 341-2;

GRUMMAN: early plane types, p. 59-60;

GUAM: amphibious landing on, p. 336-8;

GULF OF TEHUANTEPIC: p. 122; p. 127;

HALSEY, Fleet Admiral Wm. F.Jr.: p. 159-160; p. 219-20; p. 357-8; Thach's defense of Halsey's action in San Bernadino Straits, p. 387-8; p. 407; p. 410; p. 423-4; the typhoon, p. 431 ff; Thach's comments on Halsey's good relations with McCain, p. 438-41; relieves Spruance again in May, 1945, p. 445;

USS HANCOCK: damaged by a bomb from one of her planes landing on deck (1945), p. 427-9;

HARVEY, Lt. Comdr. Sid: p. 96; p. 138-9; p. 145;

HEAN, Comdr. J. H.: Ordnance Officer on staff of Admiral McCain, p. 342;

HELL DIVERS: film made by MGM with VF-1 cooperating and starring Wallace Beery and Clark Gable with Duckworth, Southwick and Thach featured, p. 40-41;

HIRUNA - Japanese BB: reported sunk by Colin Kelly in B-17, p. 304-5; p. 307;

HOKKAIDO, Japan: T.F. 38 attack on targets in mid 1945, p. 459-61; Bettys configured to carry baka bomb, p. 459-60; train ferries, p. 460; T.F. use of typhoon to follow in and attack enemy installations on the ground, p. 461;

HONG KONG: air attacks on during South China Sea Operation, p. 420-1;

HOOVER, Admiral John (Genial John): p. 133-5; p. 145;

USS HORNET: her participation in Battle of Midway, p. 226 ff; p. 258;

USS HOUSTON: cruiser hit by Japanese torpedo plane out from Formosa, p. 370; p. 373;

JACK PATROL: p. 395-6; origin of the name, p. 396;

JAPANESE MAINLAND: T.F. 38 discovers new, aggressive fighters over mainland - a new plane and new techniques, p. 451-5; raids on Hokkaido, p. 458; attack on special Bettys that carried the baka bomb, p. 459-60;

KAMIKAZE: first attack on a carrier, p. 389; a special kind of guided missile, p. 389; U. S. defense against developed - in last two months of war no carrier was hit, p. 396; jack patrols, p. 395-6; 3 strike system, p. 401-5;

KELLY, Colin: p. 304-5;

KING, Fleet Admiral Ernest: p. 60; p. 79-80; VADM McCain (and Thach) call on him in Washington (1945), p. 437-8; p. 444.

KURITA, Admiral T. (Japanese): 385, p. 387;

USS LANGLEY: damaged by bomb (Jan. 1945), p. 426;

LANPHIER, Tom: shot down the plane with Adm. Yamamoto, p. 221-2;

LEGASPI LINE: drawn by MacArthur to designate areas for the Army Air Force and Naval Air, p. 400; p. 406-7;

LESLIE, Rear Admiral Maxwell F.: Commander Dive Bombing Squadron on YORKTOWN at Battle of Midway, p. 229 ff; p. 257;

USS LEXINGTON: p. 175; VF Squadron 3 goes aboard her after SARATOGA is torpedoed - departs in Feb. 1942 for South Pacific, p. 180-1 ff; Japanese bomber attack on her, p. 192 ff; p. 209; p. 212;
the (NEW) LEXINGTON is launched in Boston Navy Yard - Thach invited to comment on design of new equipment pertaining to fighter aircraft, p. 299-300; Thach attends launching, p. 300-1; Thach joins Mitscher flagship (Apr. 1944) in time for attacks on Saipan, Tinian and Guam, p. 312 ff; p. 328; p. 367;

LEYTE GULF: the decision for Leyte landings - MacArthur influenced by Halsey, p. 357-9; McCain's Task Force joins Task Force 38 for Leyte operation, p. 379; p. 397-8;

LONGSTRETH, Lt. Thacher: on staff of Adm. McCain, p. 344-5; his desire to be dropped behind lines in China - McCain did not approve, p. 418;

LOVELACE, Lt. Comdr. Donald Alexander: p. 192; p. 199-200; joins Thach in training activities at Pearl Harbor, p. 212; p. 220; the accident that caused his death, p. 223-5;

LUZON: becomes the air target in December, 1944 - use of blanket method, p. 408; p. 410-11;

MacARTHUR, General Douglas: p. 357-8; p. 398; p. 400; p. 407; McCain calls on him, p. 449-50;

USS MADDOCKS: hit by enemy bomb (Jan. 1945), p. 426;

MARIANAS TURKEY SHOOT: comments on, p. 319 ff; Mitscher's order to turn on lights for returning planes, p. 326 ff;

MASSEY, Lt. Comdr. Lance Edward (Lem): Commanding Officer, Torpedo Squadron #3 on YORKTOWN at Battle of Midway, p. 229 ff; p. 247; his plane explodes, p. 247;

MASTER BOMBER - : qualifications for designation as, p. 113-5;

MAZARU, Japan: port on west coast of Honshu - target of T.F. 38 planes in mid 1945, p. 445; rescue of two pilots by PBY, p. 445-6; award given the army pilot, p. 456-7;

McCAIN, Vice Admiral John Sydney: p. 309; invited Thach to be his Operations Officer in the Pacific, p. 310-311; p. 340; p. 347-8; serves first as Task Force Commander before taking over from Adm. Mitscher, p. 349-50; Thach contrasts him with Mitscher, p. 351-2; Thach's duties on his staff, p. 360-1; p. 365; p. 370; p. 374; ordered to Ulithi - hears distress calls of escort carriers off Leyte and returns to give aid, p. 380-1; account of manner in which they took the scout planes aboard carriers at high speed, p. 381-5; relieves Mitscher (Oct. 1944), p. 389; p. 413; p. 418; the typhoon, p. 423-5; refueling in preparation for South China Sea operation, p. 431-4; takes Thach with him on Washington trip after being relieved by Mitscher (Jan. 1945) - calls on Adm. King - assured he will stay in Fast Carrier Command with Mitscher, p. 437-8; his good relations with Halsey, p. 438-41; McCain and Thach, p. 441 ff; relieves Mitscher again in May, 1945, p. 445; calls on MacArthur (with Thach) in Manila - also Commodore Sullivan, p. 449-5; McCain refuses to let Thach lead a strike over Japanese mainland, p. 453-4; p. 456;

McCLUSKY, Rear Admiral Clarence Wade Jr.: leader of ENTERPRISE air group attack at Battle of Midway, p. 254; p. 256;

McNAMARA, The Hon. Robert S.: his attitude towards practice with live torpedoes, p. 207;

MIDWAY, BATTLE OF: participation of Thach and his fighter squadron on the YORKTOWN in the Battle of Midway, p. 226 ff; the Army claims success of B-17s in the battle, p. 280; Thach's press conferences in Boston and Washington, D.C. dealing with navy successes at Midway, p. 301 ff;

MILLER, Rear Admiral H. B. (Min): p. 301;

USS MISSISSIPPI: Thach assigned to her upon graduation, p. 27; Thach takes elimination course in aviation, p. 28-29;

MITSCHER, Admiral Marc: p. 258-9; Thach assigned to his staff while awaiting arrival of Adm. McCain, p. 311-12; p. 325-6; Thach's characterization of him, p. 350-1; adverse to the launching of night fighters, p. 366-7; p. 370; p. 406; his reluctance to adopt innovative ideas, p. 446-7;

MOORE, Rear Admiral Edward Peerman (Country): at the Test Center, NAS Norfolk, p. 66-67; p. 71-2; p. 166; p. 168; p. 170;

MOROTAI: The rescue of pilot in the harbor, p. 354-5;

MUSHASHI - Japanese Battleship: bombing attack on her, p. 388;

MYRT: a very high level Japanese scouting plane that appeared late in 1944, p. 377;

U. S. NAVAL ACADEMY: Thach's appointment, p. 9-11; his reactions to Academy, p. 12; story of the coal burner cruise ship, p. 17-22; how he came to be called Jimmy, p. 23-24; aviation summer, p. 25-6;

NAS, NORFOLK: Thach assigned to experimental division, p. 57-58; p. 66; experiments with torpedo plane, p. 67-9; experiments with patrol seaplane, p. 69-74; experiments with 4-engined plane (XP2H-1), p. 75-81; exhaustion from long flight, p. 84-5;

NAVAL AIR ADVANCED TRAINING COMMAND: Thach reports (1942) as Asst. Training Officer under RADM A. B. Cook, p. 285 ff; use of Disney films, p. 285 ff; Thach has task of designing and producing 10 films, p. 286-296; Thach works on development of training devices, p. 297-9; Thach's comments on training in general, Japanese pilot training, etc. p. 334-6;

NAVAL AVIATION: Thach takes the elimination course p. 28-29; ordered to Pensacola for training, (1929), p. 30; p. 32-33; p. 36;

NIMITZ, Fleet Admiral Chester: ordered attack on shipping at Hong Kong, etc. p. 421-; p. 431-3;

NORDEN BOMB SIGHT: p. 114-5;

OGE (Orders for Gunnery Exercises): p. 43-4;

O'HARE, Lt. Comdr. Edward Henry: (Butch)p. 142-3; p. 152; p. 154; p. 182-3; p. 188; his role in Japanese bomber attack on USS LEXINGTON, p. 192 ff; p. 205; p. 214; gets Congressional Medal of Honor - takes over Squadron from Thach, p. 281; p. 283-4;

OKINAWA: air attack on in preparation for landing at Leyte Gulf, p. 358-9; p. 447; Thach's comments about being tied to one spot and being vulnerable to the enemy as a result, p. 448;

OLLIE BOMB: the genesis of the bomb, p. 104-5;

OWEN STANLEY MOUNTAINS - New Guinea: p. 201-2; Brett's exploit in taking torpedo planes from LEXINGTON over the mountain range, p. 204-6;

OZAWA, Vice Admiral J. (Japanese): p. 387;

PATROL SQUADRON 5 F: stationed at Coco Solo - engaged in experimental work with flares, p. 109-11; supplied with new PBYs, p. 121-2;

PATROL SQUADRON 9: p. 85; Thach attached from July, 1934 to June, 1936; p. 86; flight to the Aleutians, p. 86-94;

PEARL HARBOR: comments on exercises prior to Japanese attack that involved attacks on Hawaii, p. 170-171; the SARATOGA arrives five days after the Japanese attack, p. 173-5; p. 261-2;

PELELIU ISLAND: operation against, p. 346 ff; Bloody Nose Hill, p. 349;

PENSACOLA: see entry under NAVAL AVIATION.

PILOT TRAINING - in HAWAII: Thach put in command of special training program prior to Battle of Midway, p. 209 ff; teaching the Army pilots to use the P-39 in an overhead approach, p. 213-4; the first exchange pilot with the Army, p. 214-5;

RABAUL: early plan for air attack on island from LEXINGTON, p. 181-2; p. 200-1;

RADFORD, Admiral Arthur: relieves Bogan as Commander of High Hat Squadron, p. 60-65; backs Thach in promoting animated training films, p. 285; p. 295-6;

RAMSEY, Vice Admiral Paul H.: p. 162-3; given command of Thach's squadron on the LEXINGTON - while Thach remains in Pearl Harbor to train new pilots, p. 209-211;

ROBINSON, The Hon. Joseph T.: Senator from Arkansas, p. 10

SALUMAUA and LAE: Japanese landing there, p. 201 ff; the torpedo attack on Japanese cruisers there, p. 206;

USS SANDPIPER: BIRD class tender, p. 87; p. 92;

USS SARATOGA: p. 51; aerial gunnery, p. 54-6; VF-3 aboard her (1941), p. 157; p. 170; she sails for Pearl Harbor on Dec. 8, 1941, p. 172 becomes flagship of Adm. Fitch, p. 175; torpedoed on patrol off Hawaii, p. 178-9;

SCOUTING SQUADRON 6 B: Thach goes to this squadron in 1936 - based on USS CINCINNATI, p. 95 ff:

SOUTH CHINA SEA OPERATION: p. 409 ff; Halsey's hope for a last ditch fight with Japanese fleet remnants, p. 410-11; p. 417 ff; attacks on Canton and Hong Kong, p. 420; Japanese losses, p. 421-3;

SOUTHWICK, Rear Admiral Edward Page: (Bud) p. 40; p. 48-49;

SPRUANCE, Admiral Raymond: p. 227 ff; Spruance asks Thach to report when he lands on ENTERPRISE after loss of YORKTOWN, p. 278; declines suggestion of Thach that he should pursue the Japanese naval force, p. 278-9; p. 439; Thach's comments on Spruance's prevention of carriers from pursuing Japanese fleet off Saipan, p. 323 ff; p. 331;

STANLEY, Lt. j.g. Henry B.: skipper of VP-9 in the Aleutians, p. 86;

SULLIVAN, Rear Admiral Wm. A.: his job of salvage in Manila harbor - McCain and Thach call on him, p. 449-50;

TACLOBEN: p. 381; p. 384-5; p. 398;

TASK FORCE 38: McCain takes over from Mitscher (Oct. 25, 1944), p. 289; one of first orders put out by McCain had to do with defense against enemy suicide attacks, p. 391-4; development of 'jack patrols' against enemy torpedo attacks at dusk, p. 395-6; the 3-strike system developed, p. 401-2; McCain takes Task Force from Okinawa to Leyte Gulf in preparation for raids on Japanese mainland, p. 449; p. 451 ff;

TASK FORCE 38.1: McCain's command under Mitscher - see entries under John Sydney McCain; the development of operations plans, p. 361 ff;

THACH, VADM James Harmon, Jr.: p. 23-24; joint duty of two brothers in the CALIFORNIA, p. 30-32;

THACH, Admiral John S.: background information p. 1-9; the Thach family at home in Fordyce, Arkansas, p. 32, playing games.

p. 48-49; takes command of VF-3 as Lieutenant - becomes Lt. Comdr. Jan. 1942, p. 139-40; invited to attend launching of new LEXINGTON - after which he was awarded DSM, 1st Navy Cross and a Gold wtar in lieu of 2nd, p. 301 ff; subsequent meeting with Washington, D.C. press, p. 303-7; a review of his rank status, p. 309; his lucky escape from disaster due to bomb explosion on HANCOCK, p. 426-7; Thach and Adm. McCain, p. 441 ff; his friendship with VADM J. H. Flatley, p. 445-6;

THACH WEAVE: how Thach conceived this fighting technique, p. 146 ff; p. 155-156; p. 208; p. 238-9; use of Weave at Battle of Midway, p. 247-8;

THORBURN, Lt. Don: on staff of McCain at P.R. officer, p. 345-6;

THREE STRIKE SYSTEM: Thach develops another defense against kamikaze, p. 401-5; also called the 'thatched roof', the 'Big Blue Blanket' and the 'constant cap', p. 413; statistics on success of system, p. 414-7;

TOOTLE, III, Ensign: figures in attack of planes from YORKTOWN in Battle of Midway, p. 268-9;

TORPEDOES: proved to be duds in aerial torpedo attack on Japanese ships at Salamaua and Lae, p. 206-7;

TYPHOON (Cobra - Dec. 1944), p. 430 ff.

ULITHI: p. 380; p. 437;

VF-1 (High Hat Squadron): Thach as number one in class at Pensacola requests fighter squadron, p. 36; explanation for name of squadron, p. 38; formation flying, p. 39; p. 60-3;

VF SQUADRON 3: Thach ordered to Felix Cat Squadron, p. 132 ff; orders for gunnery exercises, p. 135-6; the camera gun, p. 137-8; Thach becomes commander of squadron, p. 139-40; some training techniques, p. 140-2; problem with oil seal leaks, p. 157-8; Halsey gives them chance for practice - excuses squadron from Fleet problem participation, p. 159-60; how they acquired necessary ammo for practice, p. 162-4; transfer of squadrons .50 calibre guns to Marines for use on Wake Island, p. 164-5; attached to USS LEXINGTON after torpedo attack on USS SARATOGA, p. 180-1; attack on Japanese EMILY off Rabaul, p. 183 ff; Fitch takes squadron on LEXINGTON but leaves Thach back at Pearl to train new flyers, - VF3 goes under command of Paul Ramsey, p. 210-210; participation in BATTLE OF MIDWAY, p. 226 ff;

WAKE ISLAND: Japanese attack - withdrawl of U. S. carriers, p. 175-7;

WEAD, Comdr. Frank Wilbur (Spig): author of HELL DIVERS, p. 39-40;

WILLIAWAW: p. 93-4;

USS WRIGHT: p. 82; p. 85; flagship for Wing Commander of Patrol Planes, p. 85; p. 130;

USS YORKTOWN: Joins LEXINGTON for attack on Japanese at Salamaua and Lae, p. 201 ff; p. 220; participation at Battle of Midway, p. 226 ff; the attack on the YORKTOWN, p. 266 ff;

ZERO: name of Japanese fighter plane - first intelligence report on ZERO - how Thach worked to offset superiority of this plane, p. 146; p. 152; p. 174; p. 233; ZERO attack on 6 U. S. fighters in Midway Battle, p. 245-6 ff.

www.ingramcontent.com/pod-product-compliance
Lightning Source LLC
Chambersburg PA
CBHW082148070526
44585CB00020B/2135